Magic and Religion in Medieval England

Magic *and* Religion

in Medieval England

Catherine Rider

Reaktion Books

Published by Reaktion Books Ltd
33 Great Sutton Street
London EC1V 0DX
www.reaktionbooks.co.uk

First published 2012

Printed and bound in Great Britain
by TJ International, Padstow, Cornwall

British Library Cataloguing in Publication Data
Rider, Catherine.
Magic and religion in medieval England.
1. Magic – Religious aspects – Christianity – History of
doctrines – Middle Ages, 600-1500.
2. Magic – England – History – To 1500.
3. England – Church history – 1066–1485.
4. England – Religious life and customs.
I. Title
261.5'13'0942'0902-DC23

ISBN 978 1 78023 035 1

Contents

C H A P. X.

How some Witches revelling in a Gentleman's Houfe, ferved the Servants who
furprifed them.

I T happened one time that a great number of Lancafhire Witches were rev-
ling in a gentleman's houfe, in his ab-
fence, and making merry with what they
found, the dogs not daring to ftir, they
having it feems, power to ftrike them
mute.—However, dnring their frolick-

1 Witches on broomsticks: an illustration from *The Famous History
of the Lancashire Witches* (c. 1780).

Introduction

Some time in the late twelfth century, a curious event happened. As Master G (we do not know his full name), a member of the Archbishop of Canterbury's household, was leaving his house one morning he met a monk, William. At once William told him to go back inside because meeting a monk on the road was a bad omen that meant there would be danger on the journey. Master G refused to listen: he dismissed the monk's advice as idle talk, 'not founded on the root of faith', and continued on his way. But later that day he and his horse fell into a deep ditch filled with water and escaped only because the same monk, William (who happened to be on the scene), mobilized people to rescue them. This incident was witnessed by several other members of the Archbishop of Canterbury's household, and it caused them to wonder. Had G been wrong? Should people trust in omens after all? One of them turned to a friend, the writer and cleric Peter of Blois, for advice, and Peter responded with a letter. In it he stated categorically that we should never put our faith in omens, even though sometimes they seem to come true.[1]

It is possible Peter of Blois simply made up this episode because it was an entertaining way to make his point about omens – the reappearance of William the monk to rescue Master G from the ditch is perhaps a little too convenient to be true – but even if he did, his letter still offers a rare insight into beliefs about predicting the future in medieval England, and the ways in which they could influence everyday life and provoke debate. Strictly speaking, official theology was on the side of the unfortunate Master G, as Peter of Blois recognized. For centuries educated medieval clergy had denounced the belief in omens as a form of magic and they sometimes claimed that only ignorant peasants took omens seriously. However, Peter's letter shows things were more complicated. William, the monk who believed in omens, was not an ignorant peasant and neither, quite clearly, was the man who supposedly turned to Peter of Blois for advice, since Peter's response is written in Latin. Moreover, clergy who believed in omens could justify their views with reference to the Bible, because the Bible contains many instances in which people predicted the future, sometimes with the help of signs from God. Peter of Blois emphasized that these Bible stories do not give us licence to try to predict the future ourselves, but other readers interpreted them differently.

Peter of Blois' letter therefore has a significance which goes beyond a group of clerics arguing over whether Master G could, or should, have taken action to avoid his soaking in the ditch. It shows how complex the relationship between religion and magic was in the Middle Ages and how even educated clergy could find it difficult to decide whether something was religious or magical. In medieval England, as in many other places and periods of history, numerous unofficial rituals and beliefs existed alongside the ones officially sanctioned by the church. Educated clergy condemned some of them as magic but it was not always easy to do this because many unofficial practices employed religious language, rituals or objects, and the people who used them could sometimes justify their actions by citing precedents from the Bible, as Peter of Blois said some people did with omens. Charms that were recited over sick people to cure illnesses often invoked God and the saints; spells for love and other purposes might use consecrated substances such as the Eucharist; and one way of predicting the future was to use a book on lot-casting called the *Lots of the Saints* or *Lots of the Apostles*, which claimed to be based on the example set by the Apostles in the New Testament. Each of these practices bore a different relationship to official religion. Healing charms shaded easily into prayers and many were seen as perfectly legitimate; but at the other end of the spectrum the misuse of consecrated substances for profane purposes was regularly condemned as magic by medieval church councils.

Medieval churchmen therefore had to draw a line between pious but unofficial religious activities and unacceptable magic. They also had to decide how strongly to oppose the practices they deemed unacceptable, given that they had limited resources and other, more urgent, priorities. These priorities are clear in the official pronouncements that medieval English bishops made in the church councils they held for their dioceses. They mentioned magic but devoted far more space to other issues. Did clergy instruct their parishioners in basic doctrines and behave as they should, observing celibacy and avoiding violence? Did laypeople go to mass on Sundays, obey the church's rules on marriage and pay their tithes?[2] Bishops were mainly interested in setting clear goals to ensure both clergy and laity met a minimum standard of behaviour. Beyond this, it was a much more complex task to start sifting through the mass of unofficial practices and beliefs, and the results were far harder to measure.

Nevertheless, the problem of how to deal with unorthodox religious beliefs and practices remained. It was a problem churchmen had always faced. The early Christians of the Roman Empire confronted it when they debated which elements of pagan culture were compatible with Christianity and which were not; and the same questions recurred whenever Christianity spread among the pagan peoples of Northern and Eastern Europe. The problem did not only arise when Christians came into contact with non-Christians, however. People who had long been Christians continued to innovate, adapting the language and rituals of religion to suit their circumstances and changing their minds about what was acceptable. This meant that the debate over where to draw the line between magic and religion focused not on pagan worship but on widespread ritual practices – the things many people did to gain health, prosperity, good fortune and protection against evil.

It is clear from reading medieval churchmen's comments on magic that there were very many of these practices, and still more have been documented in later centuries.[3] Medieval people from all parts of society – educated and uneducated, clergy and laity, men and women – tried to influence the world around them in a huge variety of ways, and their reasons are easy to understand. They lived in an uncertain world: life was short, and the risk of devastating misfortune from war, disease or famine was always present. They wanted to be healthy and they wanted their children to be healthy too. They wanted to avoid potential hazards that lay in the future. They wanted to be safe and prosperous, with reliable harvests and successful business dealings. They wanted love and the favour of people in positions of power. They did not just pursue these goals through religion, of course, but religious rituals and prayers offered a powerful tool that they believed could help. When medieval churchmen wrote about these practices, they offered glimpses of a worldview that was based on Christianity but which stretched religion beyond the minimum standards which bishops tried to enforce and used it in very diverse ways. Much of this worldview is not well known. What churchmen said about it is fragmentary and often hidden in unpublished and little-studied manuscripts. This book aims to uncover what there is, and so give a fuller picture of the religious life of medieval England and the way in which educated clergy responded to it.

Making Sense of Magic and Religion in the Middle Ages

The relationship between magic and religion in the Middle Ages has long attracted the attention of historians working both on the period of conversion to Christianity and on the centuries before the Reformation. Much of this attention has been prompted by an influential book, *Religion and the Decline of Magic* by Keith Thomas, which was first published in 1971. Thomas's book focuses mainly on the sixteenth and seventeenth centuries but it opens with a chapter on what he calls the 'magic of the medieval church'. Here Thomas argues that, in order to persuade pagans to convert, churchmen in the early Middle Ages offered them Christian 'magic' to replace the pagan sort. By magic he meant the use of sacred rituals and substances to serve everyday purposes rather than otherworldly ones; and he had in mind practices such as sprinkling holy water to bless homes, fields and domestic animals, or ringing church bells to protect against thunderstorms. Thus for many people the medieval church 'acted as a repository of supernatural power which could be dispensed to the faithful to help them in their daily problems'.[4] Thomas argues these uses of 'Christian magic' persisted in England up to the Reformation in the sixteenth century, when Protestants denounced them as pagan magic and their use gradually diminished.

Since 1971 several historians have built on Thomas's ideas. In particular, a book on magic in the period before 1100 by Valerie Flint, published in 1991, argued, like Thomas, that some Christian missionaries replaced pagan magical practices with Christian alternatives. This was the origin of Thomas's 'Christian magic', but Flint argued we should not see this as a lowering of devotional standards by clergy who were powerless to prevent magic from intruding on Christianity. Rather it was a calculated and sympathetic attempt to Christianize valued and widespread ritual practices and so to preserve what was considered good about paganism within a Christian context. Only in later and more securely Christian centuries did churchmen come to see this 'Christian magic' as unacceptable because by then, the circumstances which gave rise to it had been forgotten.[5]

These views have proved controversial – particularly Thomas's and Flint's use of the word 'magic' to describe practices which were often sanctioned by medieval clergy. For example, *The Stripping of the Altars*, Eamon Duffy's influential study of religion in fifteenth- and sixteenth-century England, has argued forcefully that much of this so-called 'magic' was not a pagan legacy. Instead it was highly Christian and formed the mainstream of medieval English religion, shared by everyone, clergy and laity, educated and uneducated alike.[6] Karen Jolly, working on the tenth and eleventh centuries, has also taken issue with the phrase 'Christian magic', pointing out that Christian clergy would never have thought of what they were doing as magic. Instead, she argues, it is more useful to talk about 'middle practices', legitimate ways of using Christian power to affect the natural world, without imposing modern ideas about what counts as 'magic' or 'religion' on medieval texts.[7]

Meanwhile other historians have explored the church's own view of 'magic' and 'superstition'. In contrast to the historians mentioned so far, these writers do not start with what medieval people were doing and ask whether we should see this as 'magic'. Instead they ask what medieval churchmen themselves were worried about. Several books on this were written in Germany in the 1970s and '80s, and more recently other historians have begun to discuss the church's attitude to 'superstition', including Euan Cameron, Michael Bailey and Kathleen Kamerick.[8] Whereas Duffy discusses practices which were widely shared among clergy and laity, these historians focus on the aspects of religious life which provoked debate and anxiety, and on the educated clergy who did worry that magic was intruding on religion.

These authors take very different approaches but they have one thing in common. All of them focus on the ends of the Middle Ages: either the early Middle Ages before 1100 or the period which stretched from 1400 into the Reformation in the sixteenth century. By contrast the period between 1100 and the fifteenth century has received far less attention, although a book by Carl Watkins does discuss (among other things) the relationship between magic and religion in twelfth-century England.[9] Instead historians who work on magic in these centuries have focused on other issues: particularly the changing attitudes to magic among intellectuals (especially academic theologians and lawyers), and the surviving medieval texts which told people how to practise magic.[10] The attitude of the medieval church to more widespread magical practices has therefore been comparatively neglected.

This is an important omission because the period between the twelfth and the fifteenth centuries witnessed several developments which profoundly affected the relationship between magic and religion. In the twelfth century texts which described how to practise magic began to appear in Christian Europe. Some of these were centuries-old works which were newly translated from Arabic and Greek while others were new compositions based on Christian rituals. At the same time Christian religious practices were coming under closer scrutiny than before as the result of a reform movement led by high-ranking churchmen. This movement sought to improve the education of the clergy and the religious knowledge of the laity, and it prompted some educated churchmen to take an interest in the sins and problems that existed in the world around them on a larger scale than before. As part of this, reformers often discussed what they claimed were widespread magical practices with new interest.

The emergence of new books about magic and the reform movement within the church forced educated churchmen to think about the relationship between magic and religion in more precise terms than they had before. They needed to find a way of deciding which practices were legitimate and which were not, and a way of explaining this to less well educated priests and their congregations. The first problem they faced was how to define magic. On the one hand they had to think about the borderline between magic and science. Did some seemingly magical phenomena really rely on natural forces, as was sometimes claimed by the Arabic magical texts? On the other hand, they had to decide what they thought about practices which looked religious. What exactly was the difference between divinely inspired prophecy and magical methods of predicting the future; or between prayers and healing charms? The second problem related to practices which did not seem to overlap clearly with either religion or science. Once churchmen began to take a deeper interest in widespread religious beliefs, they uncovered various unorthodox ideas which did not always sit easily alongside official Christianity. What should they think about the belief in fairies, for example, or the idea that strange otherworldly women flew about at night? The third and final problem related to how they put their knowledge into practice. How could they persuade other people of their views, and stop them from using magic? These problems, and the ways in which educated clergy tried to solve them, form the theme of this book.

What is Magic?

Medieval churchmen therefore faced complex problems when they thought about what magic was and how it should be distinguished from religion. Nor were they alone in this. The same issue has played an important part in modern scholarship on magic and since the nineteenth century scholars have suggested various ways of distinguishing between magic and religion.[11] Some historians have found these modern definitions of magic useful tools for shedding light on the beliefs of medieval people. As we have seen, Keith Thomas and Valerie Flint both define magic in ways medieval churchmen would not have recognized, arguing that some medieval religious practices were 'magical' even though medieval clergy did not see them that way. Their approach can be criticized for imposing modern ideas about what magic is on medieval sources but both Thomas and Flint use it as a starting point to explore the similarities between permitted religion and condemned 'magic'.

However, many historians of the Middle Ages have rejected this approach as anachronistic, as have some scholars working in other fields.[12] They argue that what matters is not whether we think something is magic, but whether it would have been understood as magic at the time. They have therefore preferred to start by asking what medieval people themselves thought magic was.[13] This book will also use medieval definitions of magic, because this is the logical starting point for exploring what 'magic' meant to medieval churchmen and it enables us to see which practices they worried about, and why. Nevertheless, Thomas and Flint draw attention to an important point. There were sometimes striking similarities between religion and magic and this posed a problem: not just for modern historians but also for medieval churchmen, who struggled to categorize some practices as one or the other.

Finding medieval definitions of magic is not entirely straightforward because there was no one word for 'magic' in the Middle Ages, any more than there is in modern English: we use magic, sorcery, witchcraft, enchantment and other words, each of which has slightly different connotations. Medieval churchmen also used various terms and the situation is further complicated because they wrote both in Latin and in their native languages. The most common Latin word for magic these churchmen used was *sortilegium*. This had originally meant lot-casting but by the twelfth century it encompassed a much wider range of practices, as we will see. More rarely they used other words includ-ing 'magic arts' (*artes magicae*), *maleficium* (which usually referred to the use of magic to harm people), *necromantia* or *nigromantia* (which had originally meant invoking the spirits of the dead but came to mean invoking demons) or, when writing in English, 'witchcraft'. Finally, some writers used the word 'superstition'. In academic theology this word did not mean quite the same thing as magic but in less learned settings clergy sometimes used the two terms interchangeably, to describe the same bundle of practices and beliefs.[14]

What were these? From the twelfth century onwards medieval churchmen often drew their lists of magical practices from the *Decre-tum*, a compilation of passages from earlier legal and theological texts which was put together by Gratian, a teacher of law in the Italian city of Bologna in the mid-twelfth century. The *Decretum* became one of the standard textbooks used to teach canon law in medieval uni-versities and so it had an enormous influence on later writers. It was structured around a series of imaginary legal cases, and Case 26 dealt with *sortilegium*.[15] Here Gratian included the following beliefs and practices: various methods of divination (predicting the future); the use of healing charms and amulets; beliefs relating to omens and mysterious supernatural beings; and unorthodox uses of religious rituals, such as reciting the mass for the dead in the name of a living person in order to make him or her die.

Equally importantly Gratian discussed why these things were magic. On this subject he copied several passages from the much earlier writ-ings of St Augustine (d. 430), a theologian who had a profound influ-ence on medieval thought. In these, Augustine listed various practices which he described as 'superstitious' and 'magic arts'. What all of these had in common, he argued, was that they did not work by any explicable, physical means. Healing incantations and amulets, for ex-ample, had no physical effects on the body, and similarly astrology and omens had no causal connection with the events they were supposed to predict. Instead these practices acted as signs to demons, who stepped in to produce the desired result. In this way, men and demons entered into 'contracts'.[16]

Most medieval churchmen did not depart significantly from Augustine's definition of magic but some writers did modify it in the thirteenth century and later, by developing a concept of 'natural magic' (*magia naturalis*) which sat alongside Augustine's view that magic relied on demons. Natural magic relied on the 'occult' (from the Latin meaning 'hidden') properties of natural substances. These were properties which could not be explained by medieval scientific knowledge but were nonetheless believed to be part of the natural world and not reliant on demons to make them work: one classic example was the power of the magnet to attract iron.[17]

So in theory the boundary between magic and religion was clear: magic relied on demons while religion appealed to God. Anything that relied on natural forces (even occult ones) was not, strictly speaking, magical or religious. But in practice it could be difficult to decide whether an unexplained phenomenon relied on demons or on occult natural forces. A further complication was that Augustine had argued demons were themselves part of the natural world and worked their magic by manipulating natural forces.[18] The boundary between magic and the natural world was therefore not as clear as it seemed.

It could be equally difficult to decide whether other practices called on God or demons. Even clearly religious phenomena, such as miracles, could superficially look similar to magic. Both magic and miracles were wondrous events which could not be explained, and throughout the Middle Ages stories about the saints played on this fact for dramatic effect. They told of early Christian saints in the period of the Roman Empire who confronted pagan magicians and defeated their magic with miracles. We will meet some of them in later chapters, including St James the Apostle, who was said to have overcome devils summoned to attack him by the pagan magician Ermogenes; and St Cyprian, a former magician who converted to Christianity after his magic was defeated by a saint's prayers. In stories such as these, the similarities between magic and miracle would probably not have challenged the audience too much, because listeners would know that, of course, the saints were not really doing magic. But in everyday life saints and magicians were not so easy to spot and unofficial religious practices were much harder to categorize.

Another term which needs explanation is 'witchcraft'. 'Witchcraft' can simply be an alternative word for 'magic' and it was often used in this way by medieval churchmen who wrote in English. However, like some other historians, I will use 'witchcraft' in a more specific way, to describe the crimes punished in witch trials in some parts of Europe from the fifteenth century onwards. Witchcraft in this sense was not found in medieval England but it is nevertheless relevant to a book on magic and religion in this period. One reason for this is because the later witch trials have affected how historians view medieval magic. Much work has gone into tracing the medieval origins of witch trials and some earlier British trials have been studied in this light, most notably the 1324 case of Alice Kyteler, discussed in chapter Seven. Another reason is because the records of witch trials contain many details about popular beliefs relating to magic, and used carefully, these can sometimes help to shed light on the more fragmentary medieval evidence.

As it came to be defined from the fifteenth century, witchcraft was about more than just magic. In addition to practising magic (usually to harm people or animals), witches were believed to have renounced God and pledged their allegiance to the devil. They were said to hold meetings called sabbaths, sometimes flying to them. There they worshipped the devil, held orgies and committed other crimes, including killing and eating children. Rather than being thought of as individual magic-users, witches were believed to be part of a secret, evil sect which committed the most terrible crimes medieval Christians could imagine. There is no evidence anyone ever went to a sabbath or committed most of the crimes associated with witchcraft, but the idea that a secret sect was working to undermine Christendom from the inside was a powerful one. From the sixteenth century onwards, books and pamphlets circulating in England began to discuss witchcraft and many of their stereotypes about witches persist to this day, in the image of an evil flying woman who does black magic. For this reason their depictions of witches can look very familiar to a modern audience. Two from the eighteenth century, drawn after witch trials had ended in England, show the stereotype in a very recognizable form, complete with pointy hats, demonic familiars and broomsticks (illus. 1 and 2).

It is telling that these images date from several centuries after the Middle Ages. The stereotype of the witch did evolve from various strands in medieval culture but it only came together at the end of the Middle Ages, in the 1430s and '40s in the Alps. The new ideas about witchcraft travelled to some parts of Europe in the fifteenth century and then spread more widely in the late sixteenth and early seventeenth centuries: the first English witch trials took place in the 1560s.[19] These witch trials are outside the scope of this book but some of the practices and beliefs mentioned in them can also be found in medieval England. For example, witch trials partly fed off a much older belief that

2 Witches with demonic familiars in an English woodcut, *c.* 1720.

magic could be used to harm others. More importantly, the existence of witch trials in later periods prompts us to ask important questions about the Middle Ages. If medieval people believed in magic, why do we not see a medieval equivalent of the later witch trials? This is a difficult question to answer but the final chapter of the book will suggest some possible reasons.

Magic and Church Reform

Many of the sources which tell us about magic and religion in medieval England were written as part of the church reform movement which has already been mentioned: a drive to improve clerical education and the pastoral care of the laity. Its aims were formally expressed at the Fourth Lateran Council of 1215, a church council convened by a dynamic reforming pope, Innocent III, which attracted clergy from all over Europe.[20] The Council aimed to rejuvenate Christendom in the broadest sense: to improve standards of behaviour among both clergy and laity, stamp out heresy and launch a new crusade to recapture territory in the Holy Land. In doing so, it responded to much larger social, economic and religious changes which were taking place. These included the growth of towns, rising levels of education, and the appearance of radical religious movements, some of which were condemned as heresies. Innocent III tried to harness this religious enthusiasm in various ways, for example by approving the creation of two new orders of friars by Saints Francis and Dominic: travelling monks whose mission was to preach to the people of Europe. But he also sought to regulate it and the Council was part of that.

The Fourth Lateran Council made several decrees connected with the pastoral care of laypeople. It ruled that 'everyone, of both sexes', should make confession to their parish priest at least once a year, at the end of Lent, before receiving communion on Easter Sunday. Two other decrees focused on how the clergy could be educated to provide effective pastoral care. This was a problem because clerical education varied a great deal in the Middle Ages. Medieval English priests were a very diverse group, from the bishops who generally came from aristocratic backgrounds, to parish priests who seem often to have come from landed gentry or upper peasant families in the local area.[21] They did not have to attend seminaries (this only became a requirement in the sixteenth century) and only a minority went to university, though the proportion rose during the Middle Ages. But they did need to be able to recite the liturgy in Latin and, equally importantly, they needed to be someone of good character whom their communities could respect.[22] Some priests learned their Latin in the schools of monasteries or cathedrals and others from schools run locally, but many may have learned mostly on the job, working for a senior priest. Educational standards therefore varied hugely, and the Fourth Lateran Council tried to make provision for some more formal training. It ordered cathedrals, and those churches that could afford it, to appoint a master to teach poor scholars, and archbishops were also to provide a master to teach theology and pastoral care. The Council also ordered bishops to provide trained preachers to preach to the laity and hold regular synods to monitor the behaviour of clergy and laity alike.

There has been much debate about how far this ambitious programme of reform was put into practice, but English bishops did try to implement parts of it.[23] They held more synods and preaching did increase, mostly thanks to the new orders of friars. Many laypeople also seem to have gone to confession once a year or more and this may have been the case even before 1215. There is less evidence of bishops and archbishops appointing masters to teach the clergy, but some cathedrals already had schools and some bishops tried to educate priests through their diocesan synods, by producing treatises on pastoral care for them to copy. Levels of priestly education in medieval England continue to be debated but it seems likely that although some parish priests were well educated, many others may not have had a very sophisticated grasp of academic theology and they may not have needed one to perform their everyday duties successfully.[24]

The Council's decrees also prompted educated clergy to write large numbers of manuals to instruct priests in how to deal with the laity, which historians have often called pastoral manuals or *pastoralia*.[25] They did not appear from nowhere in the thirteenth century: sermons and penitentials (guides to giving penance) had been written for centuries and thirteenth-century pastoral manuals drew heavily on these older works; but the volume of material surviving from after 1215 is much greater. Pastoral manuals were written by a wide range of educated clergy, including bishops, diocesan administrators, friars and the occasional parish priest. Many of their readers were drawn from the same groups.

Depending on the author and the intended readers, pastoral manuals varied greatly. In the thirteenth century most were written in Latin, the international language of the church, which meant that many works written in continental Europe circulated widely in England; but in later centuries manuals also appeared in French (which was spoken by the English aristocracy into the fourteenth century) and English, aimed at literate laypeople and at priests who preferred to read in their native language. Some of these vernacular manuals worked hard to make their contents interesting to a wide audience. For example *Handlyng Synne*, written in the early fourteenth century by Robert Mannyng, was written in easily memorable English verse and included many colourful stories that made moral points – including several dramatic, and sometimes far-fetched, stories about magic.

Pastoral manuals also varied in format. Some were large textbooks known as *summae*, reference works which summed up the theology and canon law relating to a priest's duties. *Summae* sometimes circulated very widely: for example the *Summa for Confessors* completed shortly after 1215 by Thomas of Chobham, an administrator in the diocese of Salisbury, survives in over 100 manuscripts.[26] However, long textbooks such as these were time-consuming to copy and this made them expensive. Written in Latin, they were probably also too difficult for some parish priests to read and more comprehensive than they needed to be, since they were designed to cover every possible situation a priest might encounter, however uncommon. For these reasons they were most likely to be owned by institutions such as cathedrals, friaries and monasteries and read by relatively well educated priests. But there were also cheaper and more accessible manuals which summarized key points of doctrine or the basic information a priest needed to know in order to hear confessions. They were shorter and simpler and so they were more likely to be read by parish priests or friars who had limited education. Other pastoral manuals again were aimed at preaching rather than confession. They included collections of sermons and materials which could be used to write sermons such as *exempla*, short stories which made moral points in an entertaining way.

All these pastoral manuals were designed to combat behaviour which educated churchmen found unacceptable and to encourage correct belief and practice. For this reason many of them discussed magic, in more or less detail. *Exempla* particularly favoured it, since stories about magic were a dramatic and colourful way to liven up a sermon. However, pastoral manuals' comments on magic have not attracted much attention from historians who write about the thirteenth century or later. This is surprising because earlier sermons and penitentials have long been recognized as a major source of information about magic in the period before 1100.[27] A few historians have looked at magic in late medieval German pastoral literature,[28] but the English pastoral manuals have not been much used for this, with the exception of an article written in 1957 by G. R. Owst, an expert on medieval preaching.[29] Part of the reason later pastoral manuals have been neglected is probably because they were not theologically innovative or sophisticated: they do not contain new theories about what magic is or why it works. But this very lack of sophistication makes them valuable sources for how magic was viewed by the majority of the clergy, who were not highly educated. Because they sought to correct people's behaviour, pastoral manuals sometimes also described what their authors claimed were current practices, giving us tantalizing glimpses of medieval popular beliefs.

These glimpses are not straightforward because, like all medieval writings, pastoral manuals come with limitations. One is their reliance on older texts. Many authors copied and recopied quotations from the works of church fathers such as St Augustine and other earlier texts, often taking these quotations from compilations such as the *Decretum* of Gratian. This makes it hard to establish how far they reflect the situation in medieval England. For example many English pastoral manuals mentioned 'augurs': people who predicted the future by inspecting the entrails of sacrificial animals. This was a practice which had existed in the Roman Empire but there is no evidence it was still current in thirteenth-century England. It therefore seems likely that such references were simply copied as part of a much older list of names for magical practitioners. Even within late medieval England, ecclesiastical writing on magic could be very conservative. Later pastoral manuals copied earlier ones, and thirteenth-century works were copied and printed as late as the sixteenth century.

Because pastoral manuals were so conservative, some historians have argued they tell us little about the reality of medieval magic – everything in them was copied from much older texts and therefore their comments do not reflect what was happening in their own time.[30] This is a real problem but it is nevertheless possible to learn something about current practices from these works. Even though they drew heavily on earlier sources, they did not do so blindly. Many pastoral writers copied some parts of earlier texts and omitted others, which suggests they were choosing passages which they thought were relevant. Moreover, some writers added details which do not seem to come from earlier sources. For example *Fasciculus Morum*, an early fourteenth-century preaching manual written in Latin, criticized the popular belief in 'elves' – giving the word in English, which is unusual and suggests the author was basing his comments on contemporary beliefs.[31] These variations suggest at least some pastoral writers were thinking about magic for themselves.

A second problem is that pastoral manuals are only oblique reflections of real practices. They tell us what their authors – well-educated clerics – thought people did and they discuss the issues their authors thought were most important. We cannot therefore assume they reflect widespread attitudes to magic accurately. Indeed, as we will see, there were some forms of magic which pastoral manuals did not say much about. Nevertheless, they are useful sources for a history of magic and religion precisely because they tell us which aspects of magic most concerned educated churchmen and they show how churchmen decided whether something should be classified as religion or magic.

There are also ways to overcome both of these problems, at least to some extent. We can examine a large number of pastoral manuals closely, looking for variations. Which comments were regularly copied and which were unusual? What details did individual authors add, and where did they claim to be getting their information from: from their own observation, from hearsay, or from earlier written sources? We can also see which practices caused pastoral writers most concern.

What did they discuss most often and in most detail? What did they condemn as widespread errors and what did they present as rare or exotic? In answering these questions it is helpful to compare the longer pastoral manuals, which sought to be comprehensive, with the short ones that summarized only the information deemed to be most important. Even unusual practices might be mentioned in a long pastoral manual, just in case a future reader ever needed the information. A short treatise, by contrast, was more likely to focus on the practices which were thought to be common.

Another approach is to compare the pastoral texts with other contemporary sources that mention magic. Fortunately, a range of these survive from medieval England. Magic was primarily viewed as a moral offence rather than a crime (unless it was used to harm somebody) and so it fell under the jurisdiction of the church. Cases of magic were therefore brought before the church courts, which existed in each diocese. Church court records survive from the fourteenth century onwards and although cases of magic were not particularly common, some do appear. These cases give valuable information about magical practices which can be compared with pastoral manuals and they also tell us why some practitioners ended up in court. Other sources also recorded information about magic. Medical texts sometimes included cures that could be defined as magical, and histories describe a few cases of magic, especially high-profile incidents involving the royal family. References to magic are not very frequent in these sources but when they do occur they give us insights into which practices and beliefs were current in medieval England.

Pastoral manuals, then, tell us much about the relationship between magic and religion in medieval England. Despite their reliance on earlier works, they describe unorthodox beliefs and practices which their authors thought existed in the world around them. Beyond these details, they tell us much about how churchmen approached magic. Faced with the need to instruct the laity, the authors of pastoral manuals began to give more guidance about how, exactly, magical practices could be distinguished from science on the one hand and religion on the other. Here they focused especially on magic that was used for divination and healing. Which cures worked naturally and which methods of predicting the future simply relied on observing the natural world? Which words in a charm or amulet were magical, and which kinds of people could (or could not) be trusted to use unofficial religious practices correctly? Even when pastoral writers borrowed from earlier texts, they were most likely to borrow the passages that addressed these practical concerns.

As well as focusing on practical issues, pastoral manuals also show that educated clergy were especially interested in the practices and beliefs which lay on the borderline between religion, science and magic, probably because these practices were the most difficult to detect and argue against, and so it was here that priests were thought to need most guidance. Even educated priests might take different views of what, exactly, was legitimate and what was not, as Peter of Blois' letter shows. Pastoral writing about magic therefore served to define the boundaries of legitimate religion and to reinforce the authority of the clergy as the experts who decided whether a particular practice was legitimate or not.

Nevertheless, pastoral writers did also mention other, less common problems. When they wrote about the use of magic to harm other people and the belief in fairies and other supernatural beings, they sometimes questioned whether magic was really as threatening as people thought. Here they explored the boundaries between illusion and reality, and the limits of what magicians could do. They also sometimes used less common kinds of magic as a colourful backdrop to moral stories. Here we can see a different side to the relationship between magic and religion, a side which is exotic, even playful, and which did not always take the powers of magicians too seriously. This side of magic is missing from the sober discussions of which practices can be accepted and which should be rejected, and it has received little attention from historians.

The history of magic and religion in medieval England is therefore part of the story of how people thought about their religious beliefs and devotional activities. It is the story of how educated clergy tried to decide what the dividing lines were between magic and religion when faced with real situations and beliefs. But it is also the story of a much broader range of medieval people because magic influenced people's daily lives in numerous ways. It responded to universal concerns and it could be everyday or exotic, dangerous or useful. This book is therefore about how both clergy and laity made sense of the diversity of religious ideas and practices which existed in the world around them; and how in turn they used those practices to make sense of their own lives.

3 Details of an 'experiment' to identify thieves,
from a late 13th-century medical treatise.

Predicting the Future and Healing the Sick: Magic, Science and the Natural World

Experiments for stolen goods: If you want to know who it is who has stolen your things, write these names on virgin wax and hold them above your head with your left hand, and in your sleep you will see the person who has committed the theft: '+ *agios crux* + *agios crux* + *agios crux domini*. In the name of the Father and the Son and the Holy Spirit.' [*agios* is Greek for 'holy'; *crux domini* Latin for 'cross of the Lord'.] Likewise if someone has stolen something from you or you suspect them of something, you will be able to know in this way. Take silver scum, which is thrown up from silver when it is poured, and grind it vigorously with egg white. Afterwards paint an eye like this [see illus. 3] on a wall. Afterwards call together everyone whom you suspect. As soon as they approach, you will see the guilty people's right eyes weeping.[1]

These two methods for identifying a thief were copied at the end of a collection of medical treatises in the late thirteenth century, alongside many other 'experiments': how to cut a stick in half and join it together again, how to put your hand into boiling water unharmed, how to restore harmony to quarrelling friends, prevent your enemies from acting against you or excite lust in a woman. Some of these may have been used primarily to entertain, especially the ones for tricks such as cutting and joining the stick. But identifying thieves was a serious matter, and divination which aimed to uncover this kind of hidden information or predict the future is one of the forms of magic which medieval English clergy who wrote manuals for pastoral care, preaching and confession discussed most often and in the most detail.

The scribe who copied these directions did not call them 'magic'. Instead he called them 'experiments', meaning phenomena which could not be explained by medieval science but which had been proven to work. In contrast to modern experimental science, however, medieval 'experiments' did not involve rigorous testing and it was often enough that a respectable earlier writer claimed they worked. Experiments such as these were generally assumed to work because of natural forces but medieval writers did not know exactly how they worked. This posed a problem because if the forces behind experiments were not understood, it was always possible they were not natural at all and instead worked because of demons: in other words, they might be magic. These 'experiments' to identify thieves therefore point to a crucial problem for educated medieval clergy: how do you distinguish between legitimate ways of manipulating natural forces and magic? Or in modern terms, how do you draw a line between magic and science?

Medieval churchmen faced this problem when they thought about two kinds of magic in particular: divination and healing. Both were discussed in detail by pastoral manuals and educated clergy often paid far more attention to them than to other kinds of magic precisely because in these cases it was difficult to draw firm lines between religion, magic and science. It was clear that some ways of predicting the future relied on the observation of cause and effect, and many healing practices were also believed to work purely by natural means, by affecting the balance of humours in the body. (The humours were four substances thought to be found in the body, and ancient and medieval medical writers believed the balance between them determined health and illness.) The existence of these natural methods of prediction and healing meant there was much scope to argue about what was legitimate and what was not. Educated clergy saw it as their job to define and police the boundaries, and to make sure legitimate medicine and forecasting did not shade into demonic magic.

This task fitted in well with some wider currents of thought in medieval Europe. In the twelfth and thirteenth centuries, ancient Greek scientific works, especially those of Aristotle, were being translated into Latin from Arabic and from the original Greek. These treatises prompted medieval intellectuals to study the natural world in greater depth, and also to think more precisely about what counted as 'natural' and what as 'supernatural'.[2] But this was not just a theoretical issue to be debated by a small group of educated men. Pastoral writing on magic shows that the question of where the natural world ended and magic began was relevant to everyone, because at some point in their lives almost everyone would become ill, have something stolen, become anxious about the future or want to secure good fortune. Deciding which ways of responding to these problems were natural and which were magical was therefore an important pastoral issue.

Interpreting the Universe

Many ways of predicting the future were based on observing the natural world and the seemingly random events which occurred in everyday life. Almost anything was potentially meaningful, from the motions of the stars, to the crowing of a bird, to meeting a certain kind of person on the road, as in the story of Master G and William the monk. Interpreting these signs was not necessarily seen as magic. It was widely believed that God sometimes used the natural world to communicate with mankind and so medieval chroniclers regularly noted comets, eclipses and other unusual natural phenomena alongside more ordinary events. They were well aware that some of these phenomena (such as eclipses) had predictable physical causes but despite this they also viewed them as signs from God which carried a wider meaning.[3] Even if God was not involved, it was widely recognized that some future events could be deduced simply by observation. Anyone could predict the weather with a fair degree of success if they saw grey clouds overhead, and people with specialist knowledge could do much more. For example, astrologers claimed to be able to offer long-term weather forecasts and many treatises explaining how to do this survive from across medieval Europe.[4] Doctors, too, could predict the future within their own field of expertise. Medical prognosis went back to ancient times but it took on a new significance in the Middle Ages. In medieval Christianity it was important to know whether you were dying so that you could die a 'good death': one where you had time to confess your sins and receive the last rites.[5]

Late medieval English churchmen never suggested that noting portents such as comets, weather forecasting or medical prognosis constituted magic. Quite the opposite: they stressed they were not. But beyond these recognized ways of interpreting the natural world, meanings were attached to a wide range of other natural phenomena and chance events which churchmen found far more difficult to accept. Medieval English pastoral writers gave many examples of these, sometimes adding new details to what they found in earlier sources. For example

Thomas of Chobham, an administrator at Salisbury Cathedral who wrote a *Summa for Confessors* shortly after 1215 which circulated widely in medieval England, criticized people who believed that if a dog howled in a house, someone in the house would soon become ill or die.[6] More than a century later he was quoted by Ranulph Higden, a monk from Chester, who added another belief: if a magpie crowed on the roof of a house a visitor would soon arrive.[7] Then in around 1400 Robert Rypon, a monk of Durham Cathedral Priory, complained in a sermon that 'if someone finds a horseshoe or iron key he says (as the common people do) "I shall be well today."'[8] Probably there were many similar beliefs and churchmen could always add new details if they wished.

What was wrong with believing in these omens? What was the difference between predicting the weather from grey clouds and predicting a visitor from a magpie on the roof? As early as the fourth century St Augustine had discussed the issue at length and his comments had a great influence on how later churchmen thought about divination. Augustine argued forcefully that omens such as these had no real connection with the events they portended. Instead he poked fun at people who believed in these 'utterly futile practices': quoting the Roman writer Cato, he pointed out that it was not an omen if mice nibbled your slippers; but if the slippers nibbled the mice, then you would know something strange was going on. He also denounced the use of astrology to predict people's futures for the same reason: the stars had no real connection with the events astrologers claimed to predict. After all, twins born at almost the same time could go on to lead significantly different lives so what was the use of making predictions based on the time a person was born? In the twelfth century Augustine's comments were summarized in the *Decretum* of Gratian, one of the most influential canon law textbooks, so they were known to many later educated clergy.[9]

Augustine used mockery to attack omens but he also argued they were a serious problem because demons might use people's superstitions to their own advantage. If demons saw people observing omens then they might intervene to make those omens come true, in order to distract the unwary from their faith in God: and that was why believing in omens was magic, just as other forms of trafficking with demons (knowingly or unwittingly) were.[10] Pastoral writers in medieval England knew their Augustine and they treated omens with the same combination of mockery and seriousness. Thus an *exemplum*, or moral story, told by the fourteenth-century friar John Bromyard ridiculed a belief we have already encountered in Peter of Blois' letter on omens: the idea that meeting a monk or priest on the road signified bad luck on the journey. In this story a priest became annoyed because when he passed a woman on the road, she crossed herself to ward off any misfortune that might come to her after experiencing such a bad omen. The priest responded by pushing her into a ditch, to show her that believing in omens was much more dangerous than meeting a priest![11] But putting your faith in omens could have much more serious consequences. Another *exemplum* which was widely copied told of a woman who heard a cuckoo cry five times on May Day. She took this as an omen that she had five years left to live and so when she fell ill soon afterwards she refused to make confession, assuming she would recover. Since this was a moral story she died shortly afterwards without receiving the last rites – a warning to others who might be tempted to trust in omens.[12]

Counting bird cries was simple, cheap and did not require education and so almost anyone might believe in omens like these, but a few pastoral writers also expressed concerns about a more academic way of interpreting the natural world: astrology. Astrology was a specialist skill. The practitioner had to read astrological texts, which were often in Latin, and know the positions of the planets and enough arithmetic to calculate horoscopes effectively. The level of technical knowledge involved is shown by surviving medieval astrological calculations such as the ones left by the astrologer and medical practitioner Richard Trewythian, who lived in fifteenth-century London (illus. 4).[13] Some kinds of astrology were accepted as natural, since many medieval people believed the stars could affect the natural world and even the human body: for example, the University of Paris's medical faculty pointed to a malign conjunction of planets as one of the causes of the Black Death in 1348.[14] But not all kinds of astrology were accepted as purely natural, and despite its learned trappings Augustine had denounced astrology as false and magical, just as omens were.

Because astrology was restricted to people with education and access to books, it was less of a priority for many churchmen than were more widespread beliefs about omens, and many pastoral manuals did not mention it. Nevertheless, a few did, including some which were widely read in medieval England. When they did so they took the same approach as they did to other forms of divination, focusing on whether astrology could predict the future by natural means. In the process they took pains to distinguish between legitimate and illicit kinds of astrology, in a way that Augustine had not. Their reasoning was explained in one of the most widely circulated medieval pastoral manuals, the *Summa for Confessors* written by the German Dominican friar John of Freiburg in 1297–8:

> If someone employs careful observation of the stars to predict future accidental or chance events, or even to predict people's future actions with certainty, this will proceed from a false and vain opinion, and therefore is mixed up with the opinion of a demon, and so it will be superstitious and illicit divination. But if someone employs observation of the stars to predict future things which are caused by the heavenly bodies, such as droughts and rainfall and other things of this kind, that will not be illicit divination.[15]

In other words astrology could genuinely predict certain things and it became magic only when it strayed beyond this to predict people's future actions. These could not be predicted because God had given mankind free will, which gave people the power to overrule the stars. Here John was drawing on the ideas developed slightly earlier by the theologian Thomas Aquinas, but he also reflected a more widespread consensus among many intellectuals about the possibilities and limits of astrology.[16]

In theory, then, it was clear why omens and the use of astrology to predict people's actions were magic and why weather forecasting, medical prognosis and other forms of astrology were not. With omens and astrology, the signs that people observed had no genuine connection with the events they predicted, but in prognosis and weather forecasting, the prediction was based purely on the observation of natural processes. But things were not always so clear-cut. In practice many people seem to have accepted as natural a wider variety of ways of predicting the future than the pastoral writers did; or at least they do not seem to have seen them as very wrong. The London astrologer Richard Trewythian, for example, used astrology to predict a wide range of events and uncover information about the present.[17] Most of his predictions related to the natural world, such as forecasting the weather or the quality of that year's harvest; or were predictions of general events such as wars, but some were more questionable. For example, he seems to have asked about the outcome of some political

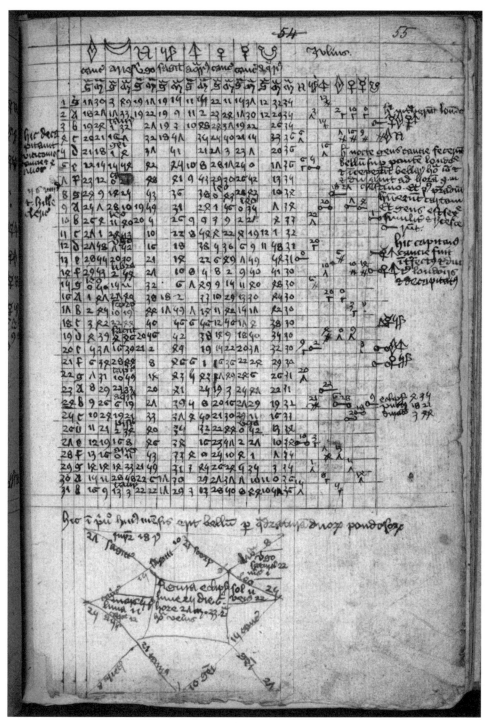

4 Astrological calculations relating to July 1450 made by the 15th-century astrologer Richard Trewythian.

events in the 1450s. This was potentially a dangerous activity because it could, in the wrong circumstances, lead to accusations of treason: it was deemed to be a short step from predicting the king's death to trying to bring it about. In other cases Trewythian asked about individual people's actions: would a missing person return? Who had committed a theft and would the stolen goods be found? If a strict pastoral writer had examined what Trewythian was doing, he would have found some of these predictions difficult to explain as natural. However, there is no evidence that either Trewythian or his clients felt such qualms. This was true of some clergy as well as laypeople. One of Trewythian's horoscopes was drawn up for an abbot whose golden cup had been stolen: probably Thomas, abbot of the small monastery of Bayham in Sussex. Trewythian provided a detailed description of the thief (ruddy complexion, greasy brown hair, pimples, a scanty beard and small eyes) but also predicted that the abbot would not find him.[18]

Other people with some education also wrote down instructions for predicting the future which strayed beyond strict definitions of what was natural. The method of thief detection quoted at the start of this chapter is one example and there are many others. Particularly attractive is a fourteenth-century chart (one of a series of charts relating to religious and astrological topics) which shows what thunder portends if it is heard in each month of the year. Thunder in January means strong winds, abundant crops and war, while thunder in December still portends abundant crops and grain but also signifies peace and concord (illus. 5).[19] Thunder predictions such as these seem to have been relatively common in medieval England. Another chart in the same set gives prognostics for the harvest based on the day of the week on which New Year's Day falls. The manuscript probably came from Worcestershire and contains portraits of two men, Harry the Hayward (pictured with his dog, Talbat) and Piers the Pinder. Haywards and pinders were officials employed on medieval manors and Harry and Piers may have been the original owners of the chart – just some of the laypeople who were learning to read in increasing numbers and who were by the end of the fourteenth century buying and owning manuscripts.

Prognostics such as these were not owned only by laypeople, however. Similar manuscripts were owned by clergy, including clergy who were interested in pastoral care, who were also the target audience of many pastoral manuals. For example an anonymous fifteenth-century collection of works relating to pastoral care contains mostly the kind

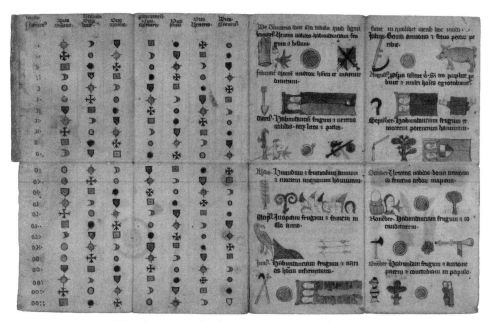

5 Thunder prognostics from an anonymous 14th-century
agricultural almanac.

of material we might expect: short treatises on confession, notes on the seven deadly sins, *exempla* and notes on theological topics. But among these there is a set of prognostications based on the day of the week on which Christmas Day falls, similar to the New Year predictions made in the chart of Harry and Piers:

> If the day of the Lord's birth occurs on a Sunday, there will be a good winter and a windy Lent, dry summer. The vines will be good and the sheep will multiply and be healthy in that year. There will be peace, the honey will be good and many healthy people will die. If [it falls] on a Monday, the winter will be changeable, Lent will be good, the summer will be windy, and it will take away from many people [the Latin text seems to be incomplete here]. The vines will not be good.[20]

These predictions were not definitely magical but they were on the edge of what could be predicted naturally. As with Harry and Piers's thunder chart, many of the predictions here are generalized statements about the weather, illnesses and mortality rates among people and animals – subjects which might legitimately be predicted by those with knowledge of the natural world. But linking thunder to war or to concord would have been harder to justify as natural, as would predictions based on the day of the week on which Christmas Day or New Year's Day falls. The Christmas Day prognostics in a compilation of pastoral texts therefore suggest that some clergy as well as laity in medieval England were less strict about divination than the pastoral writers were. This was true even of some of the educated, pastorally inclined priests who read treatises on confession and preaching.

Choosing the Right Time

From observing the natural world it was a short step to trying to engineer favourable omens to bring about the future you wanted. Richard of Wetheringsett, a pastoral writer and theologian writing shortly after 1215, complained about people who exchanged gifts and avoided performing certain actions at certain times for exactly this reason:

> People are wrong in this way when in the *hounsels* [good luck tokens] of the new year or week or day, they do not want to hand over anything to their neighbours unless they have first received a *hounsel*. They refuse [to give] fire to their neighbours while a cow is giving birth or when the breeze warms young animals [or: 'chickens'] and so forth; or they start to sow seed at weddings or even at the funerals of the dead.[21]

These beliefs are not found in earlier pastoral manuals and they may well have come from Richard's own observation. New Year's Day seems particularly to have attracted practices of this sort and had done for centuries. In the twelfth century Gratian quoted comments about New Year superstitions from earlier sources and they were still being mentioned in a New Year sermon written by the preacher John Mirk in around 1400.[22] Nor was this just a case of churchmen copying older prohibitions: practices performed at New Year and other times to secure good fortune in the future seem to have been current in medieval England. Mirk said he would not give too many details about them in case they were 'drawn into use', and Richard of Wetheringsett was not the only medieval English writer to include details not found in earlier sources. In the early fourteenth century the anonymous author of a preaching manual called *Fasciculus Morum* criticized New

Year gifts people gave 'by which they believe they will fare better or worse in the particular day, week, month, and year' and like Richard he gave English words for these: 'hansels' (again) and 'year's gifts'.[23] A few decades later Ranuph Higden described a kind of New Year divination which involved putting beans near the fire. The prediction may have been based on how the beans jumped on the hot surface, as people sometimes did with grain in earlier centuries.[24] As with omens, many other beliefs of this kind may well have gone unrecorded.

Other days also had a special significance. Several medieval English pastoral writers complained about people who performed divination and magic on the eve of St John the Baptist's day (24 June), probably because of its Midsummer position. As with New Year's Day, St John's Day superstitions can also be found widely in sources from later periods.[25]

When they thought about these practices, the key question for medieval churchmen was: was there a natural reason why some days or times might be better than others for performing certain activities? Raymond of Peñafort was the first pastoral writer to discuss the issue clearly in these terms. Raymond was a Catalan Dominican friar who compiled a textbook, or *summa*, on penance in the 1220s which was widely read and quoted by later churchmen, including many in England. He argued it was not magic to do things at particular times, if this was based on knowledge of the natural world:

> Peasants who pay attention to times for sowing seed or cutting down trees or similar things, which have a specific and natural reason why they should be done in this way, are not condemned here. Likewise physicians when they are giving medicines and letting blood and similar things for which a particular and manifest reason can be given according to medical learning.[26]

Earlier writers had not often used the word 'natural' to describe phenomena which had a physical explanation and Raymond's use of it reflected its growing use in academic circles, which was inspired by the scientific works of Aristotle. Nevertheless, Raymond's approach was similar to Augustine's: there was a physical reason why these things worked and so they were not magic. Both these exceptions also made sense. It was obvious that agriculture depended on things being done at the correct times and the idea that some medical procedures had to be done at certain times was also widespread in medieval medicine. Timing was particularly important in bloodletting, and treatises on the subject often advised physicians and surgeons to pay attention to the time of year, the day of the month, the time of day and the phase of the moon before bleeding their patients. They should also avoid the 'Egyptian Days', which were believed to be the anniversaries of the days on which God sent the plagues to Egypt in the Bible and were widely regarded as unlucky.[27] As with omens, it was not only laypeople who paid attention to these details. Some notes on good days for blood-letting in March, April and May are copied into the beginning of a manuscript belonging to Abingdon Abbey, which also includes various texts on pastoral care.[28] Raymond was therefore making sensible con-cessions to current scientific knowledge, and most later pastoral writers followed his lead.

Most, but not all. One cleric who saw things differently was John of Mirfield (d. 1407), a priest and medical writer affiliated to St Barth-olomew's Hospital in Smithfield, London, the ancestor of the modern St Bartholomew's Hospital. While at St Bartholomew's, Mirfield com-piled two books, a pastoral manual and a collection of medical recipes, and his dual background in both pastoral care and medicine gave him a unique perspective on magical cures. In his pastoral manual he used his detailed medical knowledge to debunk the idea that bloodletting had to be done on special, propitious days when the stars exerted a favourable influence:

> But such things should in no way be observed, since the benign or malign aspect of a heavenly body does not have a general influence which is fixed and determined in this way, because the influence varies according to the diversity and courses of the diverse aspects [angles between the planets] and diverse rays which descend [from the heavens]. And so they cannot always come together in a prescribed way on any particular day of the month.[29]

In other words, the influence of the planets on the human body was far too complex to reduce to a series of 'good' and 'bad' days of the month. Mirfield backed up his view by quoting the real-life experi-ence of an earlier physician, Bernard of Gordon, who wrote a treatise on bloodletting in 1308:

Gordon says of himself: 'It happened to me, however, that I calculated carefully the hour when the moon was precisely in Gemini. And afterwards I wanted to let blood from myself in the same hour but I did not remember [that it was the "bad" hour when the moon was in Gemini]. And then when everything was ready I remembered it was then the evil hour which I had previously noted. But I did not want to leave off because of that; instead I did the bloodletting and it has never gone better for me.'[30]

Mirfield's view of observing times for bloodletting was stricter than that of other churchmen and also than that of many doctors, but he approached the issue in the same way as earlier pastoral writers, asking whether the widespread beliefs about evil days had any basis in the natural world. However, the belief that there were unlucky days for bloodletting was firmly entrenched, so it is not surprising Mirfield's views were not reproduced by other pastoral writers.

Natural and Unnatural Medicines

John of Mirfield's comments about bloodletting take us into the other major area in which natural and magical activities overlapped: medicine. Some ways of curing illnesses could potentially be seen as magic, notably the wearing of amulets on the body for healing purposes and the speaking or writing of healing charms. Again medieval churchmen asked: could these practices ever work naturally? But their answers were slightly different from the ones they gave for astrology, omens and the observation of lucky times. They were less willing to mock healing charms and amulets as impossible and more willing to consider that they might have a physical effect.

Medieval pastoral writers began with a passage from St Augustine, who condemned both charms and amulets as magic:

To this category ['magic arts'] belong all the amulets and remedies which the medical profession also condemns, whether these consist of incantations, or certain marks which their exponents call 'characters', or the business of hanging certain things up and tying things to other things, or even somehow making things dance. The purpose of these practices is not to heal the body, but to establish certain secret or even overt meanings.[31]

For Augustine these practices were magic because they did not have a direct physical effect on the body, as medicine did, but instead acted as signs (the 'meanings' he talks about) to demons, who brought about the desired result. But even as he condemned magic, Augustine accepted cures which worked by physical means and claimed members of the medical profession as allies against magical cures. This recognition that medicine could work naturally meant that many medical practices were never viewed as magic because their physical effects were not in doubt. These included ointments, bloodletting, surgery and most medicines which were designed to be taken internally. All these were believed to affect the body, either directly (as in surgery) or by restoring a person's humours to a healthy balance. Instead later medieval churchmen focused on the narrow range of practices whose physical effectiveness was questionable. John of Freiburg made the point clearly in a discussion of magical cures which was quoted by many later writers:

> In those things which are done to produce some effects on the body, it should be considered whether they seem able to cause these kinds of effect naturally; and if so, it will not be illicit. But if they do not seem able to cause these kinds of effect naturally, it follows that one is dealing with certain pacts entered into with demons ... This is especially apparent when some characters or unknown names or various other observances of any kind are added, which manifestly do not have a natural effect.[32]

As he did when he discussed astrology, John of Freiburg borrowed much of this from the theology of Thomas Aquinas but both writers agreed with Augustine: some cures had a physical effect, which John, like Raymond of Peñafort, termed 'natural', and anything beyond this was magic. However, behind this broad agreement with Augustine, John's (and Aquinas's) comments show a different approach. Where Augustine had condemned all incantations, amulets and written characters, John of Freiburg and other pastoral writers from the thirteenth century onwards were more precise, singling out some amulets and incantations but not others. Thus John did not mention every incantation but only ones which contained 'unknown names' or 'characters'.

As well as trying to be more precise about what counted as magic, late medieval churchmen also had to contend with new practices which had not existed in Augustine's day. For example in the fifteenth century

Alexander Carpenter, the author of a long and detailed pastoral manual, described what he claimed was a real case of healing, although in fact he copied it from a Bible commentary by the fourteenth-century theologian Robert Holcot: 'Once in London a man was said to have been cured of a quartan fever by a gold image of a lion made according to specific constellations.'[33] Astrological images such as these were probably derived from Arabic science and astrology, and they were designed to mobilize the power of the stars to cure the sick person. Similar ideas underlay some of the Arabic astrological magic texts discussed in chapter Five, which were translated into Latin in the twelfth and thirteenth centuries. Some observers argued that healing images such as these were magic, because it was not clear how an image of a lion could cure anyone's illness naturally. However, other medical practitioners recommended them: the Catalan physician Arnold of Villanova (d. 1311) even claimed to have used one to cure Pope Boniface VIII of kidney stones.[34] For new practices such as this, Augustine did not give much guidance. Therefore, when they discussed healing, many late medieval pastoral writers in England and elsewhere departed from Augustine's views in important ways that reflect deeper shifts in medieval religious and intellectual culture. They never openly criticized Augustine – his prestige was too great for that – but they did nevertheless present their own, different ideas, designed to respond to practices which existed in the world around them.

The most important change was in their attitude to the wearing of stones or herbs on the body to cure illnesses. Augustine had labelled these amulets as magic but from the thirteenth century onwards pastoral manuals often ignored them because by this time the power of stones and herbs to affect someone who wore them was widely accepted as natural. Texts called lapidaries set out the properties of stones in detail and they circulated quite widely in medieval England (and elsewhere in Europe), both in Latin and in English, from the twelfth century onwards. They presented the wondrous properties of stones as part of the natural world, put there by God himself.[35] Some pastoral writers took a similar view. The thirteenth-century Dominican friar Thomas of Cantimpré, based in what is now Belgium, even discussed the powers of precious stones in his collection of *exempla* so that preachers could use them to illustrate the wonders of Creation and so inspire their listeners to religious devotion.[36]

Outside educated circles people also wore stones and plants for their medicinal properties. We know little about the wearing of plants because they do not survive but at the more expensive end of the scale many pieces of medieval jewellery were probably thought to have protective or healing as well as decorative functions. For example, a thirteenth-century quartz pendant found in Winchester and now in the British Museum is inscribed 'AGLA', the initial letters of the Hebrew phrase *Ata Gibor Leolam Adonai*, 'Thou art mighty for ever, o Lord' (illus. 6). It may have been designed to combine the holy words with the power of the quartz. The Middleham Jewel, discussed in chapter Four (illus. 11), a gold and sapphire pendant with prayers inscribed on it, may have worked in a similar way, combining the prayers with the sapphire's powers. Written sources from the period also mention pieces of jewellery which were used for healing. One set of healing rings even led to a court case in 1220, when Philip de Albini claimed he had lent them to Alice de Lundreford and sued her for refusing to return them.[37]

Given how accepted the wearing of stones and probably also plants seems to have been, it is not surprising that when English pastoral writers mentioned the issue (which was not often) they emphasized that this was *not* magic. Thomas of Chobham stressed that the power of stones came from nature:

> natural philosophers say the power of nature is concentrated above all in three things: in words and herbs and in stones. We know something about the power of herbs and stones but about the power of words we know little or nothing.[38]

As we will see below, Thomas was unusual in taking this view of words, but in the case of herbs and stones the idea was far more common. In the fifteenth century Robert Rypon made the same point and backed up his view by quoting the thirteenth-century pastoral writer, bishop and theologian Robert Grosseteste:

> Grosseteste says certain herbs have healing power and can be worn with the Gospel [of St John, whose opening words were often recited or written for protection and healing] or the words of the Lord's Prayer or the Creed, as long as nothing is intended other than the honour of God and the health of the sick person.[39]

For most late medieval clergy, then, wearing stones and herbs for their medicinal properties was natural and not magic, despite what Augustine had said.

6 A 13th-century silver
and amethyst pendant
bearing the magical
word 'AGLA' on its
reverse.

With other healing practices there was more room for argument, but here too the debate revolved around what was natural and what was physically possible. Thomas of Chobham went furthest when he argued, unusually, that words could affect the body naturally, just as herbs and stones could. Thomas based his view on what he claimed were real examples: the exorcisms devised by the Old Testament King Solomon, which according to legend could do many marvellous things. Almost all of Solomon's knowledge had been lost over the centuries but still, Thomas said,

> just as a certain herb has a certain effect on the human body
> and another herb an effect on something else, so the sound

of one syllable is believed naturally to have a certain effect
to do or change something which affects a certain substance,
and the sound of another syllable another effect. And just as
various herbs joined together have some power in a medicine
that none has on its own, so too several syllables or several
utterances have a certain effect on earthly things if they are
offered together which they do not have when offered individually.[40]

Combinations of words could therefore have a marvellous effect
on the body purely through physical means. This was within the bounds
of thirteenth-century science and a few scientific writers agreed with
Thomas that speaking the right words could have a physical effect
on the human body.[41] But it was always a minority position and it was
not reproduced by later pastoral writers. Indeed, in the fifteenth century Alexander Carpenter argued, quoting the fourteenth-century
theologian Robert Holcot, that King Solomon's exorcisms were a bad
example: the Old Testament king had at times lapsed into idolatry, so
he might have learned his exorcisms from demons.[42] Pastoral writers
probably failed to accept the power of words when they did accept
the powers of herbs and stones partly because there was no body of
scientific texts on the power of words to counter Augustine's condemnation of 'incantations', in the way lapidaries did for stones. In
addition to this, it is also likely that Thomas of Chobham's view of
the power of words did not gain much acceptance from other pastoral
writers because it was difficult to apply in practice. Thomas had said
perhaps some words might work through mysterious natural causes but
it was not clear which ones or how anyone could decide. By contrast
Augustine and, following him, later writers such as John of Freiburg
offered a much clearer view which was easier to apply in practice:
words could not work naturally. But what pastoral writers took away
with one hand they sometimes gave back with the other. As we will
see in chapter Two, words were used widely in medieval healing but
they tended to be viewed not as natural medicines, but as prayers.

When they thought about predicting the future and healing, then, the
clergy of medieval England who were interested in pastoral care were
faced with a wide range of very diverse beliefs and practices which
made use of the natural world. Even pastoral writers admitted many

of these were widespread and difficult to refute. Partly this was because they were useful. In the face of illness or uncertainty about the future there was a strong temptation to try any method of healing or divination that might work, without thinking too hard about whether it was natural or magical. An early fifteenth-century devotional treatise, *Dives and Pauper*, addressed this problem directly. The treatise was written in the form of a conversation between a wealthy layman, Dives, and a poor man, Pauper, described as a friar. At one point Dives says he cannot see why it is wrong to use magic to identify a thief: surely it is a good deed to catch a thief by any means possible? Pauper replies with the conventional theological position: divination involves the devil and is therefore wrong. Then he goes on to meet Dives's pragmatic objection with some pragmatic arguments of his own. The devil, who is after all the father of lies, may well point the finger at an innocent person just to cause trouble. Even without the devil's involvement, divination to identify thieves could lead to chaos: people could accuse their enemies of whatever they liked 'and say that the Fiend or the witch told it him'. But the fact that the work's anonymous author included this exchange at all suggests not everyone agreed.[43]

Predictions based on the natural world were also difficult to argue against because they seemed to work. The fourteenth-century theologian Robert Holcot, whose commentary on the Book of Wisdom in the Bible was widely read and quoted by preachers and pastoral writers (including, as we have seen, by Alexander Carpenter), emphasized that omens were based on many people's experiences. The ancients had 'proved by many experiences' that meeting a monk on the road was a bad omen for hunting, and more recent experience was also on the side of omens: 'It has been the experience of various people that certain pieces of business warn of bad outcomes: such as meeting a hare is a bad thing and meeting a toad signifies a good thing.' Similarly 'it is many people's experience that it is dangerous and irksome to begin work or journeys on certain days, such as Tuesdays'.[44] It was possible to argue that all this 'experience' was mistaken, and some pastoral writers did, but Holcot's comments point to the difficulties educated clergy faced when they argued against such diverse, widespread and useful beliefs based on the natural world.

In response to these problems, the medieval clergy who wrote about pastoral care developed clear guidelines about what was natural and what was magic. They used the new ideas about nature which were coming out of academic theology and scientific writing as a tool to carve out a sphere of future prediction and healing which was natural and therefore legitimate. Beyond this, anything that could not work naturally was magic. Thomas of Chobham's comments about the power of words and John of Mirfield's comments about bloodletting show there was scope for debate about certain practices, but individual views such as these were comparatively rare. Among most authors, a consensus emerged over the thirteenth century and it stuck. It may not have taken account of the full scope of medieval scientific writing – both Thomas of Chobham and John of Mirfield's views could be found in other writers too – but it probably corresponded to what most educated clergy found sensible and to what people actually did when faced with illnesses and other problems. It was also clear and easy to communicate to less educated clergy and to the laity.

One consequence of this approach was that it placed a high value on people who had specialist knowledge and expertise relating to the natural world. As we have seen, Raymond of Peñafort conceded that peasants who knew about agriculture and doctors who knew about illnesses could legitimately do things at specific times because they understood the natural reasons which lay behind their actions. So valuable was expertise in interpreting the natural world that these specialists could sometimes produce marvellous results which looked like magic. Thomas of Chobham made the point in detail:

> A doctor does not sin who through the subtlety of his art predicts someone's death in the future long before it comes, even though this seems miraculous to ignorant people. Similarly whoever by natural investigation of the air and planets observes fair weather or storms in the future, or fertility or sterility, or plagues or diseases, or cheerfulness or sadness in people (because people can be made sad or happy by the disposition of the air); even though he predicts this long before it happens he does not sin unless he mixes in some vanity or incantation to demons. [45]

These debates over how far divination or healing could be seen as natural show how educated churchmen tried to develop more precise ways of distinguishing between magic and legitimate activities, based on other current intellectual trends. They did this in response to practical concerns about specific activities such as medicine, astrology and agriculture. In this way we can see pastoral writers applying theoretical ideas about the natural world to what they believed was the lived experience of medieval England. They tried to navigate through this experience by using the concepts of what was natural and what was possible. But the world could also be influenced in another way: by God. Once God was involved it was irrelevant whether something was natural or possible, because God could step outside nature and do the truly impossible.

Chapter Two

Charms, Prayers and Prophecies:
Magic and Religion

St Mary enchanted her son against the bite of elves and the
bite of men, and she joined bone to bone, and blood to blood,
and joint to joint, and so the boy recovered.[1]

This charm was recorded in the mid-fourteenth century by the
Hereford friar and preacher John Bromyard. It was probably used
for healing sprains, since versions of it were still being used for this
purpose in the west of England and elsewhere in Europe as late as the
nineteenth century.[2] Bromyard condemned charms such as this one
as 'lies and contrary to the Catholic faith' but he also complained that
not everyone agreed: 'they say, both those who do them and those
who consent to them, that they speak the holy words of God and St
Mary and the other saints, and many prayers'.[3] The charm's persistence suggests this was indeed a widespread view. John Bromyard's
words point to the second major problem medieval English churchmen faced when they thought about magic: how to distinguish it from
legitimate religion. Like the borderline between magic and the natural
world, the line between magic and religion was difficult to identify, and
different people could take very different views of practices which
were close to that borderline.

The situation was still more complicated because all medieval
religious writers accepted that, in theory, it was possible for some
people to predict the future through the power of God. The Bible contained many instances of prophecy, from Joseph's ability to interpret
dreams in Genesis to the final vision of the end of the world in the
Book of Revelation. Miraculous healing was also firmly entrenched
in Christian tradition. It was especially prominent in the New Testament, which tells of how Jesus cured many ill, disabled and possessed

people. Drawing on these biblical precedents, medieval legends relating to the saints told of how God helped these special men and women to heal and prophesy, and they often modelled their stories on Christ's own healing miracles. The *Golden Legend*, a popular thirteenth-century collection of saints' lives, included many of these stories: St Remy foresaw a famine and St Dominic, 'moved by the spirit of prophecy', predicted to the prior of a monastery in Bologna that he himself would die long before the prior did, while St Agnes brought back to life a young man who was struck dead by the devil when he tried to rape her (an action which the local pagan priests mistook for magic).[4] However, despite its clear examples of miraculous prophecies and healings, the Bible also contained many warnings against false prophets. Medieval churchmen were therefore well aware that they needed to find ways to distinguish between true and false miracles and to determine when divine inspiration was present and when it was not.

From the thirteenth century onwards, clergy who were interested in pastoral care began to develop clear ideas about which practices should be regarded as magical and which as religious. Churchmen in earlier centuries had also been interested in this issue and had denounced certain unofficial healing and divinatory practices as magic, and their comments continued to be quoted by later writers. But in the thirteenth century, educated clergy discussed in more depth exactly where the line lay between magic and religion, just as they did when they thought about the borderline between magic and the natural world. They approached different practices on a case-by-case basis, offering a measure of acceptance to some while condemning others very harshly. Generally, however, the clergy was far more cautious about divination and healing that overlapped with religion than that which overlapped with ways of interpreting the natural world and manipulating natural forces.

When they dealt with these issues pastoral writers discussed a few practices in great detail: drawing lots or performing other randomized actions (such as throwing dice) to determine the will of God when important decisions had to be made; the interpretation of dreams; and the use of charms or prayers in healing, either when they were spoken over a sick person or when they were written down and worn as an amulet. Their reactions to these practices show the scope for variation which existed when clergy thought about the difference between magic and religion, and also some of the factors which led them to label some practices as religious and others as magical.

When they thought about the boundaries of magic and religion, churchmen also had to confront a further issue: who was entitled to offer religious divination or healing? When people claimed to predict the future, they were claiming they had the authority and knowledge to do so correctly – that they could reveal a future known only to God and could guarantee they were not communicating with demons. Similarly if someone claimed his or her prayers could heal then that, too, was a claim to special religious knowledge and status. Churchmen were concerned that, without the authority of the church, such people might be mistaken and might adapt Christian rituals in ways that were unacceptable and magical. Therefore when they condemned divination and magical healing they did so partly because they wanted to reserve the authority to heal and predict the future for the people sanctioned by the church, who could be trusted to act responsibly.[5]

Drawing Lots

In the New Testament the Apostles are described as drawing lots after the Crucifixion, when they elected Matthias as the twelfth Apostle to replace Judas Iscariot (Acts 1:23–6). This incident attracted much attention from later commentators because by the fifth century church councils were criticizing as magic lot-casting and other randomized activities which were used to generate answers to questions. They singled out for particular criticism a book called the *Lots of the Saints*. To use the *Lots of the Saints* you threw three dice and each combination of numbers led to a particular prediction. Three sixes, for example, generated this optimistic answer:

> After the sun the stars come out and the sun once more recovers its bright light. So too in a short while will your mind return to brightness from the point where you seem to be in doubt. And it will come to you, and you will obtain what you desire with God's help. Give him thanks. [6]

As this prediction shows, the *Lots of the Saints* was firmly Christian in its language. Combined with the precedent of the Apostles, this posed a problem for later churchmen who had doubts about lot-drawing. If it was wrong to draw lots then why had God allowed the Apostles to do it? Was it in fact wrong in all situations? Early Christian theologians took different views of this and the comments of St Jerome (d. 420), the Anglo-Saxon theologian Bede (d. 734) and others were summarized by the law teacher Gratian in his canon law text-book, the *Decretum*, in the 1140s. Gratian himself proposed a neat compromise: drawing lots was not wrong in itself and God had per-mitted people to do it in the past but now it was prohibited in case it encouraged people to turn back to pagan idolatry. The reasoning behind this was that lot-drawing encouraged people to put their faith in the lots rather than in God – an argument which expresses a deeper concern that ordinary people could not be trusted to per-form activities like lot-casting and healing responsibly.[7] Because Gratian's textbook was so widely read in later centuries, it was his view which was transmitted to later educated churchmen, in England and elsewhere in Europe.

However, Gratian's solution did not prevent other groups within the Church from thinking differently. The *Lots of the Saints* contin-ued to be copied into the later Middle Ages and by the twelfth century it had acquired a new name, the *Lots of the Apostles*, which linked it firmly with the Apostles' lot-drawing and so gave it extra legitimacy.[8] Lot-drawing also continued to be performed, most notably during the elections of bishops. Some time between 1216 and 1227 Pope Honorius III reprimanded the cathedral chapter of Lucca in Italy for doing it to decide who from the chapter would nominate candidates for the bishopric. In this case things worked out rather well: a Master Robert was duly elected and Honorius deemed him a suitable can-didate and confirmed him as bishop. But the Pope forbade the use of lot-casting in future.[9]

These debates about whether it was legitimate to cast lots were not just confined to a few isolated texts like the *Lots of the Saints/Apostles* and a few specific situations such as episcopal elections. They were part of a wider shift in educated clergy's views of whether it was legitimate to perform activities which asked God to reveal his will to mankind. The problem here was the assumption that God would intervene to answer questions relating to everyday life. For centuries many church-men had seen nothing wrong with this, even if some had qualms over the *Lots of the Saints*. From the twelfth century onwards, however, some intellectuals were beginning to see this as impious: people should not, they thought, expect God to answer questions about mundane matters, especially if they had other ways of solving the problem. It was perfectly legitimate to pray for help, but people should not perform

an activity which required God to answer or even tried to force him
to do so.[10]

Most of this debate centred on the practice of trial by ordeal. This
was used to resolve legal cases when there was no other means of proof.
It took various forms but generally the accused person was required
to undergo a dangerous or painful test, such as putting a hand into
boiling water or grasping a hot metal bar. Once the test had taken
place, it was believed God would reveal the truth of the case: if the
accused person's burned hand was healing well after three days, God
was deemed to be on their side, but if it had become infected, the
accused was guilty. Trial by ordeal was a centuries-old practice and earlier churchmen had promoted it as a religious activity, but by the early
thirteenth century it was increasingly coming under fire from educated theologians who objected to the way it apparently forced God
to intervene in human affairs. Consequently in 1215 Pope Innocent III
forbade clergy from taking part in ordeals and by the late thirteenth
century some pastoral manuals were even denouncing them as a form
of magic.[11]

It is likely that the same concern about practices which required
God to give answers lay behind Honorius III's ban on drawing lots in
episcopal elections, but for a while there continued to be scope for
debate. A few early thirteenth-century pastoral writers continued to
believe lots might be legitimate under some circumstances. For example in the 1220s, the Catalan friar Raymond of Peñafort, who wrote a
widely copied textbook or *Summa* on penance, permitted some forms
of lot-casting:

> If the cause was honest and the necessity was pressing, for
> example if there was a dispute about the election of some
> candidates and both were equal in every way, I believe that
> following the example of Matthias lots can be cast.[12]

The early thirteenth-century English writer Thomas of Chobham,
an administrator for the diocese of Salisbury who wrote a *summa* for
confessors shortly after 1215, agreed: lot-drawing might be permis-
sible if it was used to seek out information which was necessary and
not harmful to anyone, and if there was no other way of answering
the question.[13] Both Raymond's and Thomas's textbooks were widely
copied and influenced what many later writers said about magic – but
not on this point. Once Honorius III's letter reprimanding the clergy

of Lucca became an accepted part of canon law, any lingering support for lot-drawing vanished. In the light of this change William of Rennes, who wrote glosses on Raymond of Peñafort's *Summa* in the 1240s, flatly contradicted Raymond's comments on lot-drawing: 'I do not believe casting lots should have a place in elections today.'[14] No later pastoral manual claimed that lots might be legitimate under some circumstances.

A papal ban and a lack of sympathy from educated clergy did not stop every method of foretelling the future by throwing dice or drawing lots, of course. The *Lots of the Apostles* continued to be copied and it was translated from Latin into European vernacular languages, which only made it more accessible.[15] Other texts which gave instructions for fortune-telling by throwing dice or performing other chance activities also survive. Some of these may have been designed to entertain rather than to generate serious predictions: one known as the 'Chance of the Dice' refers to famous lovers from medieval literature such as King Arthur's knights and their ladies, which suggests it was written as a form of courtly entertainment.[16] Nevertheless, although guides to fortune-telling continued to be read and probably used, the idea that this was a legitimate way of discerning God's will and a religious activity had disappeared among educated clergy.

Interpreting Dreams

Educated clergy were even more suspicious of people who foretold the future by interpreting dreams, even though there were some striking parallels between lot-drawing and dream interpretation. There were solid precedents for both activities in the Bible. Again early Christian theologians were wary but they did not condemn all dream interpretation outright. Instead the most important writer on the subject, Pope Gregory the Great (d. 604) distinguished between several different kinds of dreams. Some had identifiable physical or mental causes such as hunger, drunkenness, anxiety, or memories of recent events. Some dreams came from God but others were inspired by the Devil. Because dreams could have so many different causes, Gregory advised dreamers to be extremely cautious about how they interpreted them but he did not rule out the possibility of divinely inspired dreams, and his comments were copied by later writers.[17] And again treatises which told people how to interpret their dreams circulated throughout the Middle Ages despite ecclesiastical doubts. In medieval England their owners included King Richard II and the monasteries of Reading and Bury St Edmunds.[18]

Nevertheless, late medieval pastoral writers were united in condemning dream interpretation as far as they could. They warned that dreams which seemed divinely inspired might turn out to be meaningless or, worse, demonic deceptions. Thus Richard of Wetheringsett, who wrote a manual for priests shortly after 1215, said it was stupid to hope for a divine revelation. Both Richard and the widely read French pastoral writer Guillaume Peyraut (writing in the 1230s) also stressed that dreams led many people into error.[19]

Some individual writers went even further to minimize any possibility that ordinary people might have prophetic dreams. John Bromyard, the Hereford friar who was so critical of charms, was one of the most extreme. According to Bromyard no one, under any circumstances, should ever believe in their dreams. Even if dreams did, exceptionally, turn out to be divine revelations, the events they predicted would happen (or not) at God's pleasure irrespective of whether the dreamer believed their dream.[20] Bromyard's preaching manual was widely read by later authors of sermons and at least one preacher quoted him on this point: Robert Rypon, a monk of Durham Cathedral, in around 1400.[21] However, most churchmen were more moderate and did not rule out the possibility of divinely inspired dreams altogether. For example one of Bromyard's contemporaries and fellow Dominican friars, the theologian Robert Holcot, admitted some dreams were sent by good spirits and he was quoted in the 1420s by the pastoral writer Alexander Carpenter.[22] Holcot and Carpenter also suggested another possibility: some dreams could give insight into the future for purely natural reasons. To support this they cited the scientific works of Aristotle and the thirteenth-century theologian Albertus Magnus, which said dreams could reflect physical changes in the body such as imbalances of the four humours, and so they could warn someone if he or she was becoming ill.[23] This gave further support to the idea that some dreams could predict the future but it moved them out of the sphere of divine revelation and brought them into the natural world.

However, although Robert Holcot and (following him) Alexander Carpenter were a little more willing than John Bromyard to acknowledge that some dreams were divinely inspired and others might be trustworthy for natural reasons, they were hardly encouraging. Their conclusions were: 'First, divination by dreams is licit [in some circumstances]. Second, such divination should not be expected from all dreams. Third, divination by dreams is very dangerous.'[24] Despite differences of emphasis, these writers shared an important message: dreams which appeared to predict the future should be approached with great caution and you believed them at your peril.

To underline this point many writers of preaching manuals and sermons told *exempla* about people whose dreams initially seemed to be divinely inspired but in fact turned out to have been sent by demons. In these stories the dreams either proved to be false or came true in unexpected and terrible ways. John Bromyard collected several of these, since they fitted well with his strong stance against believing in dreams. He told of one man who dreamed that if he killed a certain hermit he would become king of Sicily. He killed the hermit but did not become king and instead, predictably, was hanged for murder. Bromyard also retold the legend of Pope Sylvester II (d. 1002), who was said to have sold his soul to the Devil in exchange for magic powers. The Devil told Sylvester he would not die until he had voluntarily entered Jerusalem, so the pope thought he was safe; but when he entered the Church of the Holy Cross in Jerusalem in Rome he knew he had been tricked and was saved only by last-minute repentance.[25] Preachers also used these stories and others like them: Thomas of Chobham told one in a sermon in the early thirteenth century, while Robert Rypon retold several of Bromyard's stories about dreams in a sermon on magic.[26] Therefore, while they did not deny the possibility of divinely inspired dreams, in practice medieval English pastoral writers taught the laity to be suspicious of their own dreams and they backed this up with what they claimed were true stories.

These warnings about dreams were particularly a feature of confession and preaching manuals. In other circumstances churchmen were more willing to discuss prophetic dreams. After all, the prophetic dreams found in the Bible were well known. For example an illuminated psalter made in Oxford in the thirteenth century depicted the three Magi of the New Testament being warned by an angel in a dream not to reveal baby Jesus's whereabouts to King Herod (illus. 7). Even works written with preaching in mind might promote some prophetic dreams as a good thing: the *Golden Legend* told how the mothers of Saints Dominic and Bernard of Clairvaux both had dreams about their child's future greatness while they were pregnant.[27] However, these stories dealt with special circumstances and they were probably not seen as guidelines for everyday life. When they instructed

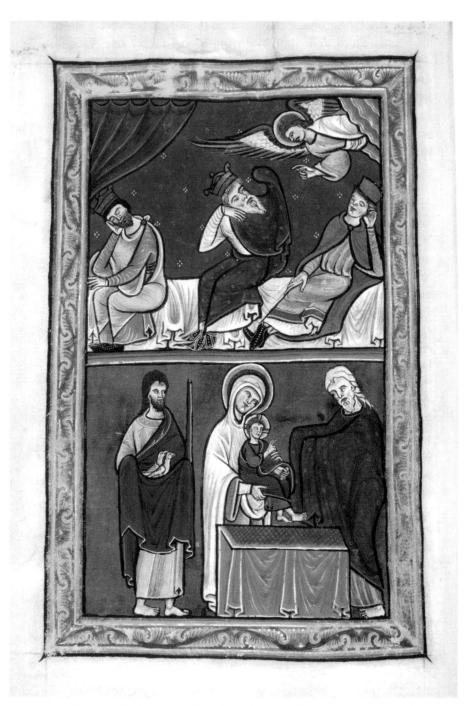

7 The three Magi are warned in a dream by an angel not to return to Herod;
from an English psalter of *c*. 1240.

the laity on the distinction between legitimate and illegitimate practices, pastoral writers were far less open-minded and more conscious
of the dangers of believing in dreams.

Words to Heal the Sick

At first glance, medieval English pastoral writers seem to have been
equally suspicious of religious forms of healing. For example several of
them quoted a criticism of medicinal 'incantations' which originated
centuries earlier and came to them through Gratian's *Decretum*:

> Nor is it permitted to give credence to certain incantations or
> observations [recited] when collecting medicinal herbs, except
> only with the divine Creed or the Lord's Prayer, so only God,
> the Creator and Lord of all things, is honoured. [28]

This was a strict view of charms: apart from a few well-known
prayers, any words recited over herbs were 'incantations' and should
be avoided. It was repeated by later writers including Thomas of Chobham (even though as we have seen Thomas believed some words could
affect the body naturally) and Raymond of Peñafort.[29] However, it
was probably too strict for many educated clergy and often later pastoral writers found ways to limit the ban. Their approach to healing
charms and prayers was therefore more flexible than their approach
to predicting the future. Thus at the same time as they became stricter
in their view of lot-drawing and dream interpretation, educated
clergy were becoming less strict in their view of healing charms. This
was largely thanks to one man, William of Rennes, who as we have
seen wrote glosses on Raymond of Peñafort's *Summa* on penance in
the 1240s. After the 1240s William's glosses were copied routinely into
manuscripts of Raymond's *Summa* as a standard commentary and
they had a great influence on how later clergy distinguished between
religious and magical cures.

On the subject of magical healing, Raymond of Peñafort himself had simply quoted the passage which banned anything other
than the Lord's Prayer and the Creed from being recited over herbs.
William of Rennes wrote a long commentary on this passage in which
he analysed much more carefully the use of both spoken and written
words in healing. First he discussed *brevia*, written amulets which contained prayers and other words and symbols and were worn to cure

illnesses or protect against misfortune. These were probably common (and they remained popular in later centuries) but because they were single sheets of parchment, they could easily be lost or worn out and only a few survive, including an elaborate one now in Canterbury Cathedral Library.[30]

For William of Rennes, *brevia* that consisted simply of quotations from the Gospels, were acceptable. This was a logical extension of the old view that only official prayers should be recited over medicinal herbs but it was no longer enough on its own to distinguish between religion and magic. William warned that even legitimate *brevia* could become magical if people put faith in the observances they performed while writing them: for example if people believed *brevia* were more effective if they were written out at a specific time, such as during Mass. *Brevia* could also be rendered magical if they combined official prayers with 'certain characters and certain unfamiliar names' or if they made sweeping promises such as 'whoever carries this *breve* on themselves will not be endangered in such and such a way, or this or that good thing will happen to them'.[31]

William therefore raised two areas of concern. First, he focused on certain identifiable characteristics: did *brevia* contain only words from the Bible, or did they combine this with unorthodox elements such as names or guarantees of good fortune or protection? Although William did not say so, his reasons for suspecting unknown names were probably the same as those set out a little later by the theologian Thomas Aquinas and repeated by another influential pastoral writer, John of Freiburg, in the 1290s: unknown names might be the names of demons, so the people who used these *brevia* could be invoking demons without realising it.[32] It is less clear why he objected to the promises of protection but he may have done so because no prayer was supposed to guarantee the future, so such promises could be seen as forcing God to act in a particular way. William's second area of concern was not about the content of the *brevia* but about the attitude of the person using them. Did they put their faith in observances which were irrelevant to a true prayer, such as writing them down at special times, rather than in the prayer itself?

William's comments marked an important departure from those of earlier clergy who had forbidden all 'incantations'. By setting out specific criteria which made *brevia* magical, he implicitly permitted other cures which used words – although with some reservations, as we will see. This more tolerant position probably reflects the attitude to healing charms found in wider society, because many people seem to have recognized at least some of these as legitimate. We know more about charms than about most medieval 'magical' practices because they were often written down, by medical writers and by other literate people who found them useful. We also know quite a lot about medieval attitudes to these charms because medical writers wrote about how they could be used. Often they were not seen as 'magic'. Instead academically trained medical writers categorized charms as *experimenta* or 'empirical' remedies, which meant that they could not be explained by medieval science and could be known only from experience (rather like the method for identifying thieves quoted at the start of chapter One).

Attitudes to charms and other empirical remedies varied. Some medical writers denounced them as 'fables', since they were based on hearsay rather than scientific theory.[33] Others were ambivalent but recorded them nevertheless, such as the priest and physician John of Mirfield, who was based at St Bartholomew's Hospital in London in around 1400, and whom we have already met criticizing the use of astrology in bloodletting. John included several charms in his collection of medical recipes, but he also expressed doubts about how effective they were.[34] Other academically trained medical writers copied them without expressing any reservations at all, including John of Gaddesden, who became court physician to Edward II.[35] Despite their religious concerns, pastoral writers moved in the same circles as other educated (and uneducated) people, and they probably shared this widespread view that not all charms were magic. Therefore, in setting out a more nuanced definition of what counted as a magical cure, William of Rennes was probably making a realistic concession to current attitudes, and other pastoral writers followed him for this reason.

In turn, churchmen's views of magical cures probably also shaped the charms that were copied in medieval England. It is difficult to know how far William of Rennes and the pastoral writers who copied him shaped attitudes to charms and how far they were themselves influenced by attitudes in the world around them but it is possible to see a broadly shared view. The majority of surviving charms do not include unknown words. Instead they used words which were known, such as Greek words like *agios* (meaning 'holy'), names for God, or the names of saints and other biblical figures: the names of the three Magi in the New Testament were believed to act as a charm against epilepsy, for example.[36] These words were unusual and powerful but they were

8 Square figure drawn within a column of text that is a healing charm; from a miscellaneous English compilation of religious and secular texts, *c.* 1320.

not unknown and an educated priest could have explained the meaning of many of them.

Very occasionally we can also see cures involving unknown words arousing suspicion in practice, as well as in pastoral manuals. In 1438 Agnes Hancock was accused in front of John Stafford, Bishop of Bath and Wells, of using (among other things) cures containing 'unknown and strange words'.[37] We will return to Agnes in chapter Three because she also claimed to communicate with the fairies, which made her cures even more suspect. This case is isolated but it suggests that when strange words were combined with other suspicious practices they might occasionally attract the attention of the authorities. It also shows they were deemed to be worth mentioning when accusations of magic were made.

This does not mean everyone shared exactly the same view. Some charms did contain unknown words: for example in around 1240 the physician Gilbert the Englishman recorded a cure for infertility which required the practitioner to write the words 'Uthihoth. Thabechay. Amath' interspersed with crosses and a quotation from the Bible on a piece of parchment and give it to the infertile couple to wear during sex. If the wife wore it they would conceive a girl, if the husband wore it they would conceive a boy. A physician who read about this cure much later, in fifteenth-century Italy, remarked that the English were the greatest sorcerers in Christendom but Gilbert himself described it as an 'empirical' remedy, not as magic.[38] Some remedies also required the practitioner to draw strange characters, such as the square design in one fourteenth-century medical manuscript, which was to be engraved on a piece of lead and laid on the sick person (illus. 8).[39] Cures which were magical by pastoral writers' standards did exist, then. But the words of many surviving charms were not obviously magical.

If charms were not obviously magical, however, they did often use prayers and religious rituals more creatively than strict theologians liked. We have already seen John Bromyard denouncing one charm which mentioned the Virgin Mary even though it contained no unknown words. Many other cures likewise mixed official prayers with additional observances. For example, one fifteenth-century collection of medical texts offered the following charm to stop a horse from bleeding:

God was born of Bethlehem, done on the rood-tree in Jerusalem, christened he was in flum [river] Jordan. Lord, as

the flood stood, so staunch this blood, be it of man or of beast,
if it be thy will.

This was to be followed by saying the Lord's Prayer and five Ave
Marias.[40] As well as adding an extra charm to the official prayers,
this cure required the prayers themselves to be said a set number of
times. For a strict pastoral writer this could be classed as magic
because it did not have any 'natural' effect and nor did it add anything to the efficacy of the prayers – just as William of Rennes had
argued for people who believed that amulets were more effective if they
were written down at particular times. However, unlike cures involving unknown words, remedies such as this are found fairly frequently
in collections of medical recipes, which suggests many people did
not see them as dangerous, in the way they may have done charms
containing unknown words.

Like charms containing unknown words, cures which combined
additional observances with prayers did at times lead to accusations of
magic. In 1527 William Brown was accused in the court of the bishop
of London of reciting the Lord's Prayer and Ave Maria five times and
the Creed three times over herbs before using them to make a medicine to cure sick horses – a practice which was in some ways similar to
the horse-curing charm quoted above. This is described in the record
as 'the magic art' and 'incantation', presumably because Brown was
speaking the prayers a set number of times, since there was nothing
wrong with the prayers themselves.[41] But cases such as this were not
common. Instead, given the number of charms which survive in medical texts and other manuscripts which require the operator to say
prayers a set number of times, it seems likely that many people were
willing to give extra observances the benefit of the doubt.

Prayers which promised certain benefits to the people who recited
or wore them also survive from medieval England despite being
denounced by William of Rennes. By the fifteenth century they were
often copied into personal prayer books known as Books of Hours.[42]
Similar protective prayers also appear in some medical manuscripts,
where they are given to ward off illnesses. An elaborate example survives in a late fifteenth-century manuscript of medical texts in English,
now in the Wellcome Library in London (illus. 9). It takes the form of
a circular diagram. In the circle are two inscriptions and the name
'Ihesu' written four times in the form of a cross. The inner inscription
is a short invocation directed to the cross, asking for protection against

the plague, or perhaps for a cure: 'Save, Cross of Christ, save me from the present straits of the pestilence, [you who] are our saviour.' The outer inscription sets out the origin of the diagram: 'A certain angel appeared to a monk, the abbot of Corby in Lincolnshire, and imprinted this figure on his hand by the command of Jesus Christ.'[43]

We do not know how the readers of the manuscript responded to this particular image, with its complex layout and angelic provenance. However, Eamon Duffy has shown that simpler protective prayers (including some which were believed to have angelic origins) were common in late medieval English culture and appealed to clergy and laity, educated and uneducated alike.[44] In this case it seems to have been the pastoral writers who judged these prayers to be magic who were in the minority. But in general, unless charms contained clearly unorthodox elements, most pastoral writers seem to have preferred not to challenge them. They concentrated instead on those which were clearly definable as magic.

Who Can Heal and Predict the Future?

In the case of charms, many late medieval English churchmen were prepared to be flexible when considering the border between religion and magic, making concessions to widespread attitudes and practices. Indeed, it is likely many of them shared the view that some charms were legitimate. But in other cases, such as dream interpretation, they were much stricter. Behind their differing responses often lay a concern about who was offering these forms of divination and healing. Who could be trusted to tell whether a dream was genuine or whether an unofficial healing charm was magic? As we saw in chapter One, several pastoral writers raised the same issues of trust and expertise when they emphasized that people with specialist skills or knowledge were the ones best qualified to predict the future by observing the natural world: doctors knew about illnesses and peasants were experts in agriculture. The same willingness to respect expertise and experience may explain why some early thirteenth-century pastoral writers allowed lot-drawing in some situations. Like medicine or agriculture, lot-drawing could be viewed as a specialist skill if it was carried out by educated clergy imitating the actions of the Apostles. However, identifying experts in dream interpretation or religious healing was much more difficult because God might grant anyone these gifts. For this reason many pastoral writers were interested not just in what people did but in what kinds of people did it.

Here their views were very varied and some writers were much more permissive than others. Perhaps not surprisingly, one of the more tolerant was William of Rennes, who took a pragmatic view of the people who used healing charms. It is worth quoting his comments in full, because of the amount of detail he gives about healing rituals and because he had such a profound influence on later writers:

> But what about enchantresses or enchanters who sing charms over the sick, children and animals? Surely they do not sin mortally? I answer that if they do not say or teach or do any-thing superstitious but use only licit prayers and adjurations (such as by the Passion and the Cross and similar things), I do not believe they sin mortally, unless they do such things after the Church has forbidden them. But I believe women and men who are accustomed to mix in very many useless and super-stitious things should be prohibited unless perhaps they are a devout and discreet priest or even a layperson, either a man or a woman, of excellent life and proven discretion, who after pouring out a licit prayer over the sick person (not over an apple or a pear or a belt and similar things, but over sick peo-ple) lays hands on them according to the Gospel of Mark, 'They shall lay hands on the sick and they shall recover.' (Mark 16.18) Nor should people of this sort be prohibited from such things unless perhaps it is feared that because of their exam-ple, indiscreet and superstitious people will see this example [the repetition is in the Latin] and practise the abuse of charms for themselves.[45]

Here William made a striking concession. He allowed some peo-ple to adapt religious rituals for healing purposes, and to go beyond official prayers if they could be trusted to do so responsibly and as long as they did not disobey a direct prohibition from the church. Moreover, William did not limit 'discretion' to any one social group. It could be found among laypeople as well as clergy, women as well as men, although the phrase 'even a layperson' suggests he thought this was rarer. In contrast to the earlier blanket prohibitions of 'incanta-tions', a priest who followed William's advice had a great deal of latitude to allow the healing practices of any parishioner who had a reputation for piety. This made the priest's task more complex but it also gave him discretion – it allowed him to use his own judgement when tackling potentially unorthodox practices which used religious language and were done for a good purpose like healing. Church court records show that in practice churchmen did sometimes consider the character and 'discretion' of healers when making judgements about their cures. This happened in the case of Henry Lillingstone from Broughton in Buckinghamshire, who was brought before the Archdeacon of Buckingham in March 1520. Lillingstone confessed to using two treatments for illnesses. One was a charm which he said was good for all conditions: 'Jesus that saved both you and me from all manner diseases I ask for saint charity Our Lord if it be your will.' The other treatment was especially good for kidney stones and colic. For this Lillingstone used the plants horehound, Alexander's foot and 'the red knoppes of marygoldes', which he mixed, ground and cooked with 'good ale and Genoese treacle' and gave to the sick person to drink. Neither of these treatments is clearly identifiable as magic from the description given in the record. The charm contained no mysterious words (although it ends quite abruptly so the court may not have recorded it in full) while the mixture of herbs involved no words or rituals. Instead the problem seems to have been Lillingstone himself. The court asked him if he was educated in Latin (*litteratus*) and where he had learned about these medicines. His reply did not inspire confidence: 'He said he was not educated but had the aforementioned knowledge only by the grace of God.'[46]

Lillingstone's trial shows that concerns about authority and status similar to those which had been raised earlier by William of Rennes could be taken seriously by bishops and their representatives, even if cases are not very numerous. Lillingstone's cures were suspect because he was not the sort of person whom the court expected to have medical knowledge, and the court did not accept that he had learned directly from God. The Lillingstone case also shows how flexible definitions of magical healing could be in practice, when they depended not on what was done but on the reputation and status of the practitioner. William of Rennes used that flexibility to allow priests to decide who could legitimately offer healing prayers. The diagram which protected against the plague, pictured overleaf, reflects the same concerns when it stresses that its source was an angel, who communicated it not just to anyone but to an abbot. This origin lent extra respectability to what could perhaps be seen as a questionable practice. For Lillingstone,

9 Talisman for protection from the plague, from a 15th-century English leech-book.

however, concerns about authority worked in the opposite way: seemingly legitimate healing practices became suspect when they were offered by a dubious practitioner.

But not every educated cleric in medieval England took this flexible approach. John Bromyard was much stricter – perhaps predictably, given his harsh criticism of people who said they used 'holy words' to heal. He required not simply discretion and a good life from people who used charms, but holy orders or even 'sanctity' (*sanctitas*, a word which could mean either general holiness or actually being a saint). God, Bromyard said,

> did not give healing power to words of any status, but where the holy orders or sanctity of the person saying them deserves it. Because just as in the words of the sacraments, the effect of the words depends more on the power of the words than the sanctity of the person quoting them, so it is the opposite for prayers and healing words and those which are associated with miracles. The effect depends more on the sanctity of the person praying or speaking than on the power of the words.[47]

These extra conditions would make it difficult for priests to sanction the use of charms by laypeople, since holiness or sanctity was a very high standard to meet. On the other hand, by implication Bromyard endorsed the use of charms by priests: sanctity *or* holy orders were enough.

It was not simply a question of trustworthy clergy against superstitious laity, however. Some laypeople were more trustworthy than others, and Bromyard was especially suspicious of the charms offered by women. Where William of Rennes discussed both male and female users of charms ('enchantresses or enchanters'), Bromyard mentioned only enchantresses.[48] His concerns about women healers were echoed by some other pastoral writers. The early fourteenth-century author of the preaching manual *Fasciculus Morum* referred to the person practising magical healing as 'some wretched old woman' and in the fifteenth century Alexander Carpenter singled out for criticism 'the invocations that elderly women make in order to cure illnesses'.[49] But not every pastoral writer singled out women and church court records suggest that in practice men and women were accused of offering magical cures in roughly equal numbers.[50] Thus although for some churchmen the use of healing charms by women was a particular concern, for many others 'discretion' and the lack of it could be found among both sexes.

The same issues of discretion, piety and good character also applied to divination, but here pastoral writers were more uniformly cautious, possibly because people who claimed to have prophetic dreams were claiming to have access to divinely inspired knowledge – a claim which carried more profound implications than using a healing charm.

Such a claim encroached dangerously on the role of the clergy, who viewed themselves as the world's mediators with God, set apart from the laity. Probably for this reason the pastoral writers worked hard to discourage people from claiming the status and authority that went with divine inspiration.

One of the ways in which they did this was by undermining the motives of people who predicted the future. For example if diviners took money for their predictions they could be denounced as false prophets. Raymond of Peñafort quoted the Old Testament prophet Micah's denunciation of prophets who took money (Micah 3:11), stating that true prophets would never do this: 'because they accepted money, their prophecy became divination; that is their divination, which was believed to be prophecy, was declared not to be prophecy.'[51] By focusing on money Raymond was probably aiming at a particular group of people: cunning folk, magical specialists who predicted the future or uncovered information for clients and also offered other services such as healing. We know little about these practitioners in medieval England but evidence from later periods suggests they were numerous. Most cunning folk probably would have made a charge for services such as identifying thieves and finding stolen goods. How much they charged varied depending on the service offered, and later examples suggest that thief detection and curing witchcraft generally cost more than simple fortune-telling.[52]

In the fourteenth century John Bromyard offered the most comprehensive medieval attack on cunning folk, criticizing them for accepting money and also attacking their characters more generally. He emphasized that cunning folk could not heal or predict the future through the power of God:

> If they were to heal people and livestock through their sanctity or predict the future by the spirit of prophecy, or name a thief through the Holy Spirit for the purpose of correcting him, and were tolerated like the other saints, both when they were alive and when they were dead . . . then the entire Church would be wrong when it teaches these people should not be believed in or revered.

That the whole church could be wrong was deeply unlikely but more to the point, cunning folk were not like saints:

For the saints, alongside all their other virtues and absti-
nences and pure life also had such humility that they fled from
those places where they performed miracles so that people's
praise would not make them vainglorious. But these [cunning
folk] gather and stay more willingly where they have more
praise and money from the people. If they have done that, even
if they had been saints before, they would lose that sanctity
which their humility did not keep under guard.[53]

Moreover, echoing Raymond of Peñafort, Bromyard emphasized that
cunning folk used their powers for profit rather than out of any
pious motives:

They do not want to do or say anything unless people bring
specific things to them, such as bread, flour, salt and similar
things, or money. Also everyone who uses this art is usually
poor, so it is presumed they use the art to make money or in
the hope of receiving it.[54]

Bromyard was unusual in giving cunning folk so much attention,
and in part it reflects his general reluctance to allow unqualified people
the discretion to adapt religious rituals. But as we have seen, the same
concerns were raised by other churchmen even if they did not take
such a strict position. Cunning folk were not the sort of people whom
God would trust with divine revelations or healing powers, and they
could not be trusted to distinguish between genuine prophecy and
the deceptions of the Devil.

The ability to predict the future or identify thieves successfully was
therefore partly a matter of authority and pastoral writers were keen
to confine that authority to the people they trusted: doctors, experts,
clergy and saints. This may explain why they said comparatively little
about forms of divination which were done by educated people, such
as astrology or lot-drawing in episcopal elections. The education
needed to do these things made them minority activities, but in addition to this, educated people were perhaps deemed more likely to be
trustworthy. By contrast churchmen were very uneasy indeed about
practices which potentially gave anybody a licence to interpret the
will of God because this infringed dangerously on the clergy's own
religious authority.

✠

Pastoral manuals therefore show that the distinction between magic and religion was a sensitive and complex issue for many educated clergy – more so than the distinction between magic and the natural world. They had to find a way of distinguishing between magic and religion which accepted the legitimacy of some forms of healing and divination because there were precedents for them in the Scriptures which it was difficult to dismiss. They also had to find a way of accommodating healing practices which were a mainstream part of their culture, and the details which pastoral manuals gave showed there were very many of these. But it was not possible to accept them all. Practices which called on God could easily become demonic if they included unorthodox elements and educated clergy did not trust everyone to adapt religious rituals responsibly.

They responded to this problem differently when faced with different practices. They forbade all forms of lot-casting and dream interpretation but acted rather differently towards healing charms. Instead of banning all healing charms, writers such as William of Rennes developed detailed criteria which set out which charms and prayers were magical. These criteria also had another side: by defining a few practices as magical, by implication they permitted anything they did not mention. Thus praying for a cure, even by slightly questionable means, was seen as less dangerous than believing that God was speaking to you directly through dreams or lot-casting, and more latitude was permitted even to ordinary pious people. As the pious parson of Chaucer's *Canterbury Tales* put it, God might tolerate the use of charms to cure illnesses so people's faith would be increased; but he did not suggest anything similar for divination.[55]

Even educated clergy who tried to offer clear guidelines to their readers therefore drew the line between magic and religion in different places in different situations. They took into account various factors: what exactly was being done, the attitude and motives of the person doing it (Thomas of Chobham emphasized that lot-drawing should not be done to uncover information which was harmful to someone, while Raymond of Peñafort criticized diviners who predicted the future for money), and the general character and status of the practitioner. This allowed them to be surprisingly flexible in their approach, leaving individual priests the discretion to judge practices and practitioners for themselves.

When they made these decisions, pastoral writers were also influenced by the world around them. Some educated churchmen took a very strict view of healing charms and the people who offered them, as John Bromyard did. However, many charms seem to have been widely used and accepted, and many pastoral writers recognized this. Outside the circle of pastoral writers, many educated people, including many clergy, were probably more tolerant still. In these circumstances it is perhaps not surprising that many pastoral writers, who shared the educated culture of their time, did not try to label every charm or protective prayer as magic. They probably found it too unlikely that all healing charms were demonic. Certainly it would have been difficult to convince their readers, let alone the laypeople whom they hoped to reach through preaching and the confessional.

CHAPTER THREE

Flying Women, Fairies
and Demons

In August 1438 Agnes Hancock appeared before John Stafford, Bishop of Bath and Wells, 'publicly defamed of the crime of magic'. Most of the accusations focused on her use of magical cures but the last one raised a separate, although related, issue:

> she herself declares that she heals children who have been touched or harmed by the spirits of the air which the common people call 'feyry'; and that she has communication with these unclean spirits and seeks answers and advice from them when she pleases.[1]

Formal accusations of trafficking with the fairies were rare but Agnes's case was not unique. In 1499 Mariona Clerk from Ashfield in Suffolk claimed to have learned how to heal and predict the future from the 'little people' called 'lez Gracyous ffayry' as well as having visions of God, the Angel Gabriel and St Stephen. She too ended up in front of the ecclesiastical authorities.[2] Even priests might occasionally claim to encounter strange beings: in 1397 John, the chaplain of Kilpeck in Herefordshire, was reported to the Bishop of Hereford's officials for not being 'firm in faith' because he had 'many times made his procession at night time with spectral spirits'.[3]

Despite the small number of recorded cases, it seems that for many people in medieval England the universe was populated by mysterious beings who existed alongside humans. Histories and works of literature described a great variety of what they claimed were popular beliefs about ghosts, walking corpses, fairies, elves and other creatures. The best overall term for these beings is 'otherworldly', since they were different from mankind and were often linked to other worlds, such as the afterlife and fairyland. These ghosts, elves and fairies were common in medieval literature and they continue to be popular in modern fiction but cases such as those of Agnes Hancock, Mariona Clerk and John of Kilpeck remind us that for some people in the Middle Ages (and in later centuries) otherworldly beings were more than good stories: they were a real part of the world.

Not surprisingly, beliefs about strange, otherworldly beings attracted the attention of educated clergy who were interested in pastoral care, in medieval England and elsewhere in Europe. Clergy who wrote confession and preaching manuals put them in their chapters on magic alongside divination, healing and other magical practices but otherworldly beings did not always fit easily into their attempts to define magic and distinguish it from the natural world on the one hand and religion on the other. As we have seen, divination and healing employed well-known practices with easily recognizable goals, and from the thirteenth century onwards churchmen were developing clear ideas about which ways of curing illnesses and predicting the future worked naturally, which were religious, and which were magic. However, beliefs about otherworldly beings were much harder to classify. There were many different kinds of otherworldly beings and while some of them could be fitted relatively easily into a Christian world-view, others were quite alien to it.

Chronicles and works of literature written in medieval England show how diverse otherworldly beings were, and also how difficult they could be to categorize. For example, in the late twelfth and early thirteenth centuries several British authors wrote descriptions of 'marvels' and unexplained phenomena for the entertainment of an aristocratic audience. They wrote in Latin but probably had in mind an audience of both clergy and educated laypeople. Three of these writers, Gerald of Wales, Walter Map and Gervase of Tilbury, told of many different otherworldly beings. They described mysterious women who were captured by human men but left them after a few years of marriage; armies of ghosts which roamed the countryside; men who turned into wolves at full moon; spirits called 'follets' which threw kitchen utensils around the house; and many more.[4] Otherworldly beings also featured prominently in romances, works of literature which told of the adventures of King Arthur and his knights or other past heroes such as Alexander the Great. These romances included beings such as giants, dwarves and fairy women who became involved with knights.[5] Both marvel literature and romances drew on folklore but they cannot be taken as accurate reflections of widespread beliefs because they were written to entertain and were almost certainly embellished. This is especially true of the romances, which were set not in their own time but in the distant past, which was portrayed as a fantasy world full of magic, marvels and glamour. Nevertheless, marvel literature and romances show that the imagination of medieval English people was populated by many different beings, and stories of those beings appealed to educated people as well as the less educated. Moreover, even educated clerics such as Gerald of Wales and Walter Map were not always too precise about exactly what these beings were, and often preferred to leave their nature ambiguous.

The wide range of otherworldly beings and their often mysterious nature posed a problem for pastoral writers. Here it was not a question of working out whether something happened naturally or by the power of God and then labelling everything else as magic. Instead there were no single, clear answers to questions such as: Could the souls of the dead return from the afterlife to interact with the living? If they could, how should the living respond to them? Were there other non-human beings out there and what was their status? The answers varied depending on what kind of beings these were and on the ways in which they interacted with people – and those things were not always obvious. Pastoral writing on otherworldly beings therefore shows how difficult it could sometimes be for churchmen to form a judgement about the relationship between magic and religion. It also shows how educated clergy who were interested in pastoral care dealt with unorthodox beliefs which did not fit neatly into their framework for defining magic.

Beliefs about Otherworldly Beings

The idea that interacting with otherworldly beings was magic had a long history in ecclesiastical writing. Medieval English clergy drew on the works of earlier churchmen to give shape to their own ideas but as with divination and healing, they added new information of their own. These additions offer a glimpse of a complicated group of beliefs about otherworldly beings: creatures who went under a variety of names and interacted with humans in ways that were both positive and negative. The starting point for most pastoral writers was a piece of canon law written by Regino, Abbot of Prüm (now in Germany) in the early tenth century. Regino claimed to have copied it from the records of an earlier church council but there is no evidence of this and he seems rather to have been describing beliefs which were current in his own time.[6] This piece of canon law is known as the Canon Episcopi, from its opening word 'Bishops' (*Episcopi* in Latin). Regino began quite generally by ordering bishops and clergy to expel from their areas any man or woman who practised the magic arts, before moving on to discuss women who had a particular set of unorthodox beliefs. This is the version of his text which was reproduced in the canon law textbook of Gratian in the mid-twelfth century, and through Gratian it became the version best known to later English churchmen:

> It is also not to be omitted that some wicked women, who have given themselves back to Satan and been seduced by the illusions and phantasms of demons, believe and profess that in the hours of night they ride upon certain beasts with Diana, the goddess of pagans, or with Herodias [the mother of Salome in the New Testament, responsible for the beheading of John the Baptist] and an innumerable multitude of women, and in the silence of the dead of night traverse many spaces of the earth and obey her commands as of their lady, and are summoned to her service on certain nights ... For an innumerable multitude, deceived by this false opinion, believe these things to be true.[7]

Regino was scathing about these beliefs. The phantasms the women saw were illusions produced by demons and the flying took place only in their dreams – and who, he asked, had not seen many things in dreams which they had never seen in the waking world? Regino's view was destined to have a long and important afterlife because from the fifteenth century onwards the Canon Episcopi was often cited in discussions of flying, devil-worshipping witches. His dismissal of the women's flying experiences as dreams posed a problem for later witchcraft writers, many of whom insisted that witches really flew and so tried to explain the discrepancy.[8] However, this aspect of the Canon Episcopi's later history does not seem to have had much impact in medieval England, where there is little evidence of beliefs about flying, devil-worshipping witches before the Reformation.

For medieval English churchmen, beliefs about flying with other-worldly ladies were part of the standard list of magical practices which they read about in Gratian's *Decretum*, wrote about in confession and preaching manuals, and occasionally prosecuted in the church courts. Quite a few pastoral writers copied the Canon Episcopi because it was a well-known piece of canon law without adding anything to it, but some added details about beliefs which they claimed were current in the world around them. These writers offer glimpses of local equivalents to the Diana beliefs, and they also show the ways in which educated clergy tried to make sense of them. Their responses were not as consistent as we might expect.

The most common beliefs about otherworldly beings which later pastoral writers described resemble the Canon Episcopi quite closely in some respects. They concerned female spirits who entered houses at night, received offerings of food and drink left by the inhabitants, and bestowed agricultural fertility or good fortune in return.[9] These ladies went under a variety of names, including the *bonae res* or 'good things', and they had several important points in common with the Diana beliefs of the Canon Episcopi. Again they were led by a goddess, sometimes now called Satia or Abundia (names which reflect the association with fertility) and again certain human beings, especially women, were believed to fly with them. In fact, it is possible the Canon Episcopi was directed against an earlier version of the same set of beliefs.

These beliefs about mysterious female spirits linked to fertility were first discussed in detail by two writers based in what is now France in the first half of the thirteenth century. One was William of Auvergne (d. 1249), a theologian who later became Bishop of Paris. William was interested in magic and even admitted to reading magical texts himself in his youth, a mistake he later came to regret. He was equally interested in other unorthodox beliefs, including beliefs relating to ghosts and other spiritual beings, and he discussed them in several of his theological works.[10] At about the same time the preacher Jacques de Vitry devised several *exempla* about mysterious ladies for his sermons. Jacques was responsible for one of the most widely copied stories about the *bonae res*. In this story an old woman told her local priest that she was able to fly at night with ladies on animals, passing through locked doors to enter houses with them. The priest's response was to lock the woman inside the church with him and beat her with the crucifix, telling her to escape through the locked door if she could. Of course she could not and the moral of the story was that anyone who claimed to fly through locked doors at night was deluded by demons.[11] Here Jacques de Vitry followed the Canon Episcopi in his view of these otherworldly ladies: they were illusions created by demons to deceive foolish, credulous women.

The *bonae res* soon transcended their origins in France. Jacques de Vitry's story about the old woman and the priest was copied by many later pastoral writers, including several in England.[12] This does not necessarily mean the belief in *bonae res* was widespread in England. English churchmen could have copied the story because they liked the way it mocked superstitious old women rather than because they wanted to combat beliefs about otherworldly beings. Nevertheless, some English churchmen described local parallels to the Canon Episcopi and the *bonae res*. For these men, the flying beings in the Canon Episcopi and in Jacques de Vitry's story were relevant to medieval England – at least in outline, if not in every detail.

Like the spirits who flew with Diana, the otherworldly beings mentioned by English pastoral writers also flew, taking their followers with them. One of the most detailed descriptions was given by John Bromyard, a friar and preacher based in Hereford in the mid-fourteenth century. Bromyard wrote a preaching manual which was widely read by later churchmen and in it he complained about women

> who say they are seized by a certain people and taken to certain beautiful and unknown places; and who also say they ride with them and in the silence of the dead of night traverse many spaces of the earth and pass over very many places.

Also to blame were 'the people who believe in these things and [believe] the women exit and enter any closed space at will'.[13]

It is probably no coincidence that the beings described by John Bromyard bear strong similarities both to the spirits of the Canon Episcopi and the *bonae res* of the *exempla*, since Bromyard knew about both of these. He placed his otherworldly beings alongside a retelling of Jacques de Vitry's story about the old woman and the priest, while the image of traversing many spaces of the earth 'in the silence of the dead of night' is a direct quotation from the Canon Episcopi. But in the introduction to his chapter on magic, where he listed the topics he planned to cover, Bromyard gave a new name for these beings: the 'beautiful people' (*pulcher populus*). Moreover, the 'beautiful people' did things which the Canon Episcopi and the *bonae res* stories did not mention. As well as flying with mortal women, they taught them divination and healing, much as Agnes Hancock's and Mariona Clerk's fairies did. Bromyard imagined magical practitioners saying 'we have not learned such things from the devil, nor do we put faith in him, but in the beautiful people.'[14] But as we will see, Bromyard's beautiful people also had a less benign side and could beat their followers. A much later series of trials, held in Friuli in northern Italy in the late sixteenth and seventeenth centuries, also refers to otherworldly beings teaching healers and beating them if they revealed their secrets, so the combination seems to have been plausible.[15]

For other English churchmen, the mysterious flying beings had yet other names. One anonymous fourteenth-century writer called them *umbrarii*. This unusual Latin word was related to *umbra*, shadow, and it was used in earlier centuries to mean a necromancer, but in this text it seems to mean a being, not necessarily human, who goes about at night: 'shadow-people' is perhaps a better translation. The priest should ask his penitent

> if he believes men and *umbrarii* go about. However it can be believed without sin that demons deceive people in such a way that they think the demons are fashioning themselves into the forms of human beings.[16]

The anonymous author of this work borrowed this passage, including the word *umbrarii*, from a slightly earlier treatise, a confession manual by the French cardinal Berengar Fredol, but he still found it worth copying. Moreover, when he did so he modified it slightly: Fredol had stated that it was not men but 'ladies' and *umbrarii* who went about, and also said they ate.[17] These details link Berengar's *umbrarii* to the female *bonae res* who were believed to consume wine in the cellars they visited, but the English version omitted this information, perhaps because the author found it less relevant. His 'shadow-people' were not obviously female and they did not eat.

Further details about otherworldly beings appear in a sermon by Robert Rypon, a monk at Durham Cathedral Priory in the late fourteenth and early fifteenth centuries. Rypon discussed beings called *phitones* or *phitonissae* who 'as it is often said by many people' put threads, ropes or bridles into people's mouths so they thought they had been transformed into the shape of horses, and rode them. 'It is said such *phitonissae* travel in one night from England to Bordeaux, from where they afterwards return, drunk on wine.'[18] Like *umbrarii*, *phitonissa* is an ambiguous and unusual word. It was ultimately derived from a seventh-century encyclopaedia by Isidore of Seville, who gave 'pythonissa' as a word for a kind of female diviner who predicted the future under the inspiration of the god Apollo.[19] Isidore's use of the word was probably known to a well-educated preacher such as Rypon but Rypon gave it a new meaning. His assertion that *phitonissae* rode people and drank wine appears to be new and it brings us back to the myths surrounding the *bonae res*, who were likewise believed to enter people's cellars and drink the wine there.

Other English pastoral manuals moved further away from the earlier written sources which told of the goddess Diana and the *bonae res*. Instead they described beings who had an English name: elves. The elves were known not for flying but for dancing with their followers. In the 1270s the *South English Legendary*, a collection of sermons on the saints written in English, talked about 'eleuene' who danced in the form of women, although the author emphasized that these elves were in fact demons.[20] Female dancing elves appeared again in an anonymous early fourteenth-century preaching manual, *Fasciculus Morum*, and the author of this work interpreted them in the light of the Canon Episcopi's description of Diana beliefs: 'superstitious wretches . . . claim that at night they see the most beautiful queens and other girls dancing in the ring with Lady Diana, the goddess of the heathens, who in our native tongue are called *elves*.'[21]

Like the 'beautiful people', elves could also be dangerous, and in particular they could carry unwary mortals off to their own world. *Fasciculus Morum* warned that elves were believed to 'change both men and women into other beings and carry them off to *elvenland*', where legendary warriors lived. [22] This seems to have been a familiar idea because works of literature also deal with the theme of abduction by otherworldly beings, for both good and bad purposes. Layamon, a poet and priest who wrote an English-language history of Britain in the early thirteenth century, tells of a beneficent otherworld abduction: when King Arthur was mortally wounded he was taken to Avalon 'to the queen Argante, fairest of fairy [or elven, *"aluen"*] women' who would heal his wounds with healing draughts.[23] But elves did not always act in the interests of mortals: in the early fourteenth-century romance *Sir Orfeo*, a retelling of the legend of Orpheus, Orfeo's queen Heurodis is abducted by the fairies very much against her will.[24]

Elves and other otherworldly creatures could also make people ill. Several tenth-century Anglo-Saxon medical texts mention them as a cause of illness, especially illnesses involving sharp internal pains.[25] Elves disappear from later medical writing, probably because late medieval academic medicine increasingly preferred to emphasize the physical causes of illnesses rather than any possible supernatural ones, but the belief that they could cause illness probably persisted in other circles: as we have seen John Bromyard quoted a charm to heal sprains which referred to 'the bite of elves'.[26] Nor was it just elves who caused illness. Agnes Hancock claimed to treat children who had been harmed by the fairies, but the most dramatic incidence of otherworldly harm happened to another Agnes, the mother of Mariona Clerk from Suffolk who saw the fairies. After talking too much with 'les Elvys' she claimed her neck and head became twisted backwards.[27]

In this way a steady stream of confession and preaching manuals in medieval England elaborated on what they found in earlier sources to give new details about fairies, elves and other mysterious beings. These beings flew or danced with their followers and they taught some people how to heal and predict the future, but they also had a dangerous side, abducting people, beating their followers, causing sickness and even sometimes making people think they had been transformed into other creatures. Beliefs similar to these seem to have been common in pre-modern Europe and in later centuries they appear in witch trials and Inquisition records from various places including Italy, Sicily, Switzerland and Scotland.[28] In these belief systems otherworldly beings often had Christian aspects. For example the Swiss herdsman Chonrad Stoeckhlin, who claimed to be in contact with a group of mysterious spirits called the 'night people', believed his spirit guide was an angel.[29] However, by the church's standards, these beliefs were wildly unorthodox. We know about the beliefs about otherworldly beings in Italy and Sicily because the Inquisition prosecuted the people who claimed to have contact with them as magicians, while Chonrad Stoeckhlin was eventually executed as a witch because the authorities believed that his 'night people' were in fact demons. The comments about otherworldly beings made by medieval English churchmen are too fragmentary to let us reconstruct a similar belief system in anything like the detail that is possible in these early modern cases. For example it is unclear how far elves, fairies, *bonae res*, ghosts, shadow-people and others were regarded as distinct beings with their own characteristics, and how far they represented a single set of beliefs which went under different names. But the sources from medieval England do point to a world in which mankind was not alone and in which various otherworldly creatures could both harm and help.

Many of the pastoral writers who included these details also gave new information about other forms of magic. *Fasciculus Morum*, John Bromyard, Robert Rypon and the *exempla* all described other magical practices which they claimed were current in the world around them. We can therefore see a group of writers who were especially interested in magical practices using the Canon Episcopi as an opportunity to discuss a wide range of unorthodox beliefs about flying and dancing beings who existed outside orthodox Christianity. Other medieval English sources, particularly romance literature, share this assumption that many different kinds of otherworldly beings existed and they expected their audiences to be familiar with terms such as 'fairy' and 'aluen'. But how did educated clergy who were concerned about pastoral care make sense of them?

What are Otherworldly Beings?

Educated clergy who wrote treatises on preaching and pastoral care worked hard to fit as many otherworldly beings as possible into an accepted Christian worldview. To do so they turned back to the Canon Episcopi and reinterpreted mysterious flying creatures either as demons or as illusions created by demons to deceive the unwary. For example, the *South English Legendary* argued that dancing elves were really demons while *Fasciculus Morum* said they were demonic illusions, 'nothing but phantoms shown them by a mischievous spirit'.[30] Berengar Fredol's comments about the 'shadow-people', quoted by the anonymous fourteenth-century English writer, also emphasized that these beings were demons in disguise.

But when they stressed how demons took human form to deceive people, pastoral writers acknowledged that not everyone saw them as demonic. In fact they often had to argue this point hard, explaining both why otherworldly beings were demons and why they were *not* something else. John Bromyard did this in the most detail:

> In the other world no people is believed to exist except a good one or a bad one. Good, such as those in Heaven or Purgatory; bad, such as demons and the damned. But the first group

cannot deceive the women [who believe they have contact with the beautiful people] in this way because the women themselves affirm that they [the beautiful people] sometimes beat them or make them ill when they speak with them. But the good do not do evil after death. Nor can they say they are the souls of the damned because those are in Hell and cannot leave at will.[31]

Therefore the 'beautiful people' were demons, because the other explanations were simply impossible. But the care Bromyard took to dismiss these alternative views suggests he saw them as serious rivals.

Sources which were written primarily to entertain also suggest that in practice people did not always identify mysterious other-worldly beings as demons. This was true even of educated clergy such as Layamon or Walter Map when they were writing marvel literature or works of history rather than treatises on pastoral care. These writers often left the nature of the beings they described undefined, although Carl Watkins has argued that Walter, at least, intended his audience to work out that they were demons, even if he did not always say so explicitly.[32] In romance literature which was set in the distant past, authors could take a still looser view of what other-worldly beings really were. Some called them 'fairies' without further explanation. Two fourteenth-century English versions of the twelfth-century Breton poem *Lanval* by Marie de France described the heroine as a fairy, or even the daughter of the king of 'Fayrye' without explaining what fairies were: they simply said she was beautiful, rich and came from another world.[33] In other cases fairies could overlap with other kinds of otherworldly being. The fairies of *Sir Orfeo* were linked with the dead, rather like John Bromyard's 'beautiful people', and the fairy realm to which Orfeo's queen Heurodis is abducted is populated by people who have died violently. However, unlike Brom-yard, the author did not try to explain this state of affairs by spelling out that these beings were really demons.[34] These writers were writ-ing to entertain rather than to combat unorthodox beliefs, so they were far more willing than the pastoral writers to leave otherworldly beings ambiguous, without explaining exactly what they were.

Moreover, unlike the confession and preaching treatises, litera-ture did not condemn the people who interacted with otherworldly beings. Romance writers sometimes presented otherworldly beings as dangerous: Heurodis is abducted by the fairies and Lanval's beau-tiful fairy mistress blinds Queen Guinevere after the queen falsely

accuses Lanval of rape. But these works do not paint their protago-
nists as sinful, deluded by demons or engaging in magic.

Given the fragmentary nature of the evidence, it is difficult to tell
how far this attitude would have been shared in real life. A few people who claimed to have contact with otherworldly beings did end up
in the church courts, although this was not very common. Since most
church court cases arose from rumours or accusations made by one
person against another, this suggests some people did regard contact
with the otherworld as suspect – or at least knew it could be made to
sound that way in court. A ghost story written down at Byland Abbey
in Yorkshire in around 1400 also implied that making contact with
the dead was frowned upon. In this story a tailor named Snowball
met a ghost on several occasions and eventually he asked it for information. What was his own greatest sin? The ghost replied that it had
caused Snowball some public dishonour itself because it had acciden-
tally given him a reputation for talking to the dead: 'people are
mistaken about you, lying and gossiping about the other dead people [whom you contact] and saying, "Either he is conjuring this dead
person, or this one, or this one."'[35] Nevertheless people who did not
have a mission to improve pastoral care and stamp out unorthodox
beliefs may have been less condemning of those who interacted with
otherworldly beings. This was perhaps especially likely if healers and
diviners who claimed they were in contact with the fairies or beautiful people were able to bring them benefits.

Medieval English pastoral writers therefore tried to impose a single interpretation on a very wide range of beliefs about otherworldly
beings. Writers who wrote to entertain audiences might exploit the
dramatic potential of ambiguous beings and healers might claim to
have otherworldly knowledge, but pastoral writers sought to close
down the ambiguities and rebrand otherworldly beings as demons.
The historian Claude Lecouteux has seen in this a process of 'diabo-
lization' which contributed to later stereotypes of flying,
devil-worshipping witches.[36] Medieval churchmen conceptualized
this association between demons and otherworldly beings in a variety of ways. Sometimes otherworldly beings were dreams inspired by
demons and sometimes they were real demons masquerading as elves
or beautiful people, but they were always demonic in one way or
another. As such it was always wrong to interact with them, whatever
benefits you might derive from doing so. The cases of Agnes Hancock, Mariona Clerk and her mother Agnes, and John of Kilpeck

show that this less tolerant attitude could lead to formal accusations of magic – but only in a few cases.

Distinguishing between Legitimate and Magical Contact

Pastoral manuals and *exempla* therefore tried hard to fit ambiguous beings into an orthodox worldview by reinterpreting them as demons or delusions and denying other possible interpretations. In this they reflected a wider trend in medieval theological writing about ghosts and apparitions. In a book on medieval ghosts, Jean-Claude Schmitt has argued that from the thirteenth century onwards theologians increasingly interpreted mysterious apparitions as demons.[37] This was clear in their commentaries on the Biblical ghost story of Saul and the Witch of Endor (1 Sam. 28). When God seemed to have stopped answering King Saul's questions about the future, the king sought out a female medium and had her raise the spirit of the dead prophet Samuel to prophesy for him. Later commentators on the Bible found this incident troubling. Was it possible for a magical practitioner to raise a dead prophet in this way? Was the apparition really Samuel or the Devil disguised to look like him? For a long time there was no consensus. From the twelfth century onwards, manuscript illumina- tors began to draw pictures of this scene and they reflected the theologians' uncertainties, depicting Samuel in many different ways: as a reanimated corpse, a pale ghostly figure or an apparition watched over by a demon. For example, in an illuminated psalter owned by John Tickhill, who was prior of Worksop Priory near Nottingham in the early fourteenth century, Samuel is depicted as a pale, hovering, shroud-clad ghost, similar in some respects to the flying dead souls (or demonic imitations of them) described by John Bromyard (illus. 10). But despite these uncertainties, over time theologians became increasingly convinced that 'Samuel' was in fact a demon.[38]

For churchmen, deliberately seeking to make contact with ghosts or demons was magic: however doubtful the status of Samuel in the story of Saul and the Witch of Endor, no medieval theologian ques- tioned whether the witch herself was doing magic. Nor was this simply a concern for biblical commentators. In the later fourteenth century when the theologian and church reformer John Wyclif (whose ideas were eventually condemned as heretical and inspired the heretical movement of Lollardy) wrote an English adaptation of

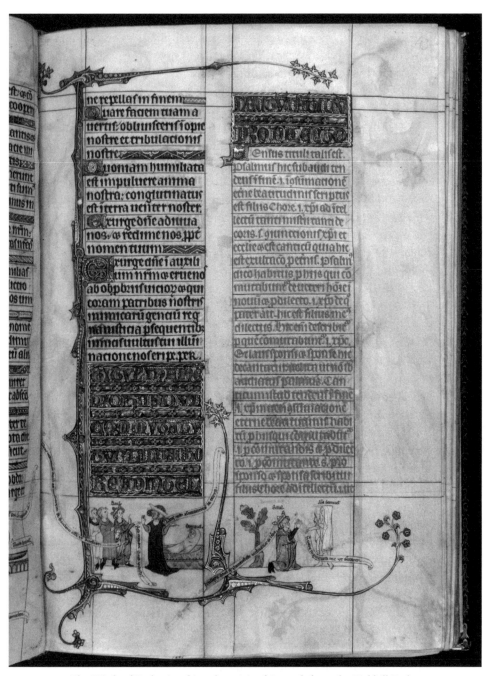

10 The Witch of Endor invoking the spirit of Samuel, from the Tickhill Psalter made for the Augustinian friar John Tickhill, *c.* 1310.

an earlier Latin work which set out what priests should know, he included among his list of forbidden magical practices a warning to 'seek not truth of dead spirits'. This detail was not in the original Latin but Wyclif thought it worth adding.[39]

However, medieval pastoral writers could not argue that all forms of contact with otherworldly beings were magic. Just as there were long-standing precedents in Christian tradition for healing or predicting the future by religious means, so too there were precedents for some kinds of contact with spirits. Despite theologians' doubts about the ghost of Samuel, ghosts had appeared in Christian writing for centuries and by the thirteenth century they featured regularly in *exempla* which were told to promote the doctrine of Purgatory. In these stories ghosts appeared to their friends and loved ones shortly after death to explain how they were suffering in Purgatory for some sin committed in life and to ask for prayers and masses to shorten their time there.[40] Ghost stories such as these fitted neatly into a Christian world view and were used to make orthodox moral points. They did not imply that the people visited by these ghosts were doing magic.

But other beings were much more difficult to categorize as either beneficent ghosts from Purgatory or evil demons. This was true even of some ghost stories influenced by the *exempla*, since a variety of old beliefs about otherworldly beings was swept up by *exempla* collectors hungry for good stories which they could adapt for preaching.[41] The ghost stories written down at Byland Abbey, for example, contained no single picture of what a dead soul might be like or how the living should interact with one. These stories lie somewhere between entertainment literature and *exempla*. They were written down in a monastery and some of them make the same moral points as *exempla*, particularly about the need to atone for sins committed during life and the power of prayers and masses to help souls in Purgatory. Nevertheless, their sources are unknown and the nineteenth-century scholar who published them, M. R. James (himself famous as a writer of ghost stories), suggested they reflected local legends and beliefs, which perhaps explains their diversity.[42] Although some of the Byland ghosts were similar to the ghosts of the *exempla*, others were not. For example the ghost of James Tankerlay, the Rector of Kereby, began to wander at night and eventually gouged out the eye of his former mistress. Instead of praying for his spirit, the story tells how the monks of Byland dug up his coffin and threw it into the water. In another story, William of Bradford was followed by a spirit crying 'how how how' and, although the author of the stories suggested this was 'a spirit which greatly desired to be conjured up and given effective help', its identity is never established and its needs never answered.[43] When faced with ambiguous stories such as these, churchmen therefore needed to decide which forms of contact with otherworldly beings were legitimate and which were not.

Pastoral writers took several approaches to this issue. Many looked at the person who was claiming to have contact with the otherworld, asking whether that person could be trusted to distinguish between a demonic apparition and a genuine ghost in need of help. This approach was similar to the one they took to religious forms of divination and healing, and it was equally useful here, since this was another situation in which religion and magic were difficult to distinguish from one another and priests needed to exercise discretion. Pastoral writers therefore focused on the status and reputation of the individuals involved, but above all they focused on gender. They often presented contact with otherworldly beings as a female activity, singling out women more than they did for any other form of magic. This emphasis on women was partly due to the Canon Episcopi, which most pastoral writers knew, but some churchmen also claimed women were the main culprits in their own time. John Bromyard declared that the belief in the beautiful people was held by 'women, who in this regard are found to be more culpable than men' and in *exempla*, too, it is usually women who claim to fly at night with the *bonae res*.[44] The association of these beliefs with women is likely to have encouraged churchmen to see them as wrong. Otherworldly beings were suspect anyway but they were probably more suspect because they were associated with a group of people whom some churchmen were unwilling to trust.

These concerns about the authority and trustworthiness of women who claimed to have contact with the supernatural were also part of wider anxieties about women's authority in spiritual matters. During the later Middle Ages churchmen in various parts of Europe raised similar concerns about female mystics who claimed to have contact with God and the saints. Some observers expressed fears that these women were in fact communicating with the devil and in the early fifteenth century this prompted several eminent theologians to write treatises on the 'discernment of spirits': how to tell whether the spirit which inspired or even possessed a person was good or evil.[45] One of the reasons discernment became a concern at this time was the emergence of several female prophets, the most famous of whom was Joan of Arc. Joan claimed, of course, to hear the voices of the angels but the theologians who condemned her at the instigation of the English in 1431 explored other possibilities. One of these was the fairies: they asked Joan what she knew about a local tree known as the 'Tree of the Mistresses' or the 'Tree of the Fairies'.[46]

In theory the discernment of spirits applied equally to men and women but often churchmen who wrote about it focused especially on possessed women, arguing that women's minds and bodies left them more vulnerable than men to the influence of both good and bad spirits.[47] This was not just a concern in the Middle Ages, and indeed the new anxiety about women and discernment which began in the fifteenth century continued into later centuries. Some early modern writers about witchcraft from this time on used similar reasoning to explain why women were more likely to be witches than men were, and concerns about the authority of women prophets persisted in England and elsewhere during and after the Reformation.[48] It has often been argued that this concern about women prophets reflects the religious uncertainties of the period from the fifteenth century onwards, which created a situation in which unlikely-seeming prophets might be taken more seriously. But pastoral writing on women's experiences of otherworldly beings show these concerns were rooted in a longer tradition which expressed suspicion of women's ability to interact responsibly with supernatural beings.

In practice, however, trustworthiness was not just a question of gender. In the few cases which came before church courts and visitations in medieval England, a person's reputation also had an important influence on how their contact with otherworldly beings was regarded, whether they were a man or a woman. The records of these cases often report that someone had a bad reputation and caused a scandal locally. John the chaplain of Kilpeck was described as 'not firm in faith'. Similarly in 1397 Nicholas Cuthlere from the parish of Ruardean in Gloucestershire was reported to the bishop's representatives for claiming that the ghost of his father walked around the parish at night. One night he held a vigil at the grave, 'to the great scandal of the Catholic faith'.[49] As the *exempla* about ghosts from Purgatory show, the idea that the dead could return to seek help from the living was not in itself unorthodox but in this case the belief was attributed to one idiosyncratic individual and apparently not shared by others. Indeed Cuthlere's neighbours (or at least the ones who spoke to the bishop's representatives) emphasized the public scandal as their reason for speaking. As we will see in chapter Seven, gossip or scandal played an important role in bringing many accusations of magic to the authorities' attention. In the case of otherworldly beings, which were particularly difficult to categorize, it may have been especially important.

In addition to considering the person who claimed to have contact with otherworldly beings, pastoral writers also looked at the circumstances in which that contact took place. If a ghost or demon simply appeared to you spontaneously, this was not wrong, but actively trying to make contact with otherworldly beings was likely to be seen as magic, as in the case of the Witch of Endor. This is shown by a particular kind of *exemplum*, which tells of people who make an agreement with a friend or relative so that whichever of them dies first will return to tell the other about the afterlife.[50] The clerics who wrote down these stories did not usually criticize these agreements and they used these stories to make the same moral points as other ghost stories: typically the dead friend comes back to describe how he or she is being punished for sins committed in life and to ask for prayers. Nevertheless, some pastoral writers raised the question of whether making this kind of agreement with a friend might be regarded as magic, probably because it was too close to trying to summon spirits to speak to you. The first pastoral writer to mention the subject was John of Freiburg, a German Dominican friar who wrote two very influential treatises on confession in the 1290s. In the longer of these treatises, John concluded that asking your dying friend to come back to you was not magic, as long as both of you accepted that any future return from the dead was subject to God's will. Thus contact with dead friends was acceptable only if it happened on God's terms, not man's: it was magic to seek to bind spirits to appear when you wanted but not if you accepted that control of these matters belonged to God. Most later writers followed John of Freiburg in allowing people to make agreements like this, but a few took a stricter view and warned that the 'dead friend' might be a demon in disguise.

Pastoral writers therefore offered clergy various ways of deciding whether someone who claimed to have contact with otherworldly beings was doing magic. They looked at the beings themselves. Were they demons? Did they fit into established understandings of how ghosts from Purgatory behaved or did they, for example, harm or beat their followers? They also looked at the people who claimed to have contact with these beings. Could they be trusted to tell demons from beneficent apparitions? Had they tried to summon a ghost or had they simply been visited? These kinds of criteria were the same as the ones pastoral writers used to categorize divination and healing magic. But whereas many pastoral writers used their discussions of healing practices and practitioners to identify a relatively wide sphere of legitimate practices, when they discussed contact with otherworldly beings their tone was much more condemnatory, as it was with people who claimed to have prophetic dreams. Pastoral writers rarely suggested that any form of contact with the otherworld was legitimate, except in the specific case of the ghost stories in the *exempla*, and even this might be questionable if it happened after you had asked your friend to come back. Instead of accepting that religion and magic might look very similar, when they wrote about otherworldly beings pastoral writers were much more cautious, and if for some reason the person claiming the contact was seen as suspect, even apparently harmless contact might be interpreted unfavourably.

When they considered otherworldly beings, medieval English churchmen therefore tried to make sense of a complex tangle of beliefs which did not always fit easily into their understanding of how the universe worked. Often they were able to make sense of these beliefs by identifying the beings as demons or as ghosts from Purgatory. In this way they were able to accept a few kinds of contact with otherworldly beings and explain what was wrong with the others. However, this interpretation of otherworldly beings was probably much stricter than many people's views. With divination and healing, pastoral writers established quite a wide space for legitimate natural or religious activities and thus found common ground with their audiences, but with otherworldly beings which were outside the Christian conceptual framework, their judgement was strict. They stressed that these creatures must be demons, or at least demonically inspired illusions, even if they looked like people, and even if they sometimes gave people useful information. The writings on otherworldly beings therefore illustrate the limits of pastoral writing on magic: both the difficulties that diverse unofficial beliefs could pose, and the difficulty of arguing against established popular views of 'magical' phenomena.

CHAPTER FOUR

Harm and Protection

On 13 January 1444 Nicholas Edmunds appeared before the court of the Bishop of Rochester to report rumours about Margery Smart:

> He reports to the official that the aforesaid Margery is suspected and defamed of the crime of magic. And he says one of his neighbours had four good horses for pulling a cart, and because she was ill-willed she said to him that in a short time he would not have one living horse. And so at once all the horses began to die.

Margery denied this and Nicholas could not prove his accusation so the court asked her to find six witnesses to swear she was telling the truth, a process known as compurgation. It is likely she found the witnesses and the case was dropped, because this is what happened in most magic cases which came to the church courts, but we do not know for certain because the record of the rest of the case is missing.[1]

Accusations such as this are common in the records of sixteenth- and seventeenth-century witch trials. People quarrel, one of them makes a sinister remark about someone's animals, family or home, and then something bad happens and he or she is accused of witchcraft. These quarrels often arose out of the tensions between people who lived in close proximity to one another – in this case Nicholas also claimed Margery had repeatedly slandered his wife.[2] Witch trial records show that by the sixteenth century it was this harmful side of magic which most worried ordinary people, and most witch trials began when one person accused another of harming them, their family or their livelihood.[3] However, harmful magic appears far less often in medieval court records. This may mean it was genuinely uncommon or less feared than in the sixteenth and seventeenth centuries but it is also possible that medieval courts were less willing to act on rumours such as the ones about Margery Smart, which were backed up by little or no hard evidence. Whatever the reason for the scarcity of accusations, Margery's case shows that some people in medieval England believed magic could be used to harm others, and occasionally this was taken seriously enough to warrant a court case.

The power of magic to harm others could be taken seriously not just in village society but also by educated clergy. In their treatises on preaching and confession, medieval English churchmen discussed the use of magic to cause illnesses, insanity or death and they also described a range of other crimes which could be committed by magic: stealing milk from cows, causing storms, and even turning people into animals. Magic which provoked love or affected a person's libido could also be seen as harmful when it led to uncontrollable and unwanted passion, or caused hatred or sexual dysfunction between married couples. Authors of pastoral manuals did not mention these practices as regularly as they did divination or healing magic and they were less ready to claim they were commonly used, but they were aware of them and some viewed them as serious matters.

Harmful magic posed a set of problems for pastoral writers different from those caused by divination, healing or beliefs about otherworldly beings. As we have seen, clergy and laity accepted that some attempts to predict the future or heal the sick, and even some forms of contact with ghosts, were perfectly legitimate, especially if they were done by experts or persons of discretion. In these cases the problem was to determine which practices were acceptable and persuade people to avoid the magical ones. In the case of harmful magic this was not the issue. There was general agreement that harming people or animals by occult means was magic rather than either natural or religious (although as we will see some kinds of harmful magic made use of religious rituals), and it was difficult for anyone to argue that it was legitimate. Instead, churchmen asked other questions about harmful magic. How seriously should they take it as a threat? Did it really work? And if it did work, what should people do about it? Their answers to these questions show us a different side of the relationship between magic and religion in medieval England.

Beliefs about Harmful Magic

When medieval English clergy in the thirteenth century and later wrote about harmful magic they often drew on earlier sources. In itself this was not particularly surprising: when they wrote about all kinds of magic pastoral writers often began with earlier texts such as the twelfth-century canon law textbook, the *Decretum* of Gratian. However, for divination and healing, and to a lesser extent for beliefs about otherworldly beings, the earlier sources were often only a starting point, and a significant number of writers went beyond them to talk about what they claimed were current practices. When it came to harmful magic, far fewer medieval English churchmen expanded on what Gratian and other earlier writers had said.

Gratian himself also said much less about harmful magic than about methods of predicting the future or healing, but he did cover the subject briefly. People who worked harmful magic appeared in a list of different kinds of magical practitioners which he copied from an encyclopaedia by Isidore of Seville, a seventh-century bishop: some magicians were called *malefici* or 'evil-doers' because 'with God's permission they strike the elements, disturb the minds of people who trust little in God, and destroy without any violence of a poisonous draft but by charms alone.'[4] As well as quoting Isidore, Gratian discussed a few specific beliefs and practices. One of these he took from a tenth-century source. It referred to the idea that some people could be harmed or even transformed into another creature by magic:

> Therefore whoever believes that some creature can be changed for the better or worse or transformed into another appearance or another likeness except by the Creator himself, who has made all things and through whom all things are made, is without doubt an unbeliever and worse than a pagan.[5]

Gratian also described one particular way of causing harm, which he quoted from an earlier church council. This condemned priests who said the mass for the dead in the name of a living person, in order to make him or her die.[6]

Some later medieval English pastoral writers reproduced these passages from Gratian. The ban on misusing the Mass for the dead was still being quoted, now translated into English, by the devotional treatise *Dives and Pauper* in the early fifteenth century.[7] Other pastoral writers took similar information from other earlier sources. For example, Thomas of Chobham quoted another piece of centuries-old advice. Priests should find out whether there was any woman thereabouts who

> says she can by some acts of harmful magic or by incantations change people's minds, for example [saying] that she converts them from love to hate or from hate to love; or that she damages or steals people's goods.[8]

Again drawing on earlier sources, Thomas also condemned people who caused storms and people who believed this was possible.[9] But these few passages did not amount to much, compared with what earlier texts – particularly Gratian's *Decretum* – said about divination or healing. They described only one magical practice in detail (using the Mass for the dead to harm the living), and even this was a practice restricted to one social group, the clergy.

Not every late medieval English pastoral writer was so brief, however, and some did give details about ways of harming people which did not come from earlier sources. These details are quite rare but they are important because they tell us much more about the practices and beliefs associated with harmful magic in medieval England than do simple quotations from earlier sources. For example a short, anonymous confession treatise written in the thirteenth century included in a list of questions which a priest could ask penitents, 'if he has consulted sorceresses or sent for them, or given gifts to such people so that their sorceries will be improved or worsened in some matter': seemingly a reference to bribing people to harm others or to lift their own spells. The same author also mentioned the evil eye, the belief that a malevolent person's gaze could harm someone: priests should ask 'if he has believed something can be weakened or worsened by other people's speech or by their look, that is *overseen*.' A second manuscript of the work added another English word, 'forespoken', to translate the harm inflicted by a person's speech.[10] The English words included in the Latin text, as well as the fact that neither sentence seems to come from an earlier source, suggest this author was recording his own observations and concerns.

Another anonymous author, who wrote a long preaching manual filled with stories called *Fasciculus Morum* in the early fourteenth century, described a different method of causing harm by magic.

'Necromancers' who 'raise devils in their circles' also 'make figures of people in wax or some other soft material in order to kill them'.[11] The mention of circles and raising devils suggests this author was thinking of ritual magic of the sort found in the magical texts discussed in chapter Five, which used circles and invoked demons. A court case from 1324, shortly after this treatise was written, suggests this was not imaginary. In this year a group of more than twenty burgesses from Coventry was put on trial for attempting to kill King Edward II, his close advisers Hugh Despenser and his son (also Hugh), the prior of Coventry Priory and two of the prior's officials. They were said to have enlisted a magician (*nigromauncer*) to make and pierce wax images of each victim. They were also accused of testing the method on one Richard de Sowe, who went mad and died as a result. The alleged plot was discovered when one of the men involved, Robert le Mareschal, revealed the details.[12] All the burghers were acquitted so we do not know how much truth there was in any of this, but the fact that the case was brought to court indicates that the use of wax images to cause harm was seen as plausible. Wax images could also be used to harm in less learned ways: the twelfth-century cleric and writer Gerald of Wales complained that people could have Masses said over wax images to curse someone.[13]

A few pastoral writers also told of love magic being used for harmful purposes, although in some of these cases what one person viewed as harmful, another might view as a legitimate attempt to preserve a relationship. For example, Thomas of Chobham described a case of magic causing impotence. Thomas had studied and lectured in theology in Paris before he took up his position at Salisbury Cathedral and he claimed to have heard of a man there who was bewitched and made impotent by his ex-girlfriend when he married another woman. The ex-girlfriend, if we had her view of this, may have seen her actions as a way of preserving her own relationship with the man, although Thomas does not say so.[14] A century later, an *exemplum* in an early fourteenth-century Franciscan collection of stories also told what it claimed was a true story about harmful love magic. It recounted how a friar on a preaching tour in the archdiocese of York was approached by a man whose wife was bewitched so that she began to rage every time she saw him, although she was perfectly sane with other people. The woman's friends had even tested how the bewitchment worked by getting various people to hide so that only their hands were visible: the woman still raged when she saw her husband's hands but remained sane when she saw other people's. The friar does not say who bewitched her or why but he reports that she was cured by making confession, after which she was able to live in peace with her husband and honour him 'as she should'.[15]

As with divination and healing, then, a few medieval English pastoral writers went beyond generalized comments from earlier sources to present a picture of harmful magic which claimed to be grounded in real practices and even in real incidents. The practices they describe do indeed have parallels in other sources so they probably were current, although they were not necessarily common. However, these writers are unusual. Many late medieval English clergy did not mention harmful magic at all, and this included some churchmen who went into considerable detail about other forms of magic, such as Richard of Wetheringsett in the early thirteenth century, who described several beliefs relating to omens, or John Bromyard in the mid fourteenth, who was so scathing about cunning folk and women who believed in the 'beautiful people'. Moreover, the information individual writers gave about allegedly real cases and practices was not widely copied by other educated clergy in the way similar comments about divination and healing were. It seems many medieval English clergy viewed harmful magic as less of a serious pastoral concern. It existed but often it was not worth going into details and for many it was not worth mentioning at all.

This seems like a surprising attitude. Surely medieval clergy, like sixteenth- and seventeenth-century villagers, would be more concerned about magic when it was used to harm than when it was used for benign purposes such as healing? Or does the lack of interest in harmful magic displayed by many pastoral writers suggest that they did not, in fact, take it seriously as a threat?

How Credible was Harmful Magic?

Sure enough, some educated clergy did express doubts about whether magic could really cause as much harm as people thought. In the early fourteenth century Robert Mannyng, the author of a long poem in English called *Handlyng Synne* which contained many edifying stories, told a spectacular tale which showed how far-fetched some forms of harmful magic could seem. A witch enchanted a sucking bag so that it would fly through the fields, attach itself to her neighbours' cows and milk them – an elaborate way of stealing milk. Eventually the neighbours realised what was happening and reported her to the local bishop, and what Mannyng says happened next is rather revealing. The bishop marvelled at the bag and asked for a demonstration, so the witch recited a 'charm' and the bag rose up. Then the bishop tried the charm himself, but nothing happened.

> 'Nay', she [the witch] said, 'why should it so?
> Ye believe not as I do.
> Would ye believe my words as I,
> It should have gone and sucken ky [cows].'[16]

In other words, the charm did not work for the bishop because he did not believe it would work. Magical milk-stealing was not unheard of, and in later periods it was sometimes mentioned in witch trials, so the bishop was probably marvelling at the self-propelled sucking bag rather than at the idea that milk could be stolen magically.[17] Mannyng told this story to illustrate the importance of faith, and particularly the importance of believing the right things and avoiding false beliefs.[18] However, it also conveys a message about magic: it was possible to doubt the efficacy of harmful magical practices, especially when the form they took seemed outlandish.

Robert Mannyng was not the only pastoral writer to cast doubt on whether harmful magic always worked as described. For centuries there had been a strand of pastoral writing which sought to combat the belief that some uses of magic were even possible rather than the practices themselves. We have already seen in chapter Three how the early medieval abbot Regino of Prüm criticized people who believed that some women could fly around at night with the goddess Diana, arguing these women were simply deceived by demons. The same strand of scepticism appeared when some other churchmen talked about harmful magic: thus as we have seen, Gratian condemned the belief that people could be changed for the better or worse or changed into other creatures by magic. From the thirteenth century onwards a few clergy went beyond earlier texts to explore the limits of what was and was not possible with magic. When they did so they examined whether magic worked at all and whether it was likely to be used in the real world – issues which were rarely raised in the more pragmatic discussions of divination or healing.

Like Robert Mannyng, many of these writers focused on forms of harmful magic which seemed particularly outlandish. One of the most outlandish is found in a long priest's manual written by a

fourteenth-century monk and historian from Chester, Ranulph
Higden. Higden discussed whether it was possible for people to be
turned into animals, or made to look like animals, by magic – an idea
which appeared in earlier theological writing and in folklore but
which was rarely discussed by pastoral writers. Earlier churchmen
had reached no clear consensus on this issue. Gratian had denied it
was possible for anyone to be 'transformed into another appearance
or likeness' but others took a different view. In the late fourth or early
fifth century, St Augustine had argued it was impossible for demons
genuinely to transform people into something else but he conceded
that demons might be able to deceive people so that they, and the
people around them, thought they had been transformed – a result
which looked identical to transformation.[19]

Folktales about people who were transformed into animals complicated the issue further. These had been told for centuries and they
appeared in several historical works written in medieval England,
including William of Malmesbury's early twelfth-century *History of the
Kings of Britain*. Higden had probably encountered them while reading for his own historical work, and this may have been what prompted
him to discuss the matter in his pastoral manual, when many pastoral writers did not bother. From William of Malmesbury he took a
story about female innkeepers in Italy who apparently transformed
their guests into beasts of burden by means of enchanted cheese, a
story which ultimately derived from St Augustine's discussion of animal transformations.[20] He also retold a story from Gerald of Wales's
Topography of Ireland, in which a man and woman were turned into
wolves.[21] Like Mannyng's story of the sucking bag, these stories often
came with scepticism built in. Augustine, for example, stated that
although it was theoretically possible to transform someone into the
likeness of an animal, stories such as these were 'either untrue or so
extraordinary that we are justified in refusing to believe them'.[22] Similarly William of Malmesbury told how when the Pope heard the
story about the innkeepers and the enchanted cheese he found it
hard to believe, until he was reminded that demons could do these
things.[23] So it is no surprise that Higden likewise presented stories of
animal transformation as hard to believe, grouping them with other
alleged feats of magicians which he deemed 'more incredible' than
most: not completely impossible but unlikely.

Flying bags and animal transformations probably stretched credibility more than most kinds of harmful magic, but a few churchmen

also criticized people who believed in more mundane practices. As we have seen, Thomas of Chobham recommended penances for believing that some people could cause storms and other kinds of harm by magic, and the anonymous thirteenth-century author quoted earlier criticized the belief that people could be 'overseen'. Similarly William de Montibus, an influential teacher and pastoral writer who was Chancellor of Lincoln Cathedral in the early thirteenth century, said in a list of penances for magical and divinatory practices that anyone who arranged someone's death by taking note of the turf from his or her footprints was guilty of murder, but that 'whoever has not done this but has believed it can be done' should do penance for twenty days, presumably for the belief.[24]

However, this strand of scepticism about harmful magic should not be exaggerated. Many of the works quoted above contain conflicting messages. William de Montibus and Thomas of Chobham criticized the people who did footprint magic or storm magic as well as the people who believed in it. These mixed messages arose because they put together material from several earlier sources and made their own additions without necessarily checking whether the final result was consistent. They may also have had reasons for condemning beliefs relating to harmful magic other than simply scepticism. If people believed something worked, they would be more likely to try it: therefore one way to combat harmful magical practices was to try to undermine the belief in them. Moreover if, as in Robert Mannyng's story, some kinds of harmful magic worked only if a person had faith in them, then it was even more important to undermine that faith. Pastoral writers did not say this explicitly but this concern may lie behind their comments that it was a sin even to believe in some forms of harmful magic.

Scepticism could also be challenged. For example, although some medieval churchmen criticized people who believed that some people could 'oversee' others or harm them with a gaze or word, in the fourteenth century one pastoral writer challenged this view from a new angle: science. Scientific and medical writers had long believed that a person's gaze could affect the people around them, a phenomenon they called 'fascination'. They also gave natural explanations for how it worked: envy might poison the brain to such an extent that noxious humours could escape from the eyes and make the surrounding atmosphere toxic, and this in turn could poison anyone who breathed it in.[25] In the early fourteenth century this explanation found its way into one pastoral manual, the *Summa* by the Italian Franciscan friar Aste-sano of Asti, which circulated in medieval England and elsewhere in Europe. Unlike many pastoral writers, Astesano treated fascination as a real phenomenon, not something that it was sinful to believe in. His evidence for this consisted mostly of quotations from medical author-ities such as the Arabic physician and philosopher Avicenna but he also claimed that 'manifold experience' showed fascination could happen when one person envied another.[26] Academic scientific writing there-fore enabled Astesano to side with what he claimed was a common belief, against a tendency among some clergy to be sceptical.

The attitude of educated clergy, both in England and elsewhere in Europe, towards harmful magic was therefore ambivalent. Often they assumed harmful magic could work but sometimes they ques-tioned it, particularly in its more dramatic forms. If this attitude was shared by others in medieval England, it may help to explain why harmful magic was not taken as seriously as we might expect. But how far was this mix of belief and scepticism shared by other people in medieval England?

It is difficult to know for sure because the evidence is fragmentary. On the one hand some people did take harmful magic seriously. This was particularly true in cases which involved the royal family, and a handful of these occurred during the fourteenth and fifteenth cen-turies. The Coventry case of 1324 was brought to court, even though the burgesses were later acquitted, and the case was probably pursued because it involved the king's welfare and an accusation of murder. A more clearly political case was that of Eleanor Cobham, the wife of Humphrey, Duke of Gloucester, Henry VI's uncle and heir.[27] In 1441 Eleanor was accused of trying to bring about the king's death by magic with the help of four accomplices: her chaplain John Home; Roger Bolingbroke, an Oxford scholar and clerk of her household; Thomas Southwell, a physician and cleric; and Margery Jourde-mayne, a woman from Eye, near Westminster, who had been arrested for magic once before and was perhaps a cunning woman of the sort denounced by some pastoral writers. Interestingly Eleanor did not deny she had dabbled in magic: instead she said she had consulted Jourdemayne for help in conceiving a child. But she was tried never-theless for using harmful magic in an ecclesiastical court presided over by the Bishops of London, Lincoln and Norwich and was ordered to do public penance, going on pilgrimage with a taper in her hand to various London churches on market days, before being imprisoned on the Isle of Man. Her accomplices were not so lucky. Home (who was accused only of knowing about the plot rather than taking part in it) was pardoned but Southwell died in prison and Bolingbroke and Jourdemayne were executed. In this case harmful magic was treated as a serious threat to members of the royal family. It is likely that the trial was engineered by Duke Humphrey's enemies as a way of discrediting him through his wife but even so, its success rested on an assumption that magic could cause harm.

Outside the royal family cases are rarely recorded but the potential for magic to cause harm was still sometimes acknowledged. The early twelfth-century laws of Henry I made provision for murders committed 'by means of a magical potion or witchcraft or sorcery practised with images or by any kind of enchantment' as well as for more conventional murders.[28] It is not known if the law led to any prosecutions but in later centuries people occasionally believed that people had tried to harm them by magical means. A rare official complaint was made by a West Country aristocrat, William, Lord Botreaux, in 1426. Botreaux petitioned Henry VI's council to act against a group of men (including a relative, Ralph Botreaux) whom he claimed had tried to weaken and destroy him by magic. We do not know what the council made of this highly unusual request but it did order commissions of knights to investigate the case in Somerset, Dorset and Cornwall, where Botreaux owned land. Sadly we do not know what came of the investigation.[29] William Botreaux in fact died some 35 years later in 1461 and he may well have felt that he had seen off the magical attempt on his life by his prompt action. There are also a few other instances in which people who claimed they had been attacked by magic were taken seriously. The Northumbrian assizes of 1279 record the case of John of Kerneslaw, who said he had been assaulted in his own home by 'an unknown woman who was a witch'. John defended himself 'as against the devil', striking the woman with a staff and killing her, and then fled. The judges ruled that John had not committed any felony so he could return but they ordered him to forfeit his possessions as punishment for fleeing.[30] Here it is significant that the judges accepted John's story and the local clergy subsequently burned the woman's body. These actions suggest that the fear of harmful magic was not just one man's paranoia but a widely held belief.

Nevertheless these were isolated cases. Overall the number of known accusations of harmful magic in medieval England is very low, though it is likely that rumours and suspicions were more common than the court records suggest. Studies of witch trials in later periods have shown that even in a period when trials were more frequent, many suspicions never resulted in formal accusations and individuals might be suspected by their neighbours of inflicting magical harm for years or even decades before a case came to court.[31] As in these later witch trials, the difficulty of proving an accusation of magic probably deterred medieval people from reporting their suspicions, since false or unproven accusations could result in the accuser being sued for defamation. For example in 1435 Margaret Lyndysay of Durham sued three men for defamation after they claimed she had made them impotent by using a stake. (They did not say how she was supposed to have done this but a much later Swiss medical book suggests one possibility: its author, the sixteenth-century doctor Bartholomaeus Carrichter, said witches could make a man impotent by sharpening a branch and sticking it into the ground where he had urinated.[32]) She won her case and the three men were warned not to spread any more rumours on pain of excommunication.[33] Nevertheless, if harmful magic was a widespread concern, it is still surprising that more evidence does not survive, either in the form of court cases for magic or in the form of defamation cases such as Margaret Lyndysay's.

Harmful magic is also rare in other sources which might be expected to mention it if it was a common concern. The records of miracles kept by saints' shrines, which described how the saints miraculously cured many illnesses, rarely said the illnesses were caused by magic. Medical treatises also said little about magic as a cause of illness: some did mention it as a possible cause of impotence but they rarely extended this to other conditions.[34]

Absence of evidence is not evidence of absence, and without more detailed records it is difficult to be sure exactly what lies behind the rarity of references to harmful magic in medieval England. Probably many suspicions were never reported but it still seems likely that harmful magic did not provoke the levels of fear which it could in later periods when trials were more numerous, although some studies of the sixteenth and seventeenth centuries have emphasized that the fear of witchcraft was not universal even then.[35] As in later centuries, some people in medieval England did fear the harm which magic could do them and made formal accusations, but they may not have been typical. Harmful magic may have been uncommon; or it may have been hard to detect and prove; or it may not have been much feared; and some combination of these factors is also possible. The witch trials of the early modern period probably show an increased interest from the authorities in prosecuting cases, but it is also likely that they reflected an increase in fear of magic in the population at large.

If this is the case, when did the fear of harmful magic begin to grow? In some parts of Europe cases of harmful magic were being tried in increasing numbers from the early fifteenth century onwards but there is little sign of this in England, except at the royal court. In part the increase in accusations relating to the royal family was probably due to the turbulent political climate of fifteenth-century England, since accusations could be used to discredit enemies, as in the Eleanor Cobham case. In part it also reflects a trend which can be seen in other fourteenth- and fifteenth-century European courts. It seems some forms of magic and astrology were genuinely on the rise in late medieval courts, prompting fears that they might be used for harmful purposes.[36] But the court was not a typical environment. Overall, although harmful magic could be taken seriously, there is little evidence of rising concern about it even at the end of the Middle Ages in England. Medieval English clergy who said little about the subject in confession and preaching manuals and occasionally questioned how dangerous it was therefore probably reflected a wider attitude which did not see harmful magic as a pressing issue.

Countering Harmful Magic

Although some people probably had doubts about how serious it was, harmful magic was still potentially a threat to a person's health, livelihood or life and not surprisingly some people sought to protect themselves against it. There were probably many commonly known ways of countering harmful magic. In later centuries the professional magical practitioners known as cunning folk identified and cured magical illnesses in addition to performing other services, and this was probably also the case in the Middle Ages.[37] Certainly churchmen such as John Bromyard criticized them for offering divination and healing, which may have included identifying witches and healing magical illnesses. Nevertheless, medieval English clergy said very little about counter-magic – either to recommend it or condemn it. This is striking when their pastoral manuals are compared with the treatises written in parts of continental Europe in the fifteenth century which discussed the new crime of witchcraft. These often emphasized that magic should not be used to counter witchcraft, and their authors tried to distinguish between legitimate and magical cures for magically caused illnesses.[38] But this new atmosphere of concern about magic and popular 'superstition' in the fifteenth century does not seem to have reflected pastoral concerns in England.

On the other hand, a few medieval English pastoral writers did suggest non-magical ways in which people could protect themselves against harmful magic. One of these was to have faith in God and behave virtuously. Their reasoning was based on medieval theologians' views of how magic worked. Magic was performed by demons, but demons were always ultimately constrained by God, so in effect magic could work only with God's permission. God might allow someone to be bewitched as a punishment or as a test of faith, but he was less likely to permit it if people lived devout and virtuous lives. Thus in the twelfth century Gratian had reported that magicians were able to disturb the minds of people 'who trust little in God', a significant addition to his source, Isidore of Seville, who had simply said magicians disturbed the minds of people.[39] Later pastoral writers agreed that faith and a pious life could protect people against magic. For example in a sermon on magic the early thirteenth-century priest and preacher Odo of Cheriton presented chastity as a defence against love magic in particular. Sometimes demons could make people fall in love, he admitted, but

> this happens because people of this sort become subject to
> the devil through mortal sin. For if they maintained chastity,
> the demons would be able to do nothing to their wills.[40]

A century later Robert Mannyng, who as we have seen emphasized the importance of faith in making magic work, also argued that faith could protect people from magic. Again he focused on love magic, telling the story of saints Cyprian and Justina to underline his point. In medieval legend Cyprian was a pagan magician who lived in the time of the Roman Empire. He was hired by a client to procure the love of a pious Christian virgin, Justina, and invoked demons to tempt her with sexual thoughts. But the demons could not prevail against Justina's faith and when Cyprian saw this he renounced magic and converted to Christianity; both he and Justina later died as martyrs. When he retold this story, Mannyng emphasized the same point as Odo: people of 'clean life' had no need to fear magical harm, whereas people who were in a state of sin were vulnerable to the Devil.[41]

Robert Mannyng added that people who found themselves be-witched could pray to Cyprian and Justina for help, and he was not alone in suggesting prayer as an appropriate response to harmful magic. Prayers to protect against magic sometimes found official acceptance at the highest levels of the English church. In 1419 Henry Chichele, Archbishop of Canterbury, asked his bishops to organize special prayers and processions to protect King Henry V against evil spells, and we know Chichele's instructions were followed in at least some dioceses because the register of Philip Repingdon, Bishop of Lincoln, records the bishop instructing his archdeacon to carry them out.[42] Lower down the social scale, laypeople could adopt similar strategies with-out the help of an archbishop. Books of Hours (prayer books which were relatively widely owned by educated fifteenth-century laypeople) sometimes include prayers for protection against a range of enemies and dangers alongside official prayers and other devotional material, including charms. 'I beseech thee Lord have mercy on me, a wretch and a sinner, but yet Lord I am thy creature and for thy precious Passion save me and keep me from all peril bodily and ghostly', ran one of these prayers.[43] Magic is not mentioned specifically but 'bodily and ghostly' peril could include the demons involved in harmful magic as well as any illnesses they caused.

In addition to prayers, religious rituals and objects could also be used to ward off evil influences. Holy water, blessings and blessed objects were all widely employed for this in medieval Europe and they continued to be used in Catholic areas after the Reformation.[44] From the sixteenth century onwards Protestants denounced them as magic and criticisms of this sort were not entirely new. Strict medieval theo-logians objected to the use of protective charms and prayers and so too did some heretics, notably the Lollards in fifteenth-century Eng-land.[45] However, as the historian Eamon Duffy has stressed, prayers and charms which offered concrete forms of protection against evil were acceptable to many medieval clerics and laypeople.[46] Even fifteenth-century treatises on witchcraft allowed these unofficial rituals against magically caused illnesses in spite of their concern about some forms of counter-magic.[47]

Religious methods of protection such as these were easily available, often cheap and probably viewed as effective, but they were not the only options. Medicine could also help against magically caused illnesses and so some medical writers, despite their general lack of interest in magical causes of illness, described ways of warding off magic and demons. These remedies are found in their chapters on sexual impotence, the health problem medical writers were most likely to blame on magic, but many of them could also be used for other illnesses. For example one widely copied collection of remedies, the *Thesaurus Pauperum* (Poor Men's Treasury) by Petrus Hispanus (d. 1277), the future Pope John XXI, recommended a range of cures for magic:

> St John's wort, if it is kept in the house, makes demons flee; therefore it is called 'demons' bane' by many people ... To take away magic theriac [a remedy against poisons made from snake meat and other substances] should be given with the sap of St John's wort and St John's wort should be put as a plaster on the kidneys ... If coral is kept in the house it will dissolve all magic spells ... Mugwort, hung above the door of the house, brings it about that no magic will harm that house.[48]

Petrus's text was translated into English and printed in the sixteenth century, and his cures were known to English medical writers even before this. John of Mirfield (d. 1407), a clerk at the hospital of St Bartholomew, Smithfield, who compiled both a collection of medical recipes and a pastoral manual, copied several of them. John was not blind to the danger that healing might overlap with magic: as we have seen, he expressed doubts about some healing charms and criticized the belief that bloodletting should be done only at certain times. Nevertheless, he recommended Petrus's methods for repelling magic without criticism.[49]

Substances such as coral and St John's wort which protected against magic could also be combined with the power of prayers and holy words to create amulets which would protect against a range of ills. One probable example of this is the Middleham Jewel, which dates from the early fifteenth century and was found near Middleham Castle in Yorkshire (illus. 11). This unusual gold pendant takes the form of a small box which once contained scraps of red silk, perhaps religious relics, but its properties do not end there. It is inscribed in Latin with the words 'Behold the Lamb of God, who takes away the sins of the world', which appear in the Mass and also in the Litany of the Saints, which asks for delivery from a range of evils, including evil spirits. The pendant is also inscribed with the words 'tetragrammaton' and 'ananizapta', which appear frequently in healing charms, especially against epilepsy, and is inset with a sapphire, a stone believed

11 The 'Middleham Jewel', a mid-15th-century sapphire and gold pendant showing the Trinity and (reverse) the Nativity; an inscription implies the pendant was a charm against epilepsy.

to possess a range of medicinal and protective powers including damping down fevers and relieving anxiety. Peter Murray Jones and Lea Olsan, who have studied the jewel, argue that it was probably designed to combine a range of protective functions.[50] With its gold and sapphire it was a very expensive piece but other less spectacular objects survive which also combine holy words and stones for healing or protection.[51] This probably included protection against magic.

There were therefore many ways to repel harmful magic and other evil influences which were rooted in religious ritual and medical knowledge, or combined the two. Since pastoral writers were interested in magic, and not generally in legitimate religious or medical practices, they probably saw no reason to discuss them. It is strange that they did not say more about forms of counter-magic which could not be seen as natural or religious, as it is known that these existed in later centuries, but perhaps they thought the subject was sufficiently covered in their discussions of healing, where they set out which charms and amulets were legitimate, and divination, where condemnations of diviners could include cunning folk who diagnosed magical illnesses. The fact that they did not single out counter-magic for special discussion is also consistent with the relatively minor position which harmful magic occupied in many medieval English pastoral writers' views of magic as a whole.

Harmful magic was believed to be a threat and it could be taken seriously by the church, the aristocracy and the general population of medieval England, but it does not seem to have provoked great concern in most people, most of the time. A few pastoral writers described what they claimed were real practices and widespread beliefs, while others focused on outlandish types of magic such as animal transformation and fantastical details such as Robert Mannyng's flying bag. Most, however, did not mention harmful magic at all or simply reproduced the brief comments made in earlier sources. It is therefore difficult to assess whether churchmen's views of harmful magic changed over the Middle Ages, in the way that one can see happening with some other magical practices such as divination and healing.

This is surprising because attitudes to harmful magic did change in some areas of medieval culture, especially in parts of continental Europe in the fifteenth century. Even in England accusations of magic against political opponents became more frequent then. Much of the other evidence for popular beliefs about harmful magic also comes from the fifteenth century, including the majority of cases in the church courts and most of the surviving prayers against evil influences. This may suggest a rise in concerns about harmful magic, but more likely it reflects the fact that more sources survive from the fifteenth century than from earlier times. Most surviving church court records are fifteenth-century or later and most prayer books also date from the late fourteenth or fifteenth centuries, when rising literacy rates created a demand for these books among laypeople. The lack of evidence from before 1400 means it is impossible to say for certain, but it seems most likely that concerns about harmful magic did not rise dramatically in the fifteenth century, in England at least. References to harmful magic are not very frequent even then, and the scattered references to it which survive from before the fifteenth century suggest it was seen as a real possibility throughout the Middle Ages – but not as a major source of anxiety.

It is possible that the existence of counter-magic was one reason why records of harmful magic are so rare. If people felt they could ward off or neutralize magic easily they may not have felt particularly threatened by it or taken drastic action. This was suggested by Keith Thomas in an important study of magic in early modern England. Thomas argued that the Reformation led to the prohibition of a wide range of religious rituals which protected people against evil. This, he suggested, left people with no recourse against harmful magic, and so anxiety about it increased and people became more willing to prosecute suspects, leading to increased numbers of witch trials.[52] This hypothesis has been criticized on several grounds. It has been argued that it overestimates the effect of the Reformation on attitudes to counter-magic: not everyone would have abandoned traditional practices so quickly. Others have pointed out that Thomas does not take into account the fact that trials often occurred only after many years of suspicion, which does not suggest they were the only available way of dealing with witchcraft, or even the preferred way of dealing with it.[53] A further criticism, less often made, is that many methods of protecting oneself against magic probably existed at a level where they did not attract the church's concern, either before or after the Reformation. Prayer and the use of substances believed to have natural protective powers would not generally have attracted the attention of medieval pastoral writers and they would not have disappeared alongside the condemned ritual practices. Some ways of countering harmful magic probably did disappear during the Reformation but many would have remained and sources which described them, such as Petrus Hispanus's *Thesaurus Pauperum*, continued to be printed and read: several editions of the English translation of the *Thesaurus* appeared between the 1550s and 1580s. The existence of ways of countering magic may therefore have been one factor which limited the number of court cases against magic in medieval England, but it was probably not the only one. It may be more significant that churchmen sometimes doubted whether harmful magic could work at all: if their doubts were shared by some of the laity this would be a powerful incentive not to prosecute magic.

Whether or not it became more difficult to combat harmful magic after the Reformation, the pre-Reformation church and its congregations appear relatively unconcerned about the subject – although there were always exceptions and special circumstances which could increase people's anxiety. It is therefore not surprising that it attracted little attention from medieval English pastoral writers. The purpose of pastoral texts was to set out clearly which practices and beliefs were wrong and to persuade others, clergy and laity alike, to avoid them. In the case of harmful magic this was relatively straightforward. It was clear why it was wrong and there is little evidence that either clerics or laypeople claimed it was legitimate. By contrast, divination, healing and even sometimes fairy beliefs seemed harmless or even beneficial and so were more difficult to argue against. Harmful magic simply did not pose the same intellectual or pastoral problems as these other forms of magic.

CHAPTER FIVE

Channelling the Stars and Summoning Demons: Magical Texts

> Once a lecherous cleric was sitting inside his magic circle and conjured the devil to come and do his will. But the devil stood far off and said: 'I cannot come any closer because of the stench of your lust. But stop for three days and I will do what you please.'[1]

This short story was told by an anonymous friar who wrote a preaching manual in the early fourteenth century. He told it to illustrate the dangers of lust: lust must be bad if even demons were repelled by it. But the story also depicts a kind of magic which is different from the ones we have met so far. It is performed by a cleric and it involves elaborate rituals such as drawing a magic circle and conjuring plus, as the cleric discovers, pious practices such as abstinence from sex. This clerical magician also invokes the Devil and talks to him face-to-face, which is unusual. In most forms of divination, healing and even harmful magic demons were not visibly present – indeed, pastoral writers had to spend time arguing that omens and some charms really were demonic precisely because this was not obvious. But like the descriptions of divination, healing and harmful magic, this description of a cleric conjuring demons had some basis in reality. Books which gave instructions on how to call up demons and achieve other effects by means of complex rituals and magic circles did exist. They were denounced and occasionally destroyed by the ecclesiastical authorities but some survive to this day.

The story therefore shows a distinct kind of medieval magic: scholarly, clerical magic. Many of the magical practices described by the educated clergy of medieval England seem to have been relatively widespread and known to both educated and uneducated people, but

12 An astrologer invoking a demon, from the entry 'Constellacio' (Constellation) in the encyclopaedic English manuscript 'Omne Bonum', c. 1370.

calling up demons was different. Magical texts were written in Latin so to read them at all you had to be educated to quite a high level. A rare picture of a magician in an encyclopaedia compiled by a treasury clerk, James Le Palmer, in the 1360s or '70s acknowledges this when it depicts an astrologer invoking a demon while reading from a book (illus. 12).[2] Moreover, many of the people who read magical books were probably clergy. Clergy were more likely than laypeople to have the education to read magical texts and the scribes who copied these works assumed the reader would be familiar with the Bible and the Christian liturgy, skills which were more common among clerics than laymen. For example one rite in a German magical manual, designed to uncover hidden treasure, instructed the reader to say 'the antiphon *Asperges me, domine, ysopo,* etc., in its entirety', followed by the Psalm *Miserere mei, Deus* (Ps. 51) again 'in its entirety'. The 'etc.' is significant: the scribe of this manuscript assumed his readers would know the psalm and antiphon so he gave only the first line of each.[3]

The people who read magical texts were therefore the same kind of people who wrote and read treatises on pastoral care: educated men, often clergy, who had the time and resources for reading and writing. The historian Richard Kieckhefer has suggested magical texts were often read by a 'clerical underworld' of men in holy orders who were not employed full-time, but other educated men also owned and read them, including monks and medical practitioners. [4] Magical texts also seem to have been common among scholars and students at medieval universities. In 1277 they were among the books banned from the University of Paris by the city's bishop, Etienne Tempier, and the university issued another prohibition in 1398.[5] Even respectable churchmen might claim to have read magical texts at university: William of Auvergne (d. 1249), a theologian who later became Bishop of Paris, said he had done so. In later life he wrote extensively to condemn them and his writings show he knew them and their contents well.[6] For some students magic may have been a form of youthful experimentation, like much of the drinking and visiting prostitutes which also went on in medieval universities, but for others it probably continued to hold its fascination in later life. Magical texts were therefore a problem within educated clerical culture, not a superstition which clergy had to eradicate from the laity.

What was in these books that simultaneously attracted and troubled the educated clergy of medieval Europe? There were in fact several types of magical text, and each kind attracted a different set of readers and different responses from the church. One group of texts concerns astrological image magic. Astrological image magic sought to channel the power of the planets to achieve particular effects on earth by means of images, pictures or symbols drawn on wax or metal. The connection between image and planet was made in several ways: by making the image at the correct astrological moment, out of the correct material (lead resonated with Saturn, for example), fumigating it with substances which corresponded to the planets, and inscribing the image with certain words, pictures and characters. In some texts the operator is also told to invoke the spirits which rule over each planet.[7] Astrological image magic was developed in the Muslim world, particularly it seems in ninth-century Syria, and it came to Christian Europe in the twelfth and thirteenth centuries when magical texts were translated from Arabic into Latin alongside other scientific, medical and philosophical works. The translations were made in areas where Christians and Muslims came into regular contact, especially Spain, so much so that Spain appeared regularly in medieval stories as the place where ambitious scholars went to learn the black arts. When these texts were first translated, intellectuals debated whether they were magic or a new kind of science. Some writers believed astrological image magic could work purely by harnessing natural forces, but for many the fumigations, inscriptions and invocations of planetary spirits looked suspiciously like acts of reverence made to demons.[8]

Other magical texts were written in Christian Europe and were based on a cosmos of God, angels and demons rather than of astrological forces and spirits. Some texts told the reader how to command demons by invoking the power of God and the angels against them, while others promised to put the operator in touch with angels. The angels and demons were invoked by means of rituals including prayers, the recitation of sacred names and ascetic practices such as fasting and sexual abstinence. As in the story at the start of this chapter, the operator was also often told to draw elaborate circles and other diagrams such as the ones depicted in an English magical manuscript now in Oxford (illus. 13). In stories about this kind of magic, the purpose of the circle was usually to give the magician a safe place to stand so that he would be protected from the demons he invoked. Because it involved complex rituals, historians call this form of magic 'ritual magic'. The theory behind it was very different from the theory behind astrological image magic but in practice it used some of the same techniques, including astrology and the making of images. The *Book of Angels, Rings, and Characters of the Planets*, a magical compendium copied in fifteenth-century England by a man named Bokenham, shows how these various elements could be combined:

> Make this of bronze or red wax in the hour of Mars, and the names of the angels who command it to be done are thus – Saliciel, Ycaachel, Harmanel – and the name of the king of demons who commands is the Red Fighter ... Say this conjuration over the image: 'I conjure you, scribes of angels, who fly through the aether ... Quickly Lataleoleas and Prolege,

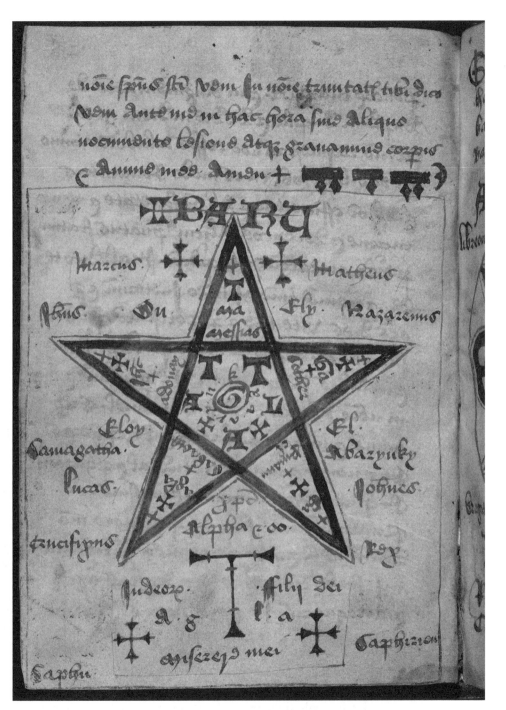

13 A diagram in a 15th-century English magical text.

Capaton, and by the one king who rules the stars and earth, and there is no other but him, and he is great and he is the most high . . . ' And with this image you can ruin or destroy whatever you wish. And it should be buried in a flowing stream.[9]

Both astrological image magic and ritual magic could be used for many of the same purposes as less learned forms of magic: predicting the future, harming others and gaining love, sex or the favour of powerful people. However, one ritual magic text, the *Ars Notoria*, promised its readers something rather different. If the reader followed a complicated programme of meditations on various diagrams and holy names, he would gain knowledge of the arts and sciences and various intellectual skills such as a good memory. These promises proved attractive to the educated and curious people who read magical texts and the *Ars Notoria* survives in more manuscripts than any other work of ritual magic. One reader, the early fourteenth-century French monk John of Morigny, even claimed he tried it because it was cheaper than going to school.[10]

Despite some overlaps, ritual magic and astrological image magic were believed to draw on different forces and they often appealed to different kinds of reader. In medieval England astrological image magic texts were often copied alongside texts on astronomy and astrology, alchemy and medicine, whereas most ritual magic texts were copied alone or with other ritual magic texts.[11] This pattern highlights how varied was the magical texts' relationship to orthodox religion. Despite the worries of some theologians about the way it invoked planetary spirits, astrological image magic seems generally to have been seen as a branch of knowledge about the natural world. Ritual magic by contrast did not sit so easily alongside other, more legitimate intellectual interests. However, even ritual magic texts shared some basic assumptions with mainstream medieval Christianity. Both assumed holy words and rituals were powerful and that demons existed and could be commanded with the aid of God – assumptions which also lay behind the official practice of exorcism.[12] There was therefore some scope to see ritual magic as a pious exercise and one ritual magic text did make this bold claim: the magicians were good men and the Pope and cardinals who forbade magic had been led astray by demons.[13] But this was very much a minority view.

Among intellectuals, then, magical texts posed a challenge. They were condemned by universities and debated by theologians. But among clergy who wrote about preaching, confession and pastoral care they were much less of an issue. Reading magical texts was clearly not a widespread activity on the scale of looking for omens in the natural world or reciting healing charms. It was also obvious to most churchmen why ritual magic, at least, was wrong. Astrological image magic might be regarded as a branch of science, but calling up demons to do your bidding was clearly magic and clearly against the rules. We might expect, therefore, to see medieval English confession and preaching manuals treat magical texts in the same way as they treated harmful magic – which was also clearly wrong – by paying it little attention and even expressing doubts about whether it really worked. To some extent this is indeed what happened, especially in treatises on confession. However, ritual magic appears much more regularly than harmful magic in one particular kind of pastoral work: collections of *exempla*, such as the story of the Devil repelled by the cleric's lust. These stories give us a different view of ritual magic. It might be un-common in practice, but the stereotype of the learned magician who called up demons was much more widespread in medieval culture. Thus even if ritual magic was not a serious pastoral problem, it held an important place in views of the relationship between magic and religion in medieval England – and in some ways a surprising one.

Pastoral Writers and Magical Texts

Not many pastoral manuals circulating in medieval England entered into detailed discussions of magical texts. It tended to be the province of the longer confession and preaching manuals, which were designed to be comprehensive and so covered the widest range of magical practices. Nevertheless the few writers who did mention magical texts are important because they show us what educated clergy who were interested in pastoral care knew about them – both what they had read in theological textbooks and what they had observed in the world around them. They are also the closest we can get to an official view of learned magic. As we will see, *exempla* present a distinctive view of ritual magic which academic theologians and the ecclesiastical authorities may not always have shared. The long pastoral manuals, by contrast, show us how their authors hoped educated clergy would treat magical texts.

Pastoral writers began to discuss magical texts relatively late. The texts themselves had been circulating in some parts of Europe since the twelfth century but they began to appear in confession and preaching manuals only at the end of the thirteenth century. Some pastoral writers were aware magical texts existed before this, since, as we will see, *exempla* were describing magicians who summoned demons earlier in the century, and thirteenth-century theologians such as William of Auvergne and Thomas Aquinas also wrote about them in their more academic works. Nevertheless, until the end of the thirteenth century, clergy who wrote treatises on pastoral care did not discuss magical texts. Instead they were more interested in deciding whether common practices such as divination and the use of healing charms were natural, magical or religious. A small group of Latin magical works, read by a minority of educated men, was probably considered less important.

The first writer of a confession manual to engage seriously with magical texts was John of Freiburg, a German Dominican friar who wrote a long confession manual, the *Summa for Confessors*, in 1297–8. In this, John summarized what the theologian Thomas Aquinas had said about the *Ars Notoria* and astrological image magic a few decades earlier. First, in question ten of his chapter on magic, John asked whether the *Ars Notoria* was acceptable and gave a categorical answer:

> The *Ars Notoria* is entirely illicit and a Christian should flee from it. For this is the art through which some people labour to acquire knowledge, but it is entirely ineffective and in it occur certain implied pacts with a demon.[14]

Then in question twelve John dealt with astrological images, both when they were used alone and when they were accompanied by invocations of demons:

> It is illicit to make the images which are called astronomical [i.e. astrological images] and they have their effect through the work of the demons. The sign of that work is that it is necessary to inscribe on them certain characters which do nothing by means of their own natural power. Therefore in these, tacit pacts are made with demons. But in the case of necromantic images invocations of demons are made explicitly.[15]

Here John of Freiburg gave his readers a more detailed view of magical texts and what was wrong with them than any earlier pastoral writer. With the help of Thomas Aquinas he also fitted them into the broader view of magic which pastoral writers had developed during the thirteenth century. The *Ars Notoria* and the characters inscribed on astrological images were magic because they could not work naturally, just as magical divination and healing could not work naturally. Therefore they must involve 'pacts' with demons – the word 'pact' echoing the much earlier comments by St Augustine about how in magic, men and demons entered into 'contracts'. If the operator invoked demons openly, the 'pact' was explicit, or obvious. If, on the other hand, he performed rituals which could not work naturally and so must rely on demons, but did not invoke them explicitly, then the pact was implicit. Later this idea of the pact became important for views of witchcraft, in which the witch was believed to have made a pact with the Devil – receiving magic power in exchange for renouncing Christ – but this was not the sense in which Aquinas or John of Freiburg used the term.[16] For them, the pact was a way of describing the more traditional view that magic relied on demons to work.

John of Freiburg's *Summa* was widely read in England and elsewhere in Europe and it became an important source of material for later pastoral writers.[17] Surprisingly, however, not many English writers copied the passages in which John discussed magical texts. Instead, if they were interested enough in magical texts to mention them at all, they preferred to give their own details. Sometimes they used alternative written sources but often they referred to what they claimed were real cases and common knowledge.

One English pastoral writer who turned to an earlier theological text to discuss the new forms of magic in depth was Ranulph Higden, a Cistercian monk and historian based in Chester who wrote a long manual for priests in 1340. When he described the kind of magic found in magical texts Higden drew not on Aquinas or on John of Freiburg but on the earlier writings of William of Auvergne.[18] As part of two unusually long chapters on magic and demons Higden quoted from William a detailed description of astrological images:

As regards the cult of images, it should be known that it is an error to think stones, gems or images can give people good things which come only from God, such as invincibility, charm, love, temperance, invisibility. For according to all the philosophers no power [in a stone] can grant something that is greater and nobler than itself ... A similar error is held by those who think that images of the stars or hanging mirrors which have been engraved or cast under the ascendant of some planet can receive and pour back power of this sort.[19]

What Higden copied from William of Auvergne was therefore a detailed description of particular practices: the use of stones and images to gain particular benefits and the making of images at particular astrological moments. His refutation of these activities also centres on a practical question: is it possible for them to work? Since they cannot, they must be magic.

The fifteenth-century pastoral writer Alexander Carpenter took a similar approach, selecting from earlier written sources passages which described particular practices and cases. Carpenter drew much of his information about magical texts from an earlier theologian based in Oxford, the fourteenth-century Dominican friar Robert Holcot. From Holcot he took various theoretical passages about why astrological images and ritual magic were wrong (many of them ultimately derived from Aquinas) but he also copied details about what he claimed were real incidents. As we have already seen, he copied from Holcot an account of how a man in London was cured of fever by means of an astrological image, and he noted that it was difficult to say whether this worked naturally or by magic.[20] He also took from Holcot a case of ritual magic which he presented in much more clearly negative terms: the case of a cleric who wrote necromancy books 'in our own days'. According to Holcot, a demon appeared to this cleric and told him he would become king of England and would ride the kingdom with a band of knights as great as the one supported by Edward I. But instead he was hanged by Parliament in Northampton.[21] The real events behind this story took place in 1318, when a man from Exeter named John of Powderham announced that he was the true son of Edward I and denounced Edward II as an impostor: he seems to have claimed the two of them had been swapped as babies. Several chroniclers who mentioned the incident said Powderham was encouraged by the Devil to make his claim, although the detail that he was a writer of necromancy books seems to be Holcot's addition.[22] Both Ranulph Higden and Alexander Carpenter therefore drew their information about magical texts from earlier written sources but they used concrete details and real examples to discuss the power and dangers of astrological and ritual magic in practical terms.

Several other fourteenth- and fifteenth-century English church-men described what they claimed were real practices and incidents without relying on earlier sources. Most striking is John Bromyard, who wrote a *Summa for Preachers* before 1352 which included an unusually long and detailed chapter on magic. As a Dominican friar Bromyard is likely to have read John of Freiburg and could easily have copied him, but he did not. Instead he ignored the *Ars Notoria* and astrological images and entered into a long discussion of whether the words and written characters that 'necromancers' used really did have the power to control demons. The practices he referred to were those of ritual magic:

> In necromancy characters and other signs seem to be made, by which demons seem to be forced to appear and answer questions. And they do not seem willing to tell the truth except when they are forced to it by the words or actions of the enchanters and conjurers, after they [the demons] have appeared to them as if to people of inferior rank and are obliged to do their will.[23]

Other pastoral writers gave similar descriptions of how ritual magicians conjured demons and commanded them. The anonymous author who told the story quoted at the beginning of this chapter also referred to 'necromancers' who raised devils in circles and made wax images to kill their victims.[24] A century later the anonymous author of the English-language devotional treatise *Dives and Pauper* also based his discussion of magical texts on what he said were real prac-tices and common knowledge. 'Often', he said, 'men know that clerks close them [demons] in rings and in other things and make them there to tell and do many wonders.' He went on to explain what really happened in these cases. Sometimes the Devil did indeed come when he was called but 'sometimes he is not ready to answer nor to do their will, and often though he would, he may not, for God will not suffer him'.[25] These writers did not invent these details. The circles, charac-ters and rings they describe can all be found in ritual magic texts and (without the circles) in astrological image magic. As we shall see, *exempla* also included numerous details about magic circles and invo-cations to add realism to their stories of ritual magic. These pastoral writers were therefore aware of what was in magical texts, or at least what popular rumour said was in them.

Only a small number of pastoral writers discussed magical texts in this way. They are a select group. They wrote long, detailed manuals and they often went into great detail about many kinds of magic, basing their comments on what they claimed was contemporary reality as well as on earlier written sources. Thus as we have seen John Bromyard and the author of *Dives and Pauper* gave many details about healing magic and divination, while Ranulph Higden and Alexander Carpenter both described what 'many people' thought about omens. For pastoral writers who were especially interested in magic, who liked to talk about contemporary beliefs and practices and who sought to be comprehensive, then, magical texts were worth discussing. But only those who were especially interested mentioned them in any detail. Apart from these few authors, most pastoral writers did not see magical texts as a priority.

Even those writers who did mention magical texts did not single them out for special attention. They added them to much longer chapters on magic, placing them alongside less specialized practices such as divination and healing rather than treating them as distinct from other types of magic. In John of Freiburg's chapter on magic, the *Ars Notoria* and astrological image magic were questions ten and twelve out of twenty-four; between them, question eleven was a more traditional discussion of healing prayers and charms. Similarly Ranulph Higden quoted William of Auvergne's description of magical images as part of a wider discussion of the use of objects for magical purposes and he placed it alongside less learned practices such as making bonfires of horses' bones on the night before St John's Day (Midsummer's Day, 24 June).

These pastoral writers also approached the question of why learned magic should be seen as magic rather than as a form of science in the same way as they did for other magical practices. John of Freiburg argued it could not work naturally and Ranulph Higden, too, denied that astrological images worked because of their physical properties. John Bromyard went further and undermined meticulously the idea that ritual magic might work either because of powers which were inherent in the natural world or by calling on the power of God. Ritual magicians, he argued, could not command demons by their own natural powers because demons were naturally superior to men and so could not be commanded by them. Nor could they do so by virtue of their own sanctity in the way Christ and the saints could because 'necromancers are not saints and cannot work miracles.' Nor were they able to control demons simply by invoking the power of God because this would not work for bad men.[26] These pastoral writers therefore did not distinguish magical texts from other, more traditional forms of magic. Instead they had an existing template for discussing magic and they fitted magical texts into this, often in a minor capacity. They were not prominent enough to require separate attention.

Stories of Demon-summoning Magicians

Magical texts were therefore not a major concern for many late medieval English clergy when they thought in terms of pastoral care. However, the magicians who used magical texts loomed much larger in their views of magic. Whereas many confession and preaching manuals did not mention the use of magical texts, most *exemplum* collections contained one or two stories about learned magicians who summoned demons with the aid of magic circles and incantations (they were much less interested in astrological image magic or the *Ars Notoria*). The way these magicians were portrayed sheds important light on how magic was viewed in medieval England. They show that magic could be seen as something scholarly, exotic and fantastical, not just as a popular 'superstition' or widespread activity which was rooted in common anxieties about health or the future. Precisely because magical texts were not accessible to the broad populace the authors of *exempla* were free to emphasize these exotic elements of ritual magic, telling stories which were colourful and outside most people's daily experience. As we will see, the ritual magic of the *exempla* was probably not as outlandish or unbelievable for medieval audiences as it seems to modern readers; nevertheless, it still hovered somewhere between fantasy and reality and it partook of both to a greater extent than did other kinds of medieval magic.

The ritual magician of the *exempla* was an exotic figure who came from far beyond the everyday world of medieval England. He had learned magic abroad, in places where Christians came into contact with people of other faiths. Spain featured regularly as a centre of magical learning and this had some basis in fact since as we have seen some magical texts were translated in Spain alongside Arabic scientific and philosophical works. This core of truth found its way into *exempla* and other stories where it was much embellished. One of the most famous of these stories is the legend of Gerbert of Aurillac, who later became Pope as Sylvester II (d. 1002). Gerbert was an expert in mathematics and astronomy but his legend grew over time. By the early twelfth century the historian William of Malmesbury was describing how he had learned magic in Spain, and by the end of the thirteenth century the story of the magician-Pope was appearing in collections of *exempla*.[27] Stories set in more recent times also portrayed Spain as the source of magical knowledge. In the 1220s the Kentish writer and priest Odo of Cheriton included in a sermon a story about an English cleric who learned how to call up demons in Spain, while a collection of *exempla* compiled in England by an anonymous Franciscan friar in the 1270s told of a Spanish magician who called up demons in Paris.[28] Occasionally other exotic settings and practitioners also appeared. One *exemplum* circulating in England featured a Jewish magician and another collection told of a young man who learned magic while he was being held prisoner by Muslims in the Middle East.[29] He brought back with him a severed human head which when he spoke the right incantations would answer questions about the future: the head, he claimed, belonged to a Muslim who had died a hundred years before.

As these stories make clear, the magician of the *exempla* was also a scholar, set apart from ordinary people by his advanced occult learning. Often, as in the story of Gerbert of Aurillac, it was the desire for learning which drove him to visit faraway places in search of knowledge not available in Christendom. Back in Christian Europe he operated above all in university towns. For this reason Paris, which was famous for its schools of theology, was also a favourite setting for *exempla* about ritual magic and even if the stories were not set there, compilers sometimes claimed to have heard them there.[30] Oxford also appeared in an English *exemplum* which claimed to describe events which had taken place there in 1298, the location described very precisely: 'in the parish of St Peter in Balliol, in a certain underground cellar next to the highway, opposite the church of that parish in the lodging called Billing Hall'.[31] Like stories of magicians going to Spain and other exotic places, this stereotype of the scholar-magician had some basis in fact because magical texts did circulate in universities.

The exotic, scholarly nature of ritual magic in the *exempla* might suggest it was remote from the experience of the average medieval English sermon audience – more a good story than an immediate possibility. This was probably true but some of these stories did describe ways in which ritual magic could spread beyond a narrow scholarly environment. The magician was a man who travelled and he brought his knowledge back from Spain or the Middle East to Christian cities

such as Paris and Oxford. On his travels he would sometimes demon-
strate his magic powers to the people he met. For example, Odo of
Cheriton's story about the English cleric who went to Spain shows how
ritual magic could spread beyond the scholarly world through personal contacts:

> A certain cleric who had learned these evil arts in Spain was
> returning to England with a certain impetuous and daring
> peasant so that he could invoke demons. They entered the cir-
> cle at the same time [from two different points] and that night
> demons appeared in the form of horses and other beasts . . .[32]

Both cleric and peasant were terrified by the demons' threatening
behaviour and the cleric ran from the circle and was carried off bodily to hell. The peasant was more sensible and stayed inside the circle
until daylight, when he was found by passers-by. Several *exempla* about
love magic likewise depict magicians doing ritual magic at the request
of clients or acquaintances and this ending, in which someone leaves
the circle and is either killed gruesomely or carried off to hell, is not
unusual. Often (and more believably) it is the client who leaves the
circle and is killed while the magician stays put and survives.[33]

These stories probably did not describe real incidents in which
people tried to summon demons. They were closer to urban myths,
but they describe a perception that ritual magic was potentially accessible to people who were not highly educated if they could persuade
a specialist to do it for them. The demon-summoning magician was
therefore an exotic, scholarly figure but he was not necessarily very
remote. Instead he was someone who came from outside the ordinary
world to operate within medieval Christendom: in an Oxford cellar or
on the road back from Spain. The stories of ritual magic in the *exempla* also reflect what we know about the readers of magical texts from
other sources. In this respect they are not as far away from the experience of a medieval English sermon audience as they initially seem. They
suggest that although very few people probably ever read or saw a
magical text, popular stereotypes existed which described ritual magic
and the magicians who performed it and showed how ordinary people
might meet these figures. The stereotypes were exaggerated but they
nevertheless had some basis in fact.

As well as being a scholar and the possessor of exotic knowledge,
the magician of the *exempla* also had genuine powers. Here he was

different from some of the less well educated magical practitioners who appear in the *exempla*, who as we will see in the next chapter are often depicted as frauds. Unlike these practitioners the ritual magician is usually able to deliver on his impressive claims. Demons appear when he summons them, sometimes in alarming or dramatic forms such as the horses and beasts in Odo of Cheriton's story. To a modern reader, the appearance of demons highlights the fantastical nature of these stories, in which ritual magic has consequences more dramatic than anything that could have happened in real life. To medieval listeners too these stories probably included an element of fantasy. However, the idea that magicians who used ritual magic texts really could sometimes invoke demons was probably accepted, at least in principle. Certainly magical texts said demons would appear if their rituals were followed correctly and some of their authors claimed to have had experiences every bit as fantastical as the events in the *exempla*, boasting of travelling on flying horses, creating illusory armies and banquets, and having sex with beautiful women in exotic places.[34] Moreover, as we have seen, mainstream medieval Christianity shared the assumption that holy words could be used to control demons during legitimate rituals such as exorcism, so stories about educated, clerical magicians who controlled demons in less orthodox ways may also have seemed believable.

Ultimately in most *exempla* magicians do not get the results they expect. Sometimes they are simply left disappointed but at worst they end up getting deceived, killed or carried off to hell. However, this is not usually because their rituals do not work. Sometimes it happens because they make mistakes, notably by stepping out of the magic circle. In other cases more powerful forces intervene. In particular, the sacraments and holy objects are shown to be more powerful than the magician's commands. For example the magician in the Oxford story summons a demon and is talking to him when a priest walks past the window carrying a consecrated Host on a home visit to a sick person. As the priest passes, the demon kneels to the Host, much to the magician's surprise. The story about the Spanish necromancer in Paris also tells of how a magician's plans were interrupted by divine power. This time the demon is slow to answer the magician's summons because it is the Feast of the Ascension. When he finally arrives, he complains, 'I marvel at you. For the angels in Heaven are celebrating the feast of Mary the Virgin and you are unable to rest on earth!'[35] The moral of these two stories is that if even demons respect the Host and observe feast days, mankind should do the same. The power of the magician to summon the demons in the first place is taken for granted.

The assumption that ritual magic works (as long as you stay in the circle and are not interrupted by a passing priest carrying the Host) appears to reflect common views of ritual magic. In fact, several medieval English treatises on confession and preaching went out of their way to argue against this view, stressing that, contrary to popular belief, magicians who performed ritual magic could not in fact command demons. As we have seen, John Bromyard took pains to argue that although it might look as if magicians really could control demons, this was just an illusion. The anonymous author of *Dives and Pauper* also wrote to contradict what he said was common opinion on this point: 'men know that clerks ... make them there to tell and do many wonders'. Like Bromyard he argued that common knowledge was wrong: demons only pretended to be bound. But both authors were forced to argue this point carefully, against what 'men know'.

The *exempla* about demon-summoning magicians therefore drew on widespread perceptions of ritual magic, even when these went against the official view that magicians could not truly command demons. In this case, however, the clergy who collected and copied *exempla* do not seem to have worried that they were conveying the wrong message and portraying ritual magic as more effective than it really was. After all, in most stories the magicians did not get the results they wanted and the stories made clear that the consequences of failure could be dire. The stories would be a lot less dramatic if the rituals were just ineffective. More practically, there was little risk that these stories would encourage people to try ritual magic because most people would not have access to magical texts or the education needed to use them.

It was therefore less necessary to persuade people not to do ritual magic than it was to persuade them not to use magic for divination or healing or to persuade them that interacting with otherworldly beings was wrong. Indeed, many *exempla* about ritual magic did not try to persuade their audiences against magic directly. Some were told to illustrate the dangers of magic, such as the story about the peasant and the cleric in Odo of Cheriton's sermon, which forms part of a longer discussion of divination, but often they are designed primarily to make other moral points, about for example the importance of revering the Host or the Feast of the Ascension or the dangers of lust. In these stories, the magic must work as described because it is necessary for the demons to appear so that they can revere the Eucharist or be repelled by the magician's lustfulness. Ritual magic adds colour and drama to these tales but is not the main point of the story. Because it was not an immediate pastoral concern, preachers were freer to take risks in how they presented it to an audience.

Pastorally-minded churchmen therefore knew about magical texts, especially ritual magic texts, even if they did not always say much about them. They assumed sermon audiences would be aware of the basic features of ritual magic, and assumed it was widely believed to work. However, it was not a major pastoral problem and does not seem to have made most churchmen very concerned. This situation led medieval English clergy to portray magical texts differently in different circumstances. When long manuals discussed magical texts they often did so in a practical tone, detailing what they claimed were real practices and cases, and debating whether ritual magic could really control demons as its users claimed. In these manuals magical texts were presented as a real and current pastoral problem but one which interested only those writers who wanted to be especially comprehensive.

Exempla, by contrast, presented ritual magic as something dramatic and effective, and they did so much more regularly because it made for a good story. It is tempting to dismiss these *exempla* as fantastical or outlandish, in contrast to the more sober details of texts and cases in the longer manuals, but it seems likely that the authors of the *exempla* reflected widespread perceptions of ritual magic more closely than did the confession and preaching manuals. Stories of demon-summoning magicians therefore provide an unusual but important perspective on magic. They show how far the presentation of magic in preaching could adapt itself to widespread beliefs which might differ significantly from the ideas developed by pastoral writers when they examined the same issues in depth for an audience of clergy.

The few cases in which individuals were accused of using magical texts in medieval England point to the same situation: a recognition that learned magic was wrong and could be dangerous but also a sense that it was rare and not much of a threat to everyday life. These accusations must be used with care because it is often difficult to know from the surviving records how much truth lay behind the accusations and exactly which practices were at stake. For example, the rumours about Alice Perrers, the mistress of Edward III in his old age, may have been just that. The chronicler Thomas Walsingham, a monk of St Albans Abbey, claimed she employed a friar who was skilled as a physician to make the king love her by means of wax effigies, potions, incantations and magical rings.[36] The rings, combined with the friar's clerical status and medical learning, suggest Walsingham was thinking of some form of learned magic. The rumours may have been baseless, concocted by enemies who resented Alice's influence over the elderly king (and there were plenty of those), but they nevertheless rest on the assumption that these forms of magic were both possible and potentially effective.

Better documented, and resting on firmer evidence, were the accusations made against Richard Walker, a chaplain from the diocese of Worcester who was brought before Convocation (the national council of the English church) in 1419.[37] Walker was accused of owning 'two books in which were written and painted many conjurations and figures savouring, so it was said, of the art of magic and sorcery, and also a box in which were contained a beryl stone artificially suspended in black leather, three small documents and two small images of saffron-coloured wax'. The two books with diagrams suggest ritual magic and Walker admitted to owning one of them as well as all the other items. After hearing the evidence, Convocation sent Walker back to prison 'until it could be deliberated by the lawyers by what penalty a magician like this should be punished according to the rigour of the law' – a delay which suggests they were not used to dealing with cases of ritual magic. Eventually he was sentenced to stand publicly at the cross in the churchyard of St Paul's Cathedral with his magical books hung round his neck 'so all the people in front and behind him can inspect and see the characters and figures made and painted in the same books' – an action which, as well as humiliating Walker himself, was designed to deter others from following his example. It must also have spread awareness of what a magical book looked like and this may have been part of the point: people would know in future what to avoid. Walker was also made to renounce magic publicly and his books and magical equipment were later burned but after this, he was permitted to go free. Similar public abjurations were used for heretics in the fifteenth century (if, like Walker, they were first-time offenders and were willing to repent of their errors), and served the same dual purpose of education and deterrence.

Ritual magic could therefore be treated as a serious sin and its users punished. However, Richard Walker's case was isolated and the bishops were not immediately sure how to deal with it, which does not suggest they were deeply concerned about the threat ritual magic posed to the spiritual welfare of medieval England as a whole. This seems to be typical of ecclesiastical attitudes to ritual magic in practice. In a recent essay Frank Klaassen points out that bishops could have sought out ritual magicians in the way they sometimes sought out heretics in fifteenth-century England, by looking for suspicious books and tracing the networks through which these books were shared, but they did not do so, perhaps because pursuing heretics was enough of a strain on their resources or perhaps because they were reluctant to prosecute fellow clergy.[38] The *exempla* suggest another possible reason for the authorities' reluctance. In these stories ritual magic could be risky but it was really a danger only to the practitioners themselves.

This has important implications for how we should interpret ecclesiastical views of magic in medieval England more generally. Pastoral writers and perhaps other churchmen too did not pay most attention to the practices which were most obviously wrong, such as harmful magic and ritual magic. Instead they focused on the ones where the overlap between magic and legitimate religion posed pastoral problems: divination which looked like prophecy or healing charms which blended unknown names with those of God and the saints. They also focused on forms of magic that were believed to be widespread among the laity. Magical texts therefore show the limits of pastoral writers' concerns about magic. When they were concerned with mass education, a limited, socially restricted practice which was obviously wrong had little place, except as an exotic, colourful background to moral stories.

CHAPTER SIX

Arguing Against Magic

In the early 1220s Thomas of Chobham offered this advice to priests on the subject of magic:

> Almost in every region and everywhere on earth certain idolatries reign, against which preachers and priests should be armed. For there are many men and women who use magic potions and sorceries and do not believe them to be idolatry.[1]

So far this book has looked at a range of individual magical practices, at how they might overlap with or differ from legitimate religion, and at the other issues which educated pastoral writers faced relating to magic. But as Thomas of Chobham's advice shows, combating magic was a practical concern as well as an area for theological discussion. For this purpose priests did not necessarily need all the information which long confession and preaching manuals gave them about magic, such as the detailed discussions of how to distinguish between prayers and magical charms, why dream interpretation was wrong, and what was in the new magical texts. This information was important for educating the clergy for pastoral care but it is unlikely that it was all used very often when they preached or spoke to the laity. A sermon could cover only so much material and it was not practical to ask penitents about every form of magic when they came to confession. How, then, did clergy convey the essentials of their view of magic to the wider population of medieval England? What did they emphasize and what did they leave out? Which arguments did they rely on? As we have already seen with magical texts, churchmen might present magic differently depending on whether they were preaching to a general audience or whether they were writing for other educated clergy.

In sermons they focused on the colourful and dramatic side of ritual magic rather than its potential overlaps with religion. Did other important changes happen when preachers and confessors adapted their material on magic for a wider audience?

To answer these questions, we must turn to the texts which were written most directly for priests to use when they were preaching and hearing confessions: sermons, *exempla* and the shortest confession manuals, which listed the important questions a priest should ask penitents. Large numbers of these survive from England from the thirteenth century onwards, as they do from other parts of Europe. Pragmatic, concise and written in a simple, accessible style, these texts are often the closest we can get to knowing what went on in medieval confessions and sermons. Nevertheless, there was still a gap between them and practice. Short confession manuals, *exempla* and most surviving sermons were not transcriptions of real events. This is not surprising in the case of confession manuals: medieval priests, like their modern counterparts, were forbidden to reveal confessions and the authors of pastoral manuals did not do so, although they sometimes wrote in general terms about what they had heard in confession, with names and details removed to protect the penitents' anonymity.[2] Sermons and *exempla*, too, were often models which priests were supposed to adapt to their needs, rather than scripts to follow exactly. But even though they are not exact records of what happened in actual confessions or preaching, sermons, *exempla* and short confession manuals tell us which practices the authors of these works thought were most important and the arguments they wanted their readers to make when speaking to their congregations. They were also copied in large numbers for several centuries, and in an age when everything had to be copied laboriously by hand this suggests they were seen as useful. It is therefore fair to assume that these texts' arguments against magic were used in sermons and confessions, even if they were not repeated in every detail.[3]

Another important question about priests' attempts to persuade their listeners not to do magic concerns their impact. Did the arguments found in short confession manuals, sermons and *exempla* really change attitudes to magical practices? It is difficult to know for sure since the people who heard sermons and made confessions did not usually write about their experiences, but it is possible to see some reactions. On the one hand, it is clear that not everyone was wholly convinced, just as not everyone is convinced by media campaigns today.

Thomas of Chobham was not the only medieval English churchman to complain that people did not see what they were doing as magic, especially if it was used for a good purpose, and as we have seen, even clergy sometimes tolerated forms of divination and healing that went beyond strict theologians' guidelines. Moreover, many magical practices persisted for centuries after the Middle Ages, which suggests the campaign against them was not very effective. But on the other hand, pastoral writers were confident that preaching and confession could influence audiences. Indeed, they were so sure of it that they warned their readers not to reveal too much. Many pastoral writers warned priests not to ask about sexual sins in detail in case they gave penitents ideas and the thirteenth-century French friar Guillaume Peyraut made the same point about magical remedies: 'The preacher should be careful that . . . he does not teach women remedies they do not know, if he believes they will use them.'[4]

There are also a few times when we know preaching against magic stirred up audiences. When the popular Franciscan preacher St Bernardino of Siena preached against magic in Rome in the 1420s, he persuaded his listeners to denounce magical practitioners to the authorities, although he was far less successful in Siena itself.[5] There is no evidence of such an extreme response to preaching against magic in England but Bernardino's success shows how a charismatic preacher could influence an audience, at least in the short term. In the long term, the less dramatic but more regular preaching by parish priests and friars may have been more effective at reinforcing the message and shaping attitudes to magic.

So preaching and confession probably did influence audiences' views of magic, at least to some extent, but their impact would have depended on how often these activities took place. The amount of preaching in medieval England is much debated but most parishes seem to have had sermons at least a few times a year, and they were probably more common in towns, where the friars were most active.[6] There were also opportunities to make confession, although as with preaching, it is difficult to determine how frequent this was. The Fourth Lateran Council of 1215 ruled that all laypeople should make confession once a year, at Lent, and most historians believe annual confession came to be regarded as the norm in England after this time and perhaps even earlier.[7] It is questionable how detailed most confessions were, however. Hearing the whole parish's confessions during Lent, perhaps with other penitents queuing nearby, priests had limited time to ask about what sins a person had committed.[8] Medieval English priests therefore did have opportunities to persuade their listeners against magic, but they were not necessarily very frequent: once or perhaps a few times a year rather than every week; and magic was just one topic among many. How then did they use these opportunities?

Arguing against Magic in Confession

The best evidence for how priests argued against magic in confession comes from the shortest confession manuals, which summarized the essential information a priest needed in order to hear a confession and listed questions for him to ask. These manuals vary in length from just a few pages to slim books. A few were issued by bishops as part of larger schemes to improve pastoral care and clerical education in their dioceses. For example Bishops Alexander Stavensby of Coventry and Lichfield, Walter Cantilupe of Worcester, and Peter Quinel of Exeter issued short confession manuals for their dioceses in 1224–37, 1240 and 1287 (Stavensby and Cantilupe produced new ones, while Quinel reissued Walter Cantilupe's). These manuals issued by bishops are particularly important because they were written directly for parish priests to use with their congregations and so they were probably what most priests were most likely to have read for information about pastoral care. Moreover, some bishops tried to make sure priests actually did own copies of these works: Walter Cantilupe ordered his archdeacons to explain any difficult points in his treatise to priests and he also threatened to fine any parish priests who were later found not to have a copy.[9] As well as these texts by bishops, similar works were written unofficially by friars and other clergy and copied by readers who found them useful. One of the most popular of these was the *Confessionale* written by the German Dominican friar John of Freiburg in the 1290s. As we have seen, John also wrote a long *Summa for Confessors* but his *Confessionale* was a much briefer guide to confession. It circulated very widely and over 150 medieval copies survive; many more were probably lost or worn out as priests and friars carried them around and used them.

Many of these short confession treatises mentioned magic, although it was not essential for them to do so and a few did not. Some simply instructed their readers to ask about magic in very general terms. For example, an anonymous thirteenth- or fourteenth-century treatise in a manuscript which once belonged to Wroxton Abbey in

Oxfordshire told priests to ask 'if [the penitent] has sometimes believed in harmful magic, sorceries and auguries, conjurations of demons and similar things'.[10] This list could cover a wide range of practices but it offered little guidance as to which practices should be classed as magic in the first place. What made something 'sorcery' or 'augury' or even a 'conjuration of demons', rather than religion or legitimate observation of the natural world? This was not always easy to decide and penitents might be unclear about it, as Thomas of Chobham recognized when he complained that many people did not believe certain things to be sorcery. However, other short confession treatises gave more details about exactly which activities they meant. A second short confession treatise bound into the same Wroxton Abbey manuscript asked:

> if [the penitent] has put faith in sorceries and divinations using the stars or using dreams or other instruments of any kind. He should also confess if he has sometimes invoked demons by verbal incantations, by inscribing characters, by burning sacrifices or similar things.[11]

Walter Cantilupe (and following him Peter Quinel) was still more specific. He advised priests to ask about:

> practising magic (that is, by resorting to incantations, as is common when something is stolen, or by using a sword or a basin, or by writing out names, sealing them in a mud plaster, and placing them in holy water, and similar things).

He also mentioned people who believed in omens and sacrificed to demons, 'as some wretches do for the sake of women with whom they have fallen foolishly in love'.[12]

Even when they went into details, most of these treatises kept their lists quite short. This is not surprising in short texts which had many sins to cover besides magic. However, a few writers said more. The list of magical practices in John of Freiburg's *Confessionale* is surprisingly long and comprehensive. It is worth quoting it in full, both because John sets out the maximum that a pastoral writer might consider to be essential knowledge about magic and because his work circulated so widely:

Then at the end [of the confession] you will be able to ask about magic and superstitions. If he has done any things of this kind or arranged for them to be done, such as the very many things which are done by many people with amulets, words, useless inscriptions and many diverse observances. Likewise, specifically if by the stars or dreams or by auguries he has wanted to have foreknowledge of matters to which things of this kind do not extend, such as human actions which are subject to free will. Likewise, if he has used some writings or written them, in which some adjuration or invocation to demons is made, or in which are included unknown names or some characters other than the sign of the cross, for things of this sort are illicit. [The 'writings' here, with their unknown words and characters, may be written amulets similar to those discussed in chapter Two.] In particular you should make him explain the magical practices he has done and at least say with what materials he did them and with what intention; for such things are often done with very unclean substances and at the risk of people's lives, sometimes even with the sacraments and other holy things, which is a most serious sin. Likewise, ask if he has taught such things or introduced someone to them. Make him remember them [or: take them back] as far as you can.[13]

John also singled out certain groups of people. Peasants should be asked about magic in general while university masters should be asked about 'necromancy' (which probably meant summoning demons by ritual magic) and particularly one of the most popular ritual magic texts, the *Ars Notoria*.[14]

But John of Freiburg was unusually comprehensive. More often short confession treatises focused on a few kinds of magic and ignored others. Divination is mentioned regularly and so is the writing or speaking of 'incantations'. This is not surprising since these practices also appear regularly in the longer confession and preaching manuals. However, the short confession texts differed significantly from the longer ones in their treatment of unorthodox beliefs rather than practices. They said very little about these. Thus they did not ask whether penitents believed in flying women or fairies, even though longer confession and preaching manuals discussed this regularly. Instead they prioritized actions over beliefs, focusing on people who tried to predict the future by divination or by reading omens, who used incantations or invoked demons. Actions were easier to identify and measure than beliefs, and with limited time in confession, it was probably more important to ensure people were behaving as they should and avoiding sinful activities than to examine every unorthodox thought.

The short confession texts also omitted many of the subtleties found in longer manuals. They did not discuss whether certain practices should be classed as magic at all. While some longer treatises explored at length whether all ways of healing or predicting the future really were magic, shorter ones simply listed what was forbidden. Their attitude to these forbidden practices was also much less diverse. As we have seen, the longer pastoral manuals offered several different interpretations of magic. Sometimes they presented it as a demonic deception which only gullible people believed in – especially beliefs relating to omens and nocturnal flying women. In other cases they acknowledged that magic might be a misguided attempt at religious practice, as when William of Rennes stated that only 'discreet' people could be trusted to use healing prayers correctly. At other times again, magic was simply trafficking with demons. The authors of the shorter manuals repeated only the last of these views. Walter Cantilupe's confession manual, the more detailed of the two Wroxton Abbey treatises, and John of Freiburg's *Confessionale* all stated explicitly that magic was about invoking demons.

Because magic invoked demons, it could be seen as a kind of demon-worship. Several short confession treatises accordingly placed magic in their lists of the Ten Commandments, categorizing it as a sin against the First Commandment, 'You shall have no other Gods before me'. Walter Cantilupe placed it here and an anonymous thirteenth-century treatise owned by Worcester Cathedral made the link between magic and demon-worship explicit. It told the priest to ask 'if [the penitent] has shown the worship due to God to a demon or creature, by sacrificing or doing magic or consulting magicians or sorcerers; which transgresses the First Commandment'.[15] The historian John Bossy has pointed out that categorizing magic as a sin against the First Commandment underlined the link between magic and demons in a way that was not so obvious if magic was placed under other headings, as it was in some longer manuals which were divided up according to the seven sins or followed the structure of canon law textbooks.[16] By classifying magic as a sin against the First Commandment, these short confession treatises further emphasized that it involved trafficking with demons, rather than presenting it as a delusion or error.

As we might expect, then, the short confession treatises simplified the longer manuals, offering a more black-and-white view of magic and religion. Magic was important enough to deserve a mention in many short confession treatises and the message was clear: it involved trafficking with demons and showing them inappropriate religious veneration. The authors of these works were far less interested in how magic might overlap with legitimate religious practice, except possibly to note (as John of Freiburg did in the *Confessionale*) that it might involve misuse of the sacraments. They also concentrated on practices, particularly practices believed to be common, such as omens, divination and healing charms, rather than beliefs. These were the clearest points of the medieval church's view of magic and it was these which most penitents would have taken away from confession.

Preaching Against Magic

Preaching gave priests the space to go into a little more detail about magic than was practicable in most confessions. Sermons on the Ten Commandments offered one opportunity to mention magic, just as lists of sins against the Ten Commandments did in confession manuals. Thus in 1281 when John Pecham, Archbishop of Canterbury, listed the topics which priests should preach to their parishioners, he included magic under the First Commandment: 'Implicitly it forbids all sorcery, incantations, and superstitious uses of written letters or other types of images.'[17] Pecham's scheme influenced later legislation on preaching and it was reissued and translated into English in 1357 on the orders of John Thoresby, Archbishop of York, including the comments on magic.[18] In keeping with these instructions, some preachers did indeed mention magic when they discussed the First Commandment. An anonymous fifteenth-century Latin sermon echoed Pecham's guidelines, noting that the First Commandment prohibited 'all idolatries and incantations and all sorceries'.[19] Robert Rypon, a monk of Durham Cathedral Priory in the late fourteenth and early fifteenth centuries, also discussed magic extensively in a sermon on the First Commandment, as we will see.

Magic was also sometimes mentioned in sermons for various feast days in the year. The most important of these was the Feast of the Circumcision of Christ, 1 January, a date which was associated with making predictions and seeking good fortune for the coming year. In around 1400 John Mirk, in a collection of sermons called the *Festial* which circulated widely in fifteenth-century England, referred to the New Year customs of pagan times, 'which be not for to tell among Christian men, lest they were drawn into use'. As we have seen, several pastoral writers claimed that taking 'hounsels' or New Year gifts which brought luck in the coming year was a current practice in medieval England.[20] Other preachers went further and said that people performed divination on New Year's Day: one anonymous New Year sermon in a fourteenth-century manuscript forbade 'all sacrileges and divinations to which false Christians are accustomed to pay attention, seeking experiences of future things with diverse operations'.[21] One other feast day was also particularly associated with magic: St John the Baptist's day (24 June), probably because of its Midsummer position. In more recent times St John's Day has been associated with various unorthodox practices to bring luck and fend off evil influences and this was probably the case in medieval England too: in a St John's Day sermon, the thirteenth-century priest Odo of Cheriton complained that 'on this night the daughters of the devil are accustomed to do harmful magic and sorcery.'[22]

Outside these feast days, magic might be mentioned on a less regular basis. *Exempla* discussed many different kinds of magic, from omens to beliefs about otherworldly beings to the ritual magic done by educated magicians, and they could be included in sermons for various days. Magic also appeared in the stories told about some saints, especially early Christian saints who lived in the days when the Roman Empire was still pagan. These early saints battled pagan magicians and overcame their magic with miracles. For example, John Mirk included in a sermon on St James the Apostle the story of how the saint was attacked by demons summoned by the pagan magician Ermogines. But angels came to James's rescue and bound the demons, prompting Ermogines to renounce magic and convert to Christianity. The story of Saints Cyprian and Justina made a similar point: it told how Justina's faith overcame the pagan magician Cyprian's magic, leading Cyprian to convert.[23]

Preachers therefore had opportunities to include magic in their sermons, but not many devoted much attention to it. It was not obligatory to mention magic on New Year's Day or St John's Day and many sermons for these days did not do so. Even sermons on the Ten Commandments did not have to mention magic because it was possible to interpret the First Commandment in other ways. For example Thomas Brinton, a fourteenth-century Bishop of Rochester, interpreted 'having

137

other gods before me' as a criticism of everyone who loved their sins more than they loved God, and he did not apply it to magic or any other specific sin.[24] Even when preachers did mention magic, their references to it were not always very detailed and some of the authors quoted above limited their comments to criticizing 'sacrileges and divinations' or 'harmful magic and sorcery'.

In fact, outside *exempla* and stories about the saints, I have found only three surviving sermons from medieval England which talked about magic at length, and two of those were written by the same author, Odo of Cheriton. Odo was a priest and minor landowner from Kent who had studied theology in Paris before returning to England. In the 1220s he wrote several collections of sermons which were copied by later writers, and were later deemed useful enough to be translated into English.[25] As well as his St John's Day sermon, Odo discussed magic in a sermon for Ascension Day. His starting point was the statement made by Jesus shortly before he ascended to Heaven, that it was not for mankind to know when he would return to re-establish the kingdom of Israel (Acts 1:6–7). Odo interpreted this as a warning against trying to predict the future and went on to condemn divination.[26] The third sermon is Robert Rypon's sermon on the First Commandment. We have already looked at some of what Rypon says about magic, such as the details he gave about magical healing, omens and mysterious flying beings called *phitonissae*. For some of this information Rypon drew heavily on a fourteenth-century treatise, the *Summa for Preachers* by the Hereford friar John Bromyard, but he also added some details of his own about magic. These three sermons were probably not preached in the form in which we now have them. All three are in Latin and the only surviving manuscript of Rypon's sermon is large and high quality, with illuminated initials and gold leaf, which suggests it was not carried about by preachers.[27] Nevertheless these sermons show us how two medieval English churchmen writing at different times in different parts of the country approached the task of preaching about magic.

The small number of sermons which discussed magic at length suggests that many preachers saw it as a low priority. They had after all many other topics to cover which were considered more important. Thus when he set out what priests should preach, Archbishop Pecham had mainly emphasized various schemes of doctrine: the Fourteen Articles of Faith, the Seven Deadly Sins, the Ten Commandments and so on.[28] Preaching on these might refer to magic but only as part of a larger scheme. Nevertheless, by putting together the passing references, stories and the occasional longer sermon on magic we can build up a picture of how magic was represented in preaching – both by preachers who were particularly interested in it and by those who were not.

Firstly, many of the sermons which mentioned magic were not primarily *about* magic. Odo of Cheriton and Robert Rypon devoted substantial chunks of their sermons to the subject, but they were unusual. Instead, most preachers mentioned magic as part of stories and *exempla* in sermons which were devoted mainly to other topics. These stories conveyed various messages about magic to their audiences but they did so incidentally. Thus stories about saints such as James who confronted pagan magicians underlined that magic could look like a miracle but was in fact fundamentally different because it relied on demons rather than God. For this reason it was always inferior to a true miracle and a magician could never overcome a saint. These dramatic stories illustrated God's power and the triumph of Christianity over paganism. However, they may not have been particularly successful at persuading their audiences to avoid magical practices. They were set in the distant past and so they presented magic as something which was far removed from medieval England and they did not deal with the practices which late medieval English clergy said were current in their own time, such as divination and healing. This meant that they did not reflect the concern expressed by many pastoral writers that magic might overlap dangerously with accepted religious practices. Little danger of that, the audience might think, when magic was the preserve of long-dead pagan magicians.

Exempla about magic told the audience more about contemporary practices. Again a few were told purely to illustrate the dangers of magic, such as the stories in which magicians who call up demons meet with dreadful fates (Odo of Cheriton told one of these stories), or in which people make terrible mistakes after believing in dreams or omens (Robert Rypon told several of these).[29] But in other cases, the magic was again incidental, background information. Thus as we have seen, stories of ritual magic could be used to show the importance of venerating the Host or the sinfulness of lust. *Exempla* about more popular forms of magic could operate in similar ways. For example, several widely copied stories told of people (usually women) who did not swallow the Eucharist when they received communion, but instead took it home to use for a range of dubious magical purposes, including love magic and increasing fertility in their crops or animals. In these stories the consecrated bread always revealed itself to be the Body of Christ eventually. If people concealed it about their persons it turned into a mass of bloody flesh, and if people put it in a beehive to increase their yield of honey, the bees built a miniature honeycomb shrine around it.[30] These stories did of course warn their listeners against misusing the Host for magical purposes but their main point was often to emphasize that the consecrated bread really was the body of Christ, as the late medieval church taught. For this reason an early fourteenth-century collection of *exempla* copied in England included a story of this kind under the title 'On the Power of the Eucharist' rather than under a title which referred to magic.[31]

Stories about magic could also be used to underline other moral lessons. For example an early fourteenth-century *exemplum* which told of a woman who was bewitched to hate her husband but was cured by making a full confession of her sins showed how confession could free people from the Devil's influence. It is clear that for the collector who copied this story, the main point was confession rather than magic, because he placed it between two non-magical stories which also illustrated the power of confession to break the Devil's hold over a person.[32] The popularity of stories such as these probably tells us more about the doubts medieval people might have about transubstantiation or confession than about magical practices in medieval England. Nevertheless, they still described particular practices which they claimed were current and they assumed some people believed in them. For example they took it for granted that ritual magic worked or that magic could cause hatred between a married couple.

Whether or not magic was the main point of the story, these *exempla* therefore portrayed magic in particular ways which were designed to influence how audiences saw it. In some respects their approach was similar to the one taken by the short confession manuals. Again they did not engage in detailed theoretical discussion about what magic was. They did not define exactly why certain practices should be classed as magic, or explore the ways in which magic could overlap with legitimate religion. Only the rare, longer sermons such as Rypon's did this. Rypon included, for example, paragraphs taken from John Bromyard in which Bromyard explained why ritual magicians could not control demons as the saints could and why people should not try to interpret dreams in the way biblical figures such as Joseph had done.[33] But most sermons and *exempla* took magic as a given, described it and showed what was wrong with it.

In other respects, however, sermons and *exempla* presented magic in rather different ways from the short confession manuals. They described a much greater range of magical practices. These included some (such as love magic and ritual magic) which appeared relatively rarely in confession manuals, especially the short ones. The *exempla* were also more willing to discuss unorthodox beliefs as well as practices. Thus as we have seen, they told of the *bonae res*, mysterious flying women who were believed to enter houses at night and bring prosperity to the owners. Beliefs about supernatural beings also appeared in sermons outside *exempla*: Robert Rypon described how beings called *phitonissae* could fly to Bordeaux, drink wine and return home. Like the *exempla* about the *bonae res*, Rypon emphasized that people who thought they flew were dreaming, quoting the old piece of canon law which stated that experiences of flying were really demonic illusions, a message which was not conveyed by shorter confession manuals.[34]

Exempla and sermons also communicated another important point which confession manuals emphasized less strongly: magic was dangerous, to both body and soul. As Odo of Cheriton put it:

> Concerning diviners, augurs and necromancers, and sorceresses, it is rarely found that they finish their life with a good end because they are either seized alive by demons, or choked with a sudden death, or they die obstinate in their malice.[35]

Exempla were able to illustrate the dangers of magic particularly effectively by depicting people who put their faith in omens and dreams and died unexpectedly as a result, or who invoked demons and ended up being dragged off to hell. One of the most dramatic of these tales about magical practitioners who met horrible fates was the story of the Witch of Berkeley. This originated in the *History of the English Kings* by the twelfth-century monk William of Malmesbury and was incorporated into preaching aids including the early fourteenth-century preaching manual *Fasciculus Morum*.[36] In this tale, a woman spent her life devoted to magic but on her deathbed she repented and asked her son and daughter (a priest and a nun) to pray for her and take precautions to stop the Devil getting hold of her body. Her body was duly placed in a stone coffin bound with three iron chains, and clerics prayed around it for three nights before her burial. But despite these precautions, on the third night demons rushed into the church, broke the chains, opened the coffin and carried her body off to hell. No simple warning against magic in confession or a sermon could convey the dreadful fate which awaited magical practitioners quite as graphically as a story like this.

Sermons and *exempla* therefore described a wide range of magical practices and beliefs, from the mundane to the exotic and the real to the illusory, but they only rarely discussed in detail the relationship between magic and religion. To some extent they reinforced the messages that medieval English clergy wanted to convey in confession, by discussing some of the same common practices, such as omens, and stressing that magic was wrong. However, they also presented magic in distinctive ways, devoting more space than the confession manuals (especially the short confession manuals) to practices and beliefs which were dramatic but perhaps more unusual: love magic, beliefs about women who flew at night, and ritual magic. These topics lent themselves to colourful stories which illustrated a range of moral points – sometimes about magic but often about other issues.

Preaching about Magical Practitioners

There is one more important difference between how magic is portrayed in sermons and especially *exempla* on the one hand, and how it appears in confession treatises on the other. Sermons and *exempla* often described the people who did magic. They were not completely unique in this. As we have seen, preaching and confession manuals sometimes described magical practitioners, and at times singled out women, peasants and, for ritual magic, scholars. Nevertheless, sermons and especially *exempla* described magical practitioners in more detail, going beyond these general comments to say who these people were and why they resorted to magic. Some of this detail was necessary because *exempla* were stories and most stories about magic needed some description of who was doing the magic and why. But in addition to this, the descriptions of magical practitioners served a further purpose. They were themselves a way of persuading people not to do magic. Apart from ritual magic, which was rather esoteric, the authors of sermons and *exempla* associated magic with low-status groups – female, old, poor and stupid – in order to persuade their audiences to reject it.

References to the kinds of people who were likely to do magic are most prominent in a particular kind of sermon, the *ad status* sermon.

These were sermons addressed to individual social groups, such as women, the clergy or knights. This type of sermon was not particularly common – most audiences were probably mixed and so most sermons had to reflect this – but a few collections of them circulated widely, notably those of the thirteenth-century friars Guibert of Tournai and Humbert of Romans.[37] Like some confession manuals, these sermons singled out women, especially poor women, and scholars as the people who were especially prone to use magic, but they gave more details about them. Thus as Humbert of Romans explained in a sermon for village women:

> women of this sort are usually greatly prone to magic, either for themselves or for various situations, or for their children when they are ill or for their animals so they will be protected from wolves, and similar things.[38]

Later, in a sermon for scholars, Humbert mentioned 'necromancy' as one of several branches of study which were forbidden because they led scholars into sin; also forbidden was studying Ovid's *The Art of Love* and other poetic 'figments' which incited lust.[39] Guibert of Tournai also singled out scholars as practitioners of learned magic:

> Scholars put faith in incredible things which they should immediately reject as unbelievable, for example [the idea] that the constellations influence our conclusion, [or] that certain characters or such and such an invocation or gazing at a diagram has such and such an outcome.[40]

The references to constellations, invocations, characters and gazing at diagrams suggest Guibert was thinking of astrological image magic and perhaps also ritual magic or the *Ars Notoria* (which required the operator to meditate on a series of diagrams). For Humbert and Guibert, these groups were led into magic by the circumstances of their lives. Scholars did magic because they had the opportunity to study magical texts which led them astray, while peasant women did so in response to the problems they faced, such as sick children and animals in danger from wolves. *Exempla* singled out the same groups of people and again they depicted them using magic for reasons which reflected the circumstances of their lives, their needs and anxieties. Scholars did ritual magic out of curiosity about the future or a desire to see demons or to seduce women. On the other hand it was women who performed magic connected to love and fertility: to get good husbands, make their marriages happier or conceive children. For example in the early thirteenth century the preacher Jacques de Vitry told a story which ridiculed old women's claims to do love magic. In this story an old woman offered to get good, rich husbands for a group of young women by magic – until one of the younger women pointed out that her magic could not be that good, since her own husband was poor.[41] Both the practitioner and her prospective clients are female: equivalent stories of men looking for good wives do not seem to exist.

Sermons and *exempla* did not say magic was done only by these groups, but they depicted scholars and women, especially poor and old women, most regularly. In the case of scholars doing ritual magic, this may well have corresponded to preachers' own experience. Scholars and clerics were the groups who did ritual magic because they were most likely to have the education this required. Preachers were probably well aware of this: many authors of sermons and *exempla*, especially the friars, had been to university and may well have heard of people using magical texts there. In their portrayal of old women, however, the *exempla* may reflect stereotypes more than reality. The stereotype of the superstitious old woman was widely used in medieval religious writing, where authors used the image of the 'little old lady' to represent both simple faith and credulous superstition.[42] By contrast, the surviving evidence for many common magical practices indicates that they were used not just by little old ladies but by many different social groups.[43]

There was also another strand to the way in which *exempla* depicted women magical practitioners in particular. They often argued that some women's magical beliefs were delusions and the women who believed in them were simply wrong and stupid. This idea can be found in other treatises on confession and preaching and in canon law, for example when learned clergy discussed beliefs about women who flew around at night with strange otherworldly beings. Nevertheless, it is especially prominent in *exempla* and their authors applied this reasoning to many different kinds of magic. Some stories told of how believers in magic made mistakes and deceived themselves: for example, in the story of the woman who believed that the crying of the magpie would tell her how long she had to live and who ended up dying without receiving the last rites as a result.[44] In other cases they depicted fraudulent practitioners who tried to deceive other people, as in Jacques de Vitry's story of the old woman who offered to find other women rich husbands by means of love magic. For preachers this was a useful way of persuading audiences to avoid magic. Who, they imply, would be stupid enough to believe such obvious frauds? As Robert Rypon put it:

> for some people (both men and women) are so stupid that they believe trifles of this sort more than the Scriptures or the words of the saints, and [believe] an old woman more than the best doctor of theology.[45]

Here Rypon was echoing the earlier writer and preacher John Bromyard, who had said something similar.[46] In doing so, both men placed a great emphasis on the education and religious authority of the clergy and contrasted this with the stupidity of the old women and the people who believed in them.

The *exempla* did not dismiss all kinds of magic as ineffective. As we have seen, they often stressed that ritual magic could really work, even if it did not always work in the way the magician expected. Nevertheless, they emphasized the fraudulent and ineffective side of magic more strongly than other preaching and confession manuals did – especially when magic was practised by uneducated women. This view of magic as a fraud or delusion offered preachers an entertaining way of debunking the claims of diviners. It may also have resonated with sermon audiences because there are a few court cases in which diviners were accused of fraud. For example, a magical practitioner who had promised to identify a thief but failed to do so was brought before the courts in London in 1375, when his client sued him for breach of promise.[47] It is hard to know how far most magical practitioners truly believed in their own powers, but cases such as these show that people were aware of the possibility that some might be frauds, and the *exempla* played on this.

Ridicule was therefore a powerful means of persuading people not to engage in magical practices. It sat alongside the more traditional argument that all magic was wrong because it involved trafficking with demons and it was probably especially useful against magical practitioners whose activities were not obviously demonic, or who adapted Christian rituals and prayers. Here it allowed educated clergy to claim that only they could be trusted to offer legitimate religion and to belittle less educated people who acted unofficially.

Thus while short confession manuals offered a simplified message which focused on demons and on a few magical practices, sermons and *exempla* gave their audiences a more varied view of magic. Magic could be a conscious human fraud, a mistaken belief, a demonically-inspired illusion or a real and dangerous attempt to summon demons. It might even be more than one of these things simultaneously. In every case, the people who offered it could not be trusted. Scholars who performed ritual magic were shown clearly to be trafficking with demons and the risks they ran were graphically described. Meanwhile less well educated practitioners were exposed as frauds or fools.

In these ways the educated clergy of medieval England tried to persuade their audiences – clergy as well as laity – not to do magic. It is not clear how far they succeeded. Audiences probably heard about magic only from time to time, in disconnected snatches: as part of an *exemplum*, in a story about a saint or as one of several ways of going against the First Commandment. In confession, too, they may not have heard about it routinely or in any great detail. However, the snippets in these sources convey the outline of ecclesiastical views: magic was demonic, it was wrong, and (in sermons and *exempla*) it was often practised by unsuitable and foolish people, or by scholars who should know better than to take risks with demons. With repetition, this message would have reached at least some of the people of medieval England. Moreover, although there were variations between individual writers and preachers, the overall message does not seem to have changed substantially over time. Individual preachers elsewhere in Europe in the fifteenth century, such as Bernardino of Siena, did stir up campaigns against magic but there is little evidence of this reforming zeal in the English sermons and *exempla*.

The church did therefore use the opportunities it had to spread its messages about magic, but its teaching was sporadic and this is likely to have limited its effectiveness. The final chapter of this book will examine what happened when reforming churchmen went beyond persuasion and sought actively to prevent and punish laypeople and clerics who took part in magic.

CHAPTER SEVEN
Action Against Magic

Much of the time senior churchmen in medieval England seem to have been content simply to tell the laity and also other clergy not to do magic. They asked about it in confession and sometimes told stories in sermons which warned against it but usually they left the matter there. They had many other concerns besides magic and limited time and resources with which to persuade people of their views, and they may not have taken all forms of magic very seriously, especially the more outlandish ones which seemed to stretch credibility. As we have seen, they sometimes expressed doubts about the reality of magic which allowed women to fly around at night or turned people into animals, arguing that these things were impossible or at least very unlikely. But there were times when educated clergy did take magic more seriously than this, and tried to suppress it and punish the people who were caught using it. The church's role in taking action against magic was crucial because there is little evidence the secular authorities were interested in it, except when it was used against the king. For the most part magic was regarded as a moral offence and so left to the church.

Here England is part of a much larger history of action taken against magic by the medieval church. Many of the measures which English churchmen took – preaching against magic, asking about it in confession and prosecuting it in the church courts – were taken by clergy across much of Europe. In many cases these clergy were reading the same canon law textbooks, sermons and pastoral manuals as their English counterparts. However, against this general background, important changes were taking place in some circles and in some parts of Europe in the fourteenth and fifteenth centuries, which led to magic being taken more seriously and punished more harshly. In universities from the thirteenth century onwards, theologians were beginning to place increasing emphasis on the Devil's role in making magic work.[1] Some of them were also coming to see magic as a form of heresy: not just a sinful activity but a rejection of God and the Church in favour of wrong religious beliefs. These theologians argued that magic appealed to the Devil rather than God and therefore magical practitioners were showing reverence to him – only a short step away from devil-worship. The turning point came in the early fourteenth century, when Pope John XXII (1316–34) was especially instrumental in classifying some forms of magic as heresy, particularly ritual magic (since invoking demons could be seen as a kind of devil-worship) and magic which involved misusing the sacraments (because misusing the Host or other holy objects could be seen as a rejection of accepted religion). This also had important implications for the ways in which these kinds of magic could be prosecuted. By classing them as heresy, John XXII brought them under the jurisdiction of the Inquisition, which had been set up in the thirteenth century to investigate heretics.

Initially this did not have much effect and the Inquisition continued to focus on heretics rather than magicians.[2] But a century later, Western Europe was feeling the effects of a schism in the papacy, with two and then three rival popes from 1378 to 1417. Church reformers became convinced that not just the church but the whole of Christendom needed to be purified and reformed, and for some magic was a part of this programme. Thus several theologians wrote treatises against 'superstition' as part of an effort to improve pastoral care and religious observance. This was new: previously churchmen had written about magic and superstition within larger pastoral manuals rather than singling it out as a special problem.[3] Reformist preachers also denounced magical practitioners in violent terms, alongside other groups who were believed to be polluting Christendom such as heretics, Jews and homosexuals. These new fears did not wholly replace earlier views and they were not shared by everyone, but in the hands of a charismatic preacher like the Italian Franciscan friar Bernardino of Siena they sometimes led to trials and executions.[4] Outside reforming circles there was also rising concern about the use of magic at royal and aristocratic courts, particularly in France, where the long-term mental illness of King Charles VI led to accusations that he was bewitched and magical attempts were made to cure him.[5]

Together these changes contributed to the creation of a new crime which historians often call 'witchcraft' to distinguish it from other forms of magic.[6] 'Witchcraft' conflated magic, devil-worship and heresy into a powerful cocktail. Witches were believed not just to do harmful magic but also to have renounced God in favour of the Devil. They were said to perform a range of terrible crimes which had earlier been linked to heretics, including holding secret meetings called sabbaths where they worshipped the Devil, held orgies and killed and ate babies. Often they were believed to fly to these sabbaths, a detail borrowed from earlier beliefs about women who flew at night with otherworldly beings. The first trials for witchcraft seem to have taken place in the Alps in the 1420s and '30s (where they developed out of earlier campaigns against magic and heresy) and shortly afterwards the new crime was described in several treatises written by clergy and lay judges who had been involved in the trials. As the fifteenth century went on, trials became a little more widespread and witchcraft began to be more widely written about. It also attracted attention from artists, and fifteenth-century pictures of witches show how magic, heresy, devil-worship and flying came to be combined. An illustration drawn in the margin of one of the earliest treatises on witchcraft depicts two women flying on broomsticks but labels them 'Vaudoises', that is, Waldensian heretics rather than witches (illus. 14). (The Waldensians were a heretical sect which originated in the twelfth century and proved very persistent: inquisitors were still pursuing them in the Alps in the early fifteenth century.) At the end of the fifteenth century, a Flemish artist was depicting a group of witches, again with broomsticks, worshipping the Devil in the form of a goat while other witches flew through the air behind, almost invisible against the dark background of the sky (illus. 15).

This general picture varied considerably in different regions. Even in the Alpine areas, which saw the earliest trials, attitudes to witchcraft varied, in the fifteenth century and later. Since the 1990s, research into the fifteenth-century Swiss witch trial records has also shown the importance of the local factors which lay behind individual trials.[7] Sometimes trials were started by the people in authority for their own reasons: an especially zealous Bishop of Lausanne encouraged witch trials in his diocese in the 1440s to 1460s, while in other cases local lords or clergy might use witch trials to establish their own authority. Not all of the impetus came from above, however, and a variety of quarrels and jealousies led people to accuse their neighbours of witchcraft.[8] Moreover, not everyone in authority was willing to prosecute witchcraft. Some people remained sceptical about it and trials sometimes

14 Female witches / heretics flying, from Martin le Franc's *Le Champion des Dames* (*c.* 1450).

met with opposition: the inquisitor Heinrich Kramer, the author of one of the most notorious treatises on witchcraft, the *Malleus Maleficarum*, was ordered to leave the Austrian city of Innsbruck in 1486 when the local bishop accused him of conducting trials wrongly and causing a scandal.⁹

At first glance it is not clear where England fits into this picture. In fact, comparatively little attention has been paid to magic in fifteenth-century England. Was the relationship between magic and religion changing there too, with magic coming to be seen as a kind of heresy

ieu tout puiſſant créateur du
monde vniuerſel fiſt et créa
tous les céleſtiens eſperitz bon
et vertueux leur donnāt les
hauls dons de nature et de ꜫrace · Car
comme dit ſaint Auꜫuſtin auecꜫ la
noble nature quil leur bailla il les
dōma auſſi de vertu et ꜫrace · Mais
comme ilz euſſent en leur premiere in
ſtitucion receu de dieu boulenté frāce

15 Witches / heretics flying and worshipping the Devil in the form of a goat, from
a 15th-century Flemish manuscript.

and the authorities increasingly willing to prosecute and execute suspects? In 1977 the historian and English literature scholar H. A. Kelly suggested this could have happened.[10] He pointed out that some of the conditions which historians have identified as important in the Alps were also present in England. There was heresy in the shape of the Lollards. The teachings of this group were based broadly on the ideas of the theologian John Wyclif (d. 1384) and they criticized many established religious practices as superstitious. In England as in the Alps, the presence of heresy prompted the church and the government to oppose religious deviance through preaching, trials and some executions. There was also at least some fear of harmful magic, as shown by political trials such as that of Eleanor Cobham, Duchess of Gloucester. In addition to this, senior English churchmen may well have heard about the new crime of witchcraft through their links with the Continent. Several English bishops attended the Council of Basel in Switzerland in the 1430s, a reforming church council which seems to have been responsible for spreading the new concept of witchcraft among educated clergy.[11] But despite all this, there is no evidence that the new image of the devil-worshipping witch had a significant impact in England before the Reformation.

How, then, did the church in medieval England try to suppress magic? Which methods were available to them and how did they work? The answers to these questions offer us an insight into an important aspect of how medieval English clergy viewed the relationship between magic and religion: how they viewed the duty of pious clergy and laity to repress magic. They also shed light on a broader issue in the history of medieval magic which has often been neglected by historians who study witch trials: the church's treatment of magic in places and periods where the new fears of witchcraft had not yet taken hold.

Action in the Parish

An anonymous thirteenth- or early fourteenth-century confession manual owned by Durham Cathedral Priory included among the questions which priests could ask 'almost everyone' in confession, 'whether he has practised magic arts, taught them or consented to them'.[12] Confession was one of the most powerful ways in which the church could combat magic. It gave priests the opportunity to explain to penitents individually which practices were magic and why they were wrong, and to give them penances. The penances which confession manuals suggested for magic varied considerably but for some kinds of magic they could be severe. For example, the thirteenth-century confession manual of Master Serlo reproduced a passage from earlier sources which said a woman who mixed menstrual blood into her husband's food or drink so he that would love her more should do penance on certain days for a period of seven years.[13]

The penitential system also acted as a deterrent in other ways. Seeking absolution for magic is likely to have involved publicity and inconvenience because many bishops from the thirteenth century onwards categorized magic as a 'reserved sin', one of a group of serious sins which parish priests were not qualified to absolve. Absolution for these sins could be granted only by the bishop or his representative, the penitentiary; and going to these men would require effort and would also advertise to a person's neighbours that he or she had committed a serious sin. Confessing to magic might also lead to further penalties. The parish priest and penitentiary William of Pagula (from Paull in Yorkshire), whose priest's manual circulated widely in four-teenth-century England, set out some of these in a passage taken from earlier canon law: as well as doing penance for 40 days, laypeople who practised magic could be excommunicated and clerics could lose their benefices.[14]

Refusing to confess may not have been very easy either. Some people did avoid it, but the evidence suggests that in later medieval England going to confession was regarded as the norm and so absences would probably have been noticed.[15] If penitents refused to confess or do penances, or were judged by the priest not to have made a full confession, the priest had a further sanction. Confession took place in Lent, to prepare Christians to receive Communion on Easter Sunday. (In the Middle Ages Communion was often an annual event, and on most Sundays Christians were expected simply to attend Mass.) On this special Sunday, the priest could refuse Communion to penitents who were still in a state of sin, a very public way of singling someone out and mobilizing social pressure against them.

The risk of being denied communion or getting serious penances suggests confession was potentially a powerful way of discouraging people from doing magic. But the word 'potentially' is crucial, because many unanswered questions remain about how medieval confession worked in practice. Priests probably did ask about magic in confessions, since it appears in many short confession manuals, but it is hard to tell exactly how often they did so or in how much detail. There is also much we do not know about how penitents responded to this questioning. In theory, everyone was supposed to go to confession regularly but this meant only once a year. Also, they may not necessarily have confessed every sin despite the priest's efforts: indeed, the risk of getting heavy or inconvenient penances may well have discouraged people from doing so. Finally, we do not know how the penances worked in practice: for example, how often penitents who confessed to magic or other serious sins were sent to the bishop's penitentiary. One author of a thirteenth-century confession manual complained that, despite the rules, many priests absolved reserved sins themselves. The friars were particularly guilty of absolving any sin confessed to them: 'God', the author complained, 'is witness'.[16] In practice, therefore, although confession would have influenced people's attitudes and behaviour, we do not know how effective it truly was as a means of detecting or deterring magic.

The same is true of the other methods of opposing magic (and other serious sins) available to priests. From the early thirteenth century onwards *sortiarii*, a word which could describe either diviners or magical practitioners in general, were one of the groups of sinners listed in the General Sentence of Excommunication which priests were supposed to pronounce in their parishes three or four times a year.[17] This was a declaration that anyone who committed certain sins was automatically excommunicated. Some versions of the General Sentence also included anyone who knew someone who was guilty of magic (or other serious sins such as heresy) and did not report them.[18] Excommunication was a serious matter, since other Christians were supposed to shun the excommunicated person. It was not always observed in practice but some people did try to avoid excommunicates and worried when they could not.[19] The threat of excommunication might pressure people into making a confession or reporting their neighbours, but it required priests to be conscientious in pronouncing the General Sentence and parishioners to pay attention to it.

There is also a more fundamental problem. The General Sentence listed *sortiarii* without saying who these people were or what they did. As we have seen, some short guides to confession did the same, telling priests to ask if people had done 'sorcery' or 'magic arts' without expanding on this. Without further details about what magic was, the people who heard these condemnations may not have identified

themselves or other people as *sortiarii*, especially if they were performing practices which used religious rituals and were seen as beneficial.
For example, in 1431 John Stafford, Bishop of Bath and Wells, complained about simple people who mistook magical healers for medical
practitioners.[20] Authors of confession and preaching manuals made
the same point: people mistook magical charms for 'holy words' and
diviners for divinely inspired prophets. Without extensive education
through preaching and confession, therefore, broad prohibitions
such as the General Sentence could have only limited efficacy; but
once there was a consensus about what magic was, they could be far
more effective.

A further way of combating certain kinds of magic may have been
more reliable because it was less dependent on education and persuasion. Churchmen had long worried that people might steal consecrated
substances, especially the Eucharist, chrism (consecrated oil) and the
holy water in the font, and use them for magical purposes. *Exempla*
warned against this and in 1215 the Fourth Lateran Council ordered
priests to keep these substances locked up. The message was reinforced
by several thirteenth-century English bishops, who repeated the instructions in their church councils.[21] It also seems that some parishes
put this into effect, which gives us a rare insight into how one way of
acting against magic may have worked in practice. St Paul's Cathedral
in London conducted visitations (inspections) of the parishes under
its jurisdiction in 1249–51 and again in 1297. In both visitations the
visitors noted the state of the church's equipment, including the
pix (container for the Host), font and chrismatory (container for the
chrism). Of the fourteen churches surveyed in 1249–51, five were
reported as having no locks on their fonts, seven had no locks on
chrismatories and four had no lockable pix. Although the state of
these items in the other churches is seldom recorded, none was said
to have a lockable font, only one was said to have a lockable pix and
only one had a lockable chrismatory. Of the twenty two churches surveyed in 1297, by contrast, ten had locks on their fonts, fifteen had
locks on their chrismatories, and eleven had lockable pixes.[22] This is
a small sample but it suggests locks were being used more commonly
in this area and that bishops' representatives had begun to check for
them. Much later a visitation of parishes in the diocese of Hereford
in 1397 includes only ten cases of unlocked fonts and one unlocked
chrismatory, out of a total of 281 parishes (in the parish of Weston
one of the priests, John, had taken the lock from the font).[23] These

figures may not be complete, since visitations depended on parishioners reporting defects in their churches, but again they suggest that holy substances were increasingly locked away and that bishops were asking about this.

The church therefore had some ways of opposing magic and other sins at parish level, in addition to the preaching and questions in confession discussed in chapter Six. Such measures would have been most effective when they were able to mobilize social pressure and individual consciences against people who were doing things which everyone agreed to be wrong. Against practices which were widely accepted, however, and which made use of religious language and objects in ways that were not obviously magical, broad condemnations of magic in confession manuals and the General Sentence of Excommunication probably made little headway.

Action by Bishops

Bishops were also responsible for taking action against magic, either themselves or through the administrators of their dioceses. Occasionally they attacked magic directly because (they claimed) it was especially prevalent, sinful or threatening. Thus in August 1311, the Bishop of London issued a mandate ordering one of his archdeacon's officers to preach against magic and report to him the names of individuals rumoured to be magicians, because these crimes were becoming more common.[24] One of the earliest known cases which combined accusations of magic and devil-worship was also instigated by a bishop. This was the case of Alice Kyteler in Kilkenny, Ireland, in 1324. The local bishop, Richard Ledrede, had spent time at the court of Pope John XXII and seems to have absorbed the Pope's view that magic was a serious matter and a form of heresy. When he was appointed Bishop of Ossory he was determined to root out heresy in his new diocese and he succeeded in launching a trial for harmful magic and devil-worship against Alice, her son William and her servants. Ledrede had the support of Alice's stepchildren, who felt they had been dispossessed in favour of Alice's own son, but he also faced strong local opposition from Alice's relatives and supporters. Alice and William escaped but one of her servants, Petronella of Meath, was burned – the first person to be burned for witchcraft in the British Isles.[25] This trial shows one determined bishop taking harmful magic very seriously, but equally striking is the reluctance of many local notables to help him.

The Alice Kyteler case is highly unusual and it seems to have been the result of one bishop's persistence. But in the fifteenth century bishops tried to act against magic more often, perhaps because they were more sensitized to religious deviance than in earlier centuries as a result of Lollardy. They were probably also more alert to magic because of the growing number of accusations arising in the royal court. Sometimes it is obvious that the concern came from the court. For example in 1406, Philip Repingdon, Bishop of Lincoln, was ordered by the Privy Council to inquire into reports of magic in his diocese.[26] In other cases the action was initiated by the bishops themselves, but since many bishops were involved in politics, political and religious concerns were often interlinked. Thus in 1431, Bishop John Stafford, who would become Lord Chancellor the following year, ordered the archdeacons in his diocese to organize preaching against magicians, perjurers and Lollards.[27] Stafford claimed to be following the injunctions of a recent church council held in London but it seems likely that his concern about magic was also motivated by the arrest of seven people in London a year earlier for allegedly plotting to murder the young king Henry VI by magic.[28]

The language which these bishops used to describe magic implies they were seriously concerned about it. The 1311 mandate complained 'in our city and diocese of London we have found that the impious crime of sorceries, incantations and the art of magic has become stronger, so much so that great ruin threatens for very many of our subjects, as does danger to their souls.' According to Stafford in 1431, magic occurred with 'execrable frequency' and those who took part in it had 'abandoned God their Creator'. However, there is a significant gap between the bishops' rhetoric and their actions. There is no evidence any of these pronouncements led to trials, although it is always possible that records have not survived. After the investigations of 1406, only one case of magic appears in Philip Repingdon's register, and it dates from eleven years later, in 1417: the case of a diviner named John Smith from Alconbury in Cambridgeshire, who identified thieves by magical means.[29] Similarly, despite his strong language in 1431, John Stafford's register contains only one case of magic, from 1438: the case of three female healers, including Agnes Hancock who claimed she could make contact with fairies.[30] The time which had elapsed makes it unlikely that these cases were the direct results of the bishops' earlier demands for action against magic.

In addition to these rare, direct measures, each diocese had more routine mechanisms for detecting and punishing magic along with other sins. Most important were the church courts. A large number of church court records survives from medieval England, mostly from the fifteenth and early sixteenth centuries, though they vary greatly in the amount of detail they give about cases and in the offences that were tried there. Most church court cases resembled modern civil lawsuits in that they were brought by one of the parties against the other. Canon law textbooks often embellished their columns of text with illustrations of these cases, showing the parties arguing in front of the bishop: one, in a manuscript of Gratian's *Decretum* which was in England in the fourteenth century, shows a wife claiming her husband is impotent, depicted at the heading of the chapter on impotence caused by magic (illus. 16). There are also a few cases in which people came to court voluntarily, to clear their names after rumours were spread about them. In both these types of case, the courts responded to the demands of laypeople and local clergy, rather than to the bishop's initiative. But some cases were initiated by the bishop's administrators, acting on general rumours or on reports they had received during visitations.

Visitations were periodic inspections of parishes and monasteries which bishops or their representatives were supposed to undertake. The bishop's men would inspect the state of the parish church and its equipment (sometimes checking for locks on fonts and chrismatories) and then question a group of prominent parishioners about whether there were any problems in the parish, either with the priest or with laypeople who habitually committed moral offences. The questions varied considerably and so did parishioners' answers. Quite often they simply said *omnia bene*, 'everything's fine' – and perhaps it was, but some parishioners may simply have been unwilling to stir up trouble by reporting their neighbours or a priest they liked. Like church court records, visitation records vary in their contents and level of detail but they say much about what concerned late medieval parishioners including, occasionally, magic. Finally, magic cases also appear occasionally on their own in bishops' registers (records of business), as did the cases of John Smith and Agnes Hancock. These were probably cases which were regarded as particularly serious or which for some reason could not be dealt with by the usual methods of church court and visitation.

Formal action against magic through any of these mechanisms was not very common. Many bishops' registers and visitation records

16 Husband and wife arguing a case before the bishop at his Consistory Court: illustration at the top of the chapter on impotence caused by magic in a 13th-century French manuscript of Gratian's *Decretum*, the handbook of canon law.

do not mention it at all and those that do include only a handful of cases. This does not necessarily mean magic was rare, but it does suggest bishops did not routinely pursue it. Cases were more frequent in the church courts, with an average of one to three people per year accused in those dioceses that have been studied in depth. Although not negligible, these numbers are far lower than the numbers of people prosecuted for some other sins, such as sexual and marital offences.[31] Again this suggests magic was not a high priority either for bishops or for the laypeople who initiated many cases.

The ways in which cases came to bishops' attention suggest the same. Often, magic did not come to the attention of church courts or visitations in isolation. Many of the recorded cases are not only about magic and in some it is not even the primary allegation. For example, in January 1280 Archbishop William Wickwane of York conducted a visitation of Selby Abbey in Yorkshire. The monks there reported that their abbot, Thomas of Whalley, had very many faults. He did not (they said) observe the Rule of St Benedict or participate in the communal life of the monastery as he should. He had given away part of the monastery's property to his kinsmen and he had slept with two women. Furthermore, he had been involved in magic. At the end of a long list of misdemeanours, it is reported:

> the abbot procured Elias Fauvelle, an enchanter and magical practitioner, to search for the body of his dead brother, which had sunk in the water of the River Ouse. He spent a great sum of money on this.[32]

Thomas's consultation of a diviner is only one of a long list of reasons why he was an unsuitable abbot and even then, part of the problem was that he had spent a large sum of money on it, perhaps the abbey's money. If it were not for his other shortcomings, it is doubtful whether Thomas's attempt at divination alone would have been reported to the Archbishop. Faced with these accusations, Wickwane deposed Thomas and ordered him to do penance at Durham Cathedral Priory; but he was still at Selby two months later when he took some of the abbey's horses and possessions and ran off in the night.[33] This is the last we hear of him.

The next Archbishop of York also had to deal with a wayward monk accused of magic. In 1286, Archbishop John Le Romeyn ordered the rector of Birkin in North Yorkshire to seek out Godfrey Darel, a monk of Rievaulx Abbey who had left the monastery and was practising 'nefarious harmful magic spells and incantations', 'to the harm of his own salvation and, alas, the manifest scandal of the orthodox'.[34] In this case Darel seems to have come to the Archbishop's notice initially not because of the magic but because he had absconded from his monastery: the letter asking the rector to find him is described in the Archbishop's register as a 'letter to recall an apostate', that is, a runaway monk. Bishops routinely asked monasteries about runaways during visitations and sometimes took action against them themselves, so Darel's case would probably have reached the Archbishop sooner or later even without the added scandal of magic.[35]

The church courts also heard cases in which magic appears as just one of many allegations. The most striking example of this is the case of William Netherstrete, a chaplain in Fulbourn, near Cambridge, who was summoned to the Bishop of Ely's court in 1377. Netherstrete was accused of having sex with several women, cutting one of them in her private parts because he suspected her of sleeping with another man, and hitting three other clerics in Fulbourn church. He was also charged with going to taverns with suspicious persons, day and night, and trading in wheat. On top of this, he was accused of using magic on yet another woman:

> The same Sir William ['sir' is the honorific title for a priest] performed magic, that is, by employing conjurations and incantations with which he implored and solicited Katherine, the wife of Henry Molle of Fulbourn, to come to his chamber by night so that he could violently oppress her in adultery.[36]

Faced with this host of accusations, William admitted sleeping with some of the women some years previously and hitting one of the clerics, but he denied the other charges, including the charge of magic. He was ordered to find twelve witnesses who would swear he was telling the truth, a process known as compurgation. People who denied accusations in the church courts were very often asked to do this and the number of witnesses required varied depending on the person and the offence: twelve was relatively high, which reflects the serious nature of the charges. If you failed to find enough witnesses to swear to your truthfulness, the courts assumed you were guilty. At a later session of the court Netherstrete duly produced his witnesses, though he continued to pursue a separate dispute with one of the other Fulbourn clerics whom he had been accused of hitting.[37]

William Netherstrete had probably not behaved well and he had made enemies. Two years before these accusations he was one of a group of men who sued William Fool, the vicar of nearby Hinton: they claimed Fool had accused them of theft and excommunicated them unjustly.[38] It is not impossible that he had dabbled in love magic since a few clerics did own magical texts, but the accusation may simply have been a convenient way of further blackening an already unpopular priest's name, while at the same time explaining any strange behaviour on the part of Katherine Molle. If this was the case, then the accusation of love magic reflected existing perceptions of who was at fault, reinforcing the image of Netherstrete as a violent and sexually aggressive man.

Laypeople might also be accused of magic as one of several crimes which drew them to the attention of their neighbours. In 1482, Joanna Beverley of London was accused of using love magic on two men as well as being a whore and procuress.[39] In 1445 a woman called Christina East took pre-emptive action when she was rumoured to be guilty of a similar combination of crimes. She came before the Bishop of Rochester's court to clear herself of adultery, prostitution and magic. Specifically she said a malicious rumour was being spread that she was a 'hagge' – a word which could mean a witch, a female evil spirit, or just an ugly and malicious old woman.[40] She produced several witnesses to her good character, all of them women, and left with her reputation officially restored.

A few cases of magic were also linked to heresy. This is not surprising because, as we have seen, from the early fourteenth century onwards some forms of magic were deemed heretical by theologians and canon lawyers. In 1417 the diviner John Smith was made to abjure heresy as well as magic after he falsely named another man as a thief. The three women including Agnes Hancock who were accused of magic in front of John Stafford in 1438 were also made to abjure heresy, while in 1491 Isabel Gartrygge from the diocese of Winchester was accused of believing and teaching 'heretical ways of sorcery'.[41] In these cases, the combination of heresy and magic may have arisen because the accused had combined their magical practices with teaching false beliefs. John Smith had 'openly and publicly declared and preached that it is licit to use conjurations and magic, for St Peter and St Paul had done this',[42] while Isabel Gartrygge had taught sorcery and so may have been seen as leading others astray. Cases such as these could potentially have paved the way for church courts to conflate magic and heresy into the single crime of witchcraft, but in England they remained a minority. Usually the ecclesiastical authorities adhered to the older view that magic was a separate issue from doctrinal deviance.

In all these cases magic was not the sole reason these people came to the attention of the authorities. Often we can also see why they ended up in court. Some of the people accused, notably Thomas of Whalley and William Netherstrete, seem to have alienated many of the people around them, so they were liable to be reported for something sooner or later. It is also unlikely to be a coincidence that several cases involved members of the clergy. Monks were more closely supervised by the bishop than laypeople, and runaways such as Godfrey Darel would be noticed. Outside the monastery, priests were expected to adhere to higher standards of conduct than laypeople, so the misbehaviour of a priest such as William Netherstrete was more likely to provoke complaints from parishioners than the misbehaviour of a layperson.

Magic was also more likely to come to the bishop's attention if it caused a scandal. Studies of the church courts have emphasized how selective prosecutions were and stressed the importance of community disapproval in determining which accusations were reported, and this was equally true of magic.[43] Godfrey Darel was said to have caused a scandal by his divination, and scandal was also sometimes noted in church court records. For example Elena Dalok, a London woman who was accused in 1493 of (among other things) being an enchantress and saying anyone she cursed would soon die, was described as a 'scandalizer' of her neighbours – not surprisingly if she was claiming she could curse them to death.[44]

In Elena Dalok's case and other similar ones, there was not only scandal but publicity. In Whalley, Lancashire, in 1519, Elizabeth Robynson was alleged to have 'declared openly in public and widely that she intends to keep a fast, called the black fast, to invoke vengeance against Edmund Parker'.[45] A case which came before the court of the deanery of Wisbech in Cambridgeshire in 1462 shows how public threats such as these could turn into formal accusations:

> The churchwardens [of Leverington parish] present that Agnes, wife of William Chamberlain has publicly asserted that whoever she curses will die a bad death, thereby incurring the crime of magic.[46]

In this case the local churchwardens transformed Agnes's public statement into a charge of magic, probably by reporting her to the bishop's
representatives during a visitation.

As well as declaring their powers publicly, Elena Dalok, Elizabeth
Robynson and Agnes Chamberlain had all claimed they could use
magic to harm others – claims which were especially liable to create
both publicity and scandal. But publicity could also cause people
who practised more benign forms of magic to end up in court. 'The
wife of John Herryson, as reported by common knowledge, makes
charms and tells fortunes', recorded the court held by Whalley Abbey
in Lancashire for the parishes under its jurisdiction in 1519.[47] Similarly, in March 1520 Henry Lillingstone from the parish of Broughton
was brought before the court because 'he is commonly said to use the
art of magic to cure diverse persons'.[48] Healers such as Herryson's wife
and Henry Lillingstone trod a fine line: they needed some publicity in
order to get clients, but too much could lead to unwanted attention
from the church. Nevertheless, it is often unclear why these particular healers ended up in court when, presumably, others did not. As we
have seen, Henry Lillingstone's case seems to have been a focus for
the court's concerns about whether an uneducated practitioner had
the right to offer healing charms, but this does not explain why he
came to the attention of the bishop in the first place. Perhaps he, and
John Herryson's wife, had such widespread reputations that the
bishop's representatives were bound to hear about them in visitations.
Alternatively they may have been reported by a client or neighbour if
a patient they were treating grew worse, or if they became involved
in the kinds of arguments which led to witchcraft accusations. Both
of these occasionally happened to healers in later centuries.[49]

A final way in which accusations of magic came to the church
courts was when people who had been publicly accused of magic sued
their accusers for defamation. Thus in 1435 Margaret Lyndysay sued
three men in the church courts of Durham for saying she had made
a man impotent by magic.[50] Occasionally it is clear where the charge
of defamation came from because we find someone who was accused
of magic in court immediately launching a defamation suit against
the person who accused them. For example, in the records of the
Bishop of London's court, one Eleanor Dulyne was cited for using
'divinatory arts' in an attempt to kill her husband. She underwent
compurgation with two witnesses and the next case in the record was
a defamation suit by Eleanor against Anna Miller, who had accused

her of trying to poison her husband, an accusation which suggests Anna was also the source of the magic charge.[51]

These suits point to a world of rumours and accusations of magic which were not followed up automatically by the ecclesiastical authorities and came to court only when the defamed person chose to sue or approached the court voluntarily in order to clear themselves, as Christina East did. Magic was probably not the most common accusation in local gossip-defamation cases which concern sexual insults or accusations of crime were much more frequent.[52] Nevertheless, rumours and accusations of magic were probably far more common than the number of formal accusations suggests, and they were plausible and serious enough to prompt some of the people on the receiving end to sue their accusers.

These cases suggest that most of the time, the church did not seek out magic for its own sake, although bishops occasionally made attempts to do so. Instead there were in many cases clear reasons why individuals were accused – reasons which drew some people to the attention of the authorities or encouraged their neighbours to report them. Many other cases probably went unreported if people did not sue for defamation or if they were less prominent or had greater levels of support within the community.

Penalizing Magic

How did bishops and their representatives treat those cases which did come to court? Like the pattern of accusations, the penalties given suggest that typically magic was not viewed as a major concern, but under certain circumstances it could be taken much more seriously. Accusations connected with the royal family were treated especially seriously and could lead to harsh punishments, including death, but they are hardly typical of most magic prosecutions in medieval England: they were high-profile, there were often clear political motivations at work, and even in the fifteenth century they were relatively infrequent. There is also little evidence they had any impact on the regular prosecution of magic at diocesan level.

A few magical practitioners at lower social levels did receive heavy penances in the church courts, however. The healer John Wilmot from Winchester was given a substantial penance for using healing magic, equivalent to the penance for heresy, perhaps because he had a large clientele and claimed to be successful.[53] Henry Lillingstone also

17 A church court record from the deanery of Wisbech, Cambridgeshire, with later updating by a scribe.

received a relatively heavy penance, again perhaps because of his wide clientele. He was ordered to swear publicly not to use his medicines any more; to offer a candle, barefoot and wearing only a shirt, at his parish church every Sunday in Lent; to fast on bread and water every Wednesday and Friday for a year; and to make a pilgrimage barefoot to the shrine of the Virgin Mary at Walsingham. But these cases were not the norm and often the people who were convicted of magic in the church courts received light penances.[54]

Moreover, if defendants failed to appear in court when summoned, they were not rigorously chased. This was a general problem for the church courts: if people ignored summonses to come to court, they could be excommunicated, but if they ignored that or left the area, then there was little the church could do.[55] Nevertheless, the church courts did follow up cases of magic as far as they could. In the Ely records, William Netherstrete's case reappeared in several later court sessions until it was eventually resolved. In the deanery of Wisbech in Cambridgeshire, a scribe went back to the original record of two cases of magic from November 1463 to note how they had ended. Beside the case of Hugo Rokysby, who had been accused of doing magic with 'diverse persons', he noted when the case was closed with the word 'recessit', 'he withdrew', squeezed almost invisibly into the margin. Further down the page, where Robert Mabley had been accused of speaking incantations over fishing nets, the scribe noted that on the appointed day Robert cleared himself by compurgation and so the case was dismissed (illus. 17).[56] Overall, then, although the church courts did not make a point of pursuing magic cases especially rigorously, they dealt with them as carefully as they dealt with any other offence.

There are several reasons magic generally attracted no special attention. Bishops were busy and had limited resources, and in the fifteenth century they probably regarded Lollardy as a much greater threat than magic. Under these circumstances, prosecuting magic was not a priority unless someone made a complaint or a case provoked widespread rumour or scandal. It is also possible that many people did not identify their own or their neighbours' practices as magic at all, deeming them to be legitimate religious rituals, or that they took a less strict view of them than theologians did, especially if the intention behind a given practice seemed pious and the practitioner 'discreet' (in the widely quoted words of the thirteenth-century pastoral writer William of Rennes) and not scandalous.

But toleration was not universal and some people who used healing charms which included religious language were reported to the church courts. Some people therefore classed these practices as magic; or at least knew they could give them as grounds for accusations of magic in a church court. An exact boundary between magic and religion may at times have been difficult to identify but some people at least were aware of which practices lay near the borderline and could lead to accusations. It is also clear that the action taken against magic does not always correspond neatly with the comments made about it in treatises on confession and preaching. It was not simply a case of assessing whether particular practices met theologians' definitions of 'magic', although no doubt this played a part. Equally if not more important were the many specific factors which led the ecclesiastical authorities to act, or not act, against magic in individual cases.

The church's response to magic in medieval England therefore remained conservative into the sixteenth century. There is little evidence that magic and heresy were becoming fused together in the way they were in some parts of Europe. Nor is there much evidence that magic was regarded as an unusually horrible crime in the way witchcraft was. Despite occasional attempts by bishops to launch action against magic, there is also little evidence that concern was increasing overall. Even in the fifteenth century bishops were usually reactive rather than proactive, dealing with cases when they arose rather than seeking out magical practitioners. Bishops could feel strongly about magic: some wrote about it in heated terms and when cases came to their attention they dealt with them as carefully as they did other offences. But they did not regard it as worthy of special attention.

In medieval English society more generally, cases of magic appear regularly enough in the records to suggest that the accusation was a recognized, if not necessarily frequent, part of local gossip. There were also some circumstances which made formal accusations more likely: widespread rumours, defamation suits, or when magic appeared as one of a group of accusations against an unpopular individual. However, the records are often brief and the individual circumstances behind many cases remain obscure. As in later periods, local relationships, tensions and reputations are likely to have been crucial in determining when people chose to label certain practices as 'magic' and report them in a visitation or in the church court, and also in determining whether the local authorities deemed such accusations worth pursuing.

Even though most educated English clergy probably believed magic could have real effects, then, patterns of prosecution do not suggest they believed it was so dreadful that it needed to be actively rooted out. Mechanisms existed by which serious cases could be reported and dealt with, and they probably coexisted with less formal ways of protecting oneself against harmful magic, of the sort described in chapter Four. The attitude to magic in medieval England therefore appears much like the attitude to most other crimes and sins. This is perhaps not surprising. The witch trials of the early modern period may have distorted our view of how magic was regarded by most people in most periods of history, leading us to expect that magic will be seen as an unusually threatening and serious sin, one that provokes especial horror. Some studies of witch trials have questioned how far this picture is true even for the sixteenth and seventeenth centuries, pointing out that many places did not see large numbers of witch trials and often local elites did not give witchcraft a high priority.[57] In medieval England, before harmful magic was commonly linked with other terrible crimes, it might be expected that local elites would give it a similarly low priority most of the time. This seems to have been more typical of medieval attitudes to magic than the intense fears found in some places in the fifteenth century and later.

CONCLUSION

Religion and Magic: Medieval
England and Beyond

This book has traced the attitudes of the educated clergy of medieval England to various practices and beliefs which were seen as magic. Some of these bordered on orthodox religious practices or on legitimate ways of interpreting and manipulating the natural world, especially methods for healing the sick or predicting the future. But others differed more radically from official religious rituals. The use of magic to harm people and animals, the belief in elves, fairies and otherworldly ladies who flew around with their followers at night, and the ritual magic done by educated magicians who tried to call up demons, were all much harder to integrate with official Christian belief. We can learn about all these practices and beliefs, and more, from the treatises which were written to educate medieval clergy about how to preach and how to hear confessions. These treatises describe some of the kinds of people who used magic, what they did and why. The information they give is sometimes patchy and it is written to serve a particular agenda: to condemn the practices which most bothered educated clergy. Nevertheless, these treatises on pastoral care give us glimpses of a world of practices and beliefs which we would otherwise know little about.

It is clear both from confession and preaching manuals and from other sources that magic took many different forms. It could be as mundane as speaking incantations over fishing nets or predicting good or bad fortune for the day, or as outlandish as the ritual magic which aimed to call up demons and which was presented by *exempla* as having spectacular effects and a tendency to misfire badly. But whether it was commonplace or exotic, much magic responded to everyday hopes and fears which were shared by almost everyone: gaining prosperity and good fortune; predicting and avoiding bad luck; finding lost or stolen goods; curing illnesses; explaining misfortune; and warding off evil influences that might harm you or your livelihood. Other kinds of magic answered the more specific concerns of particular social groups. For example, ritual magic responded to the anxieties of its learned male users, such as their desire to be better educated or more successful with superiors and with women, while many churchmen portrayed love magic as a response to women's desire to find a good husband, maintain a happy marriage, or conceive children.[1] In most cases magic was therefore a pragmatic response to widespread concerns, a way of trying to control events and improve your life.

It was probably also common. Medieval English churchmen often acknowledged that magic was widespread, although they sometimes found it convenient to denounce it as the preserve of ignorant laypeople or superstitious old women. Methods for predicting the future and healing charms were copied by many different kinds of people, including clergy, and many others were probably transmitted orally to a broader audience. Harmful magic and beliefs relating to fairies could also be taken seriously by both clergy and laity, although there was some scepticism. The historian Richard Kieckhefer has described these practices as a 'common tradition' of magic, known and practised by a wide range of people, and medieval English churchmen also seem to have thought this was the case.[2] But even ritual magic, which was restricted to the educated, is likely to have formed part of common knowledge about magic, and preachers used stereotypes about exotic, scholarly, demon-summoning magicians to add colour to a variety of moral stories.

When they wrote about these common practices, medieval English churchmen borrowed some of their information from earlier sources. Textbooks such as the twelfth-century *Decretum* of Gratian shaped educated clergy's ideas about which practices should be viewed as magic, setting out why these things were condemned when others were not. But medieval English clergy who wrote about pastoral care did not just copy earlier texts. A significant number of them also gave new details about magical practices which they said existed in their own time. Some writers described what they claimed were real cases and beliefs – although some of these 'real' cases of demon-summoning magicians and superstitious old ladies were probably closer to urban myths than real events. Other writers copied these details about specific practices and incidents. Even if they did not record their own first-hand observations, then, it is clear that many educated churchmen placed a high value on examples and experience, which gave their discussions of magic a practical tone. Moreover, they continued to do this into the fifteenth century despite having an ever-growing pile of earlier works to draw on. Information about current practices, or what were believed to be current practices, remained an important part of pastoral writing.

The details about current practices in pastoral manuals reveal much about magic and its practitioners in medieval England, although the information they give is often fragmentary. Medieval English confession and preaching manuals are nowhere near as extensive as, for example, the records kept by the Inquisition in sixteenth- and seventeenth-century Italy, which many historians have used to reconstruct early modern magical practices in depth and examine what they meant to the people who enacted them or feared them.[3] There are also too few recorded trials for magic for us to generalize safely about how common different kinds of magic were or why particular instances came to court when, probably, many others did not, though we can see some factors which made court cases more likely. Later sources such as the Inquisition records and the records of early modern witch trials alert us to how much may have gone unrecorded in the Middle Ages, and we should be wary of assuming that the magical beliefs and practices of medieval England were any less rich or complex than those of later centuries. Nevertheless, pastoral manuals, church court records and other sources do allow us to sketch the outlines of magic in medieval England: both some of the beliefs and practices which existed and educated churchmen's attitudes to them.

As the more detailed records from later periods show, many of the magical practices which medieval English clergy faced were not unique to medieval England. Indeed it would be surprising if they were, since magic often addressed universal needs and anxieties. Clergy in other parts of Europe found many of the same treatises on pastoral care useful, and they probably confronted similar kinds of magic, subject to local variations. Clergy in other periods of history also encountered similar practices, from the early church to well after the Reformation. As late as the 1890s the Reverend John Christopher Atkinson, who ministered for many years in rural North Yorkshire, published an account of his time there which included descriptions of magical healers and the belief in malevolent magic – although unlike medieval clergy, who viewed such things as popular superstitions which should be eradicated, Atkinson wrote in order to record the last traces of a vanishing world of folk belief.[4] Our understanding of magic in medieval England, and the church's attitude to it, therefore has implications for how we view magic in other periods and places in pre-modern Europe. What did churchmen resist, where did they accommodate, and how did they make these decisions?

When medieval clergy wrote about magical practices, they did so as part of a much broader mission to spread what they saw as correct religious belief and observance. As we have seen, many 'magical' practices had a religious dimension: healing charms often invoked God and the saints; divination, especially from dreams, recalled the prophetic dreams of the Bible; and otherworldly beings might be interpreted as ghosts from Christian Purgatory. Even ritual magic made use of religious language in order to control demons, although it was less easy to argue that this was a legitimate religious exercise. Writing about southern Italy in a later period, the historian David Gentilcore has described this range of practices as a 'system of the sacred', in which religious language, rituals and ideas were adapted unofficially to provide order and security for people's everyday lives.[5] Other historians have pointed out that in medieval England, too, Christian language and rituals were widely used to provide help with everyday concerns, stretching legitimate religion further than strict theologians liked. Keith Thomas called this 'the magic of the medieval church' but more recent historians have stressed that much of this unofficial ritual would not have been seen as magic at the time.[6]

Pastoral writers and other clergy interested in pastoral care therefore faced a situation in which the boundaries of religion were permeable and magic was not always easy to define. This was not a new problem but medieval churchmen from the thirteenth to the fifteenth centuries approached it in a distinctive way. First they developed clear definitions of magic so clergy could apply these to the practices they encountered in the world around them. They also set out in more detail than most earlier writers exactly which practices should be categorized as magic and, just as importantly, why. On the one hand they distinguished magical practices from practices which worked naturally, here reflecting a growing interest in the natural world in intellectual circles. On the other hand they identified specific factors which rendered apparently religious activities magical: the most important was the insertion of unknown names into otherwise orthodox prayers. These criteria for defining magic were developed not just in England but in conjunction with other educated, pastorally concerned clergy across western Europe. The most influential pastoral manuals circulated internationally, and international institutions such as the orders of friars, universities and the papacy encouraged the movement of clergy, and with them moved texts and ideas.

This focus on establishing clear criteria for defining beliefs and practices as magic also had a reverse side: it concentrated priests' attentions on a relatively narrow group of practices which fitted their definitions. Practices which did not meet these criteria were by implication accepted and were rarely discussed. As we have seen, many charms, in particular, did not meet pastoral writers' definitions of magic and were copied by medical writers, some of whom were clergy themselves.

Medieval English pastoral writers were therefore not unsure of the boundaries between magic, religion and the natural world. Rather they developed a rough consensus about where those boundaries should lie and they worked hard to close down some of the ambiguities and to offer clear ways of distinguishing between magic and legitimate practices. Their approach was essentially practical, and aimed to equip their readers with the tools to define magic when faced with a range of questionable practices. In this way, alongside the diversity of possible views, we can see a single church attitude to magic taking shape.

What, then, was this attitude? First, it is striking that pastoral writers did not usually mention many of the practices which Protestants later denounced as superstitious or magical and which Keith Thomas termed 'the magic of the medieval church'. These included the use of blessings and sacramentals (consecrated objects such as holy water and blessed salt) to heal, ward off evil spirits or promote agricultural fertility; and the miracles associated with saints' shrines. Medieval English clergy could have viewed some of these practices as magic if they had chosen to, since there were intellectual currents, especially in the fifteenth century, which raised doubts about them. In parts of Continental Europe, some fifteenth-century theologians who wrote treatises on superstition and witchcraft did worry about the appropriation and misuse of sacramentals and blessings by the laity, and in England the Lollards went further and denounced them as magic from the late fourteenth century onwards. But this was not the case with most English clergy. Indeed, once Lollards began to take a less tolerant view of blessings and sacramentals, this probably discouraged other English clergy from criticizing them because to do so was too close to heresy. But it was not only Lollardy which discouraged most educated clergy from discussing sacramentals and blessings. Many pastoral writers had taken the same approach long before the fifteenth century, both in England and in continental Europe. For these writers the use of officially promoted rituals to protect against misfortune or secure blessings on earth was not even worth discussing in the context of magic. Instead of focusing on the blessings and sacramentals which could be found in liturgical books and which were generally supervised by priests, pastoral writers were primarily concerned with what happened when religious rituals or substances were taken out of this official setting and adapted unofficially.

Because they were concerned with the ways in which people adapted religious rituals and ideas unofficially, many pastoral writers focused on the issue of personal authority and trust. Could the people who adapted religious rituals be trusted to do so responsibly? A priest was more likely to be deemed responsible and other experts such as physicians were also seen as more trustworthy than most, but many pastoral writers acknowledged that some laypeople, both men and women, could possess the 'discretion' and good character which qualified someone to use healing charms. There was no absolute consensus about this, however, and some writers expressed particular suspicions about women and the poor; the fourteenth-century friar John Bromyard, who attacked poor women who acted as cunning folk or believed they flew around at night, was one of the most extreme. As Kathleen Kamerick has suggested, these conflicting attitudes about how far different groups of laypeople could be trusted to adapt religious rituals reflect a wider debate within medieval clerical culture about how competent laypeople were to understand religious matters.[7] With no single official view, pastoral writing on the boundaries between magic and religion reflects the same tension.

For medieval English clergy, and clergy elsewhere in late medieval Europe, then, part of the concern about magic was a concern about how much religious diversity could be tolerated. Their answer to this was not always clear-cut but, as we have seen, a general consensus did emerge which singled out particular practices as magical and others as not worth discussing. This consensus worked best for the borderline practices, the ones which might arguably have been seen as legitimate religious beliefs and rituals or as ways of manipulating the natural world: healing charms and amulets, lot-drawing and omens, and to a lesser extent contact with the spirits of the dead. Pastoral writers spent a great deal of time discussing these borderline cases, probably because they were difficult to categorize and argue against and probably also because they were the most common: more people are likely to do something they think is acceptable than something which is thought to be demonic and sinful. Here the English evidence reflects wider ecclesiastical attitudes to magic: for example Mary O'Neil has pointed out that the Inquisition in sixteenth-century Modena, northern Italy, prosecuted healing, divination and love magic more often than other forms of magic which we might expect them to have taken more seriously.[8]

However, this was not the only way in which medieval churchmen approached magic. Not every practice that appeared in the pastoral manuals' discussions of magic can be seen so easily as part of a 'system of the sacred', a potentially legitimate adaptation of religious ritual. It was harder to argue that harmful magic, ritual magic and to a lesser extent beliefs about otherworldly beings bordered on religion (although a few ritual magic texts tried), and yet all held a recognized place in pastoral writing even if they were less commonly mentioned than divination and healing. These kinds of magic prompt us to look beyond debates about the 'magic of the medieval church' and about how medieval churchmen decided whether to sanction particular ritual practices as religious or reject them as magic. When we do so, other patterns start to emerge.

With harmful magic, ritual magic and sometimes with otherworldly beings, churchmen did not try to draw fine distinctions between magic and religion. Instead they presented them as uniformly demonic (though there was some scope for flexibility in the case of ghosts). They also approached these beliefs and practices with greater scepticism, sometimes casting doubt on how far they really worked: whether harmful magic could do all the things claimed for it, whether ritual magicians really could control demons, and whether people who claimed to have contact with the fairies were just dreaming or deluding themselves. Pastoral writers allowed few overlaps here between magical and religious practices.

As we have seen, these practices attracted less attention from clergy. One reason for this was probably that it was not so difficult to persuade people they were wrong. Another reason may be that, although harmful magic and ritual magic seem especially disturbing to modern readers, medieval people may not have seen things that way. Anthropological studies of some twentieth-century societies which believe in magic have argued that it is possible to take the dangers of harmful magic seriously without being permanently anxious about it, particularly if there are well-established methods for countering hostile magical attacks.[9] The strand of scepticism running through educated churchmen's views of these practices may also have encouraged some people, both clergy and laity, to regard them as a lesser threat. This scepticism was not total or consistent but it may have been just enough to raise doubts in people's minds. In fact, some churchmen may have thought that denouncing and prosecuting the people who claimed to do harmful magic or talk to the fairies would give them more credence than they deserved.

Prosecutions launched against magical practitioners also show that, although there could be uncertainty about the overlap between magic and religion, this uncertainty had limits. Some trials of healers such as Henry Lillingstone in the church courts do reflect the fact that the boundary between religious, natural and magical healing could be questionable, and in these cases decisions about what was legitimate were sometimes based on factors such as the status and education of the practitioner as well as on the exact practices they performed. However, other cases, like that of Richard Walker, the chaplain from Worcester who dabbled in ritual magic, or the women who claimed to heal with the help of the fairies and elves, fit this pattern much less well. Some clergy and laypeople went well beyond bending the rules and instead indulged in practices which were generally acknowledged to be wrong, and the bishops who tried Walker and the female healers never argued that their activities could be misconstrued as religious. Educated churchmen did not therefore see every 'magical' practice as needing to be rigidly defined and distinguished from religion. Rather their responses varied from painstaking assessment to mockery and outright rejection.

Above all, it is clear that the educated clergy of medieval England, and medieval Europe more generally, were interested in magic but there is little evidence it was a major source of concern for most of them, most of the time. It was not an essential part of confession and preaching manuals, although many writers included at least a brief reference to it and some said much more. It is also relatively uncommon in church court records and in other sources, including chronicles and the records of miracles performed at saints' shrines, which might be expected to mention magic more often if it was a widespread concern. A few accusations of magic did lead to violent punishments, particularly when the magic was alleged to have been used against the king, but overall, magic's lack of prominence suggests that it was familiar but not obtrusive. Instead the educated clergy of medieval England focused on other problems. These included making sure that priests were properly ordained and behaved as they should (the target of many church councils); that laypeople made confession regularly and in full (the target of many *exempla*); that the rules on marriage were followed (the target of many church court cases); and that, in the fifteenth century, Lollards were detected and forced to recant. Compared with these concerns, magic was a relatively low priority.

The low profile given to magic by English churchmen seems to have persisted through the fifteenth century, despite the changes which were occurring elsewhere in Europe. There are a few indications of change, notably the greater prominence of political accusations of magic in the fifteenth century. Some scholars have also identified changing attitudes in particular kinds of writing. For example Heidi Breuer has suggested that Sir Thomas Malory, who wrote a famous version of the King Arthur legend, the *Morte Darthur*, in the fifteenth century, presented the many magicians in the legend as more demonic than earlier versions of the story did.[10] However, these changes are not found in pastoral writing on magic or, so far as we can tell, in the records of the church courts. They may reflect changing attitudes among some members of the elite, rather than the wider population.

Confession and preaching manuals therefore shed light on the range of attitudes to magic found in medieval England and in other parts of medieval Europe. In many cases these attitudes persisted in later periods, and so too did the practices which medieval churchmen described. For centuries after the Middle Ages (and probably also before) people used magic to identify thieves and stolen goods, used powerful words and objects to cure illness and ward off evil influences, and sometimes feared the harm which malevolent neighbours could do them. The history of these magical practices and beliefs sometimes involved repression and prosecution but more often it did not. Instead the usual concern, at least for the clergy, was to establish which practices should be seen as magic, and set this out clearly so that it could be preached to the laity. Beyond that, they condemned and sometimes mocked other magical practices but without much persecution. From this perspective the witch trials appear anomalous. The typical attitude of many medieval clergy and laity to magic was less anxious and more concerned to situate it within wider under-standings of religion and the natural world, and this was probably characteristic of many people in the pre-modern past.

References

All translations are my own unless a translation is mentioned in the References. In quotations from primary sources, I have given the Latin original if the text only survives in manuscript or in an early printed book. I have also modernized the spelling of English works. Many medieval works on penance were divided into books and then further subdivided, perhaps several times, to help readers find their places in different manuscripts where there would be no consistent page numbering. For ease of reference, where there is not a modern edition of a text I have noted these subdivisions as well as the page and folio numbers where these are given. For example 'Gratian, *Decretum,* 26.1.3' refers to Gratian's *Decretum*, Case 26, question 1, chapter 3; 'John of Freiburg, *Summa Confessorum*, 1.11.21' refers to book 1, title 11, chapter 21 of the *Summa* while 'John Bromyard, *Summa Praedicantium*, 'Sortilegium' 1 refers to the chapter on *sortilegium*, article 1 in Bromyard's *Summa*.

BL = London, British Library
CUL = Cambridge University Library
OBL = Oxford, Bodleian Library

Introduction

1 J.-P. Migne, ed., *Patrologia Latina* (Paris, 1855), vol. 207, cols 190–95.
2 Norman Tanner and Sethina Watson, 'Least of the Laity: the Minimum Requirements for a Medieval Christian', *Journal of Medieval History*, 32 (2006), pp. 395–423.
3 See Stephen Wilson, *The Magical Universe: Everyday Ritual and Magic in Pre-Modern Europe* (London and New York, 2000).
4 Keith Thomas, *Religion and the Decline of Magic* (London, 1971), p. 32.
5 Valerie Flint, *The Rise of Magic in Early Medieval Europe* (Oxford, 1991), pp. 83–4.
6 Eamon Duffy, *The Stripping of the Altars: Traditional Religion in England, 1400–1580* (New Haven, CT, 1992), ch. 8.
7 Karen Jolly, *Popular Religion in Late Saxon England* (Chapel Hill, NC, 1996), pp. 15–18, 89–90.

8 Dieter Harmening, *Superstitio: Überlieferungs- und Theoriegeschichtliche Untersuchungen zur Kirchlich-Theologischen Aberglaubensliteratur des Mittelalters* (Berlin, 1979); Karin Baumann, *Aberglaube für Laien: zur Programmatik und Überlieferung Mittelalterlicher Superstitionenkritik* (Würzburg, 1989); Michael D. Bailey, 'A Late-Medieval Crisis of Superstition?' *Speculum*, 84 (2009), pp. 633–61; Michael D. Bailey, 'Concern over Superstition in Late Medieval Europe', in *The Religion of Fools? Superstition Past and Present*, ed. S. A. Smith and Alan Knight, *Past and Present*, Supplement 3 (Oxford, 2008), pp. 115–33; Euan Cameron, *Enchanted Europe: Superstition, Reason and Religion, 1250–1750* (Oxford, 2010); Kathleen Kamerick, 'Shaping Superstition in Late Medieval England', *Magic, Ritual and Witchcraft*, 3 (2008), pp. 29–53.

9 C. S. Watkins, *History and the Supernatural in Medieval England* (Cambridge, 2007), chs 3–4.

10 On magical texts see the works cited in chapter 5. On academic writing see Jean-Patrice Boudet, *Entre science et nigromance: astrologie, divination et magie en l'Occident médiéval* (Paris, 2006) and the works cited by Cohn and Peters in ch. 7.

11 On approaches to defining magic since the nineteenth century see Stanley Jeyaraja Tambiah, *Magic, Science, Religion and the Scope of Rationality* (Cambridge, 1990).

12 Hildred Geertz, 'An Anthropology of Religion and Magic, I', *Journal of Interdisciplinary History*, 6 (1975), pp. 76–7. For Thomas's reply see Keith Thomas, 'An Anthropology of Religion and Magic, II', *Journal of Interdisciplinary History*, 6 (1975), pp. 91–109.

13 Richard Kieckhefer, *Magic in the Middle Ages* (Cambridge, 1989), pp. 15–16; Richard Kieckhefer, 'The Specific Rationality of Medieval Magic', *American Historical Review*, 99 (1994), pp. 822–3; Karen Jolly, 'Medieval Magic: Definitions, Beliefs, Practices', in *Witchcraft and Magic in Europe: the Middle Ages*, ed. Karen Jolly, Catharina Raudvere and Edward Peters (London, 2002), pp. 11–12.

14 Bailey, 'Late-Medieval Crisis', p. 633.

15 Gratian, *Decretum*, ed. E. Friedberg, *Corpus Iuris Canonici*, vol. 1 (Leipzig, 1879, repr. Graz, 1959), Case 26.

16 Augustine, *De Doctrina Christiana*, ed. and trans. R.P.H. Green (Oxford, 1995), pp. 91–101.

17 Kieckhefer, 'Specific Rationality', p. 819.

18 Robert Bartlett, *The Natural and the Supernatural in the Middle Ages* (Cambridge, 2008), p. 20.

19 J. A. Sharpe, *Instruments of Darkness: Witchcraft in England, 1550–1750* (London, 1996), p. 108. For the 15th-century Alpine trials see my ch. 7.

20 On the reforms see Colin Morris, *The Papal Monarchy: The Western Church from 1050 to 1250* (Oxford, 1989), pp. 433–8, 489–96.

21 C. H. Lawrence, 'The English Parish and its Clergy in the Thirteenth Century', in *The Medieval World*, ed. Peter Linehan and Janet Nelson (London, 2001), p. 655; Nicholas Bennett, 'Pastors and Masters: the Beneficed

Clergy of North-East Lincolnshire, 1290–1340', in *The Foundations of Medieval English Ecclesiastical History*, ed. Philippa Hoskin (Woodbridge, 2005), pp. 47–8.

22 Leonard Boyle, 'The "Oculus Sacerdotis" and Some Other Works of William of Pagula', *Transactions of the Royal Historical Society*, 5th ser. 5 (1955), p. 92, repr. in Boyle, *Pastoral Care*.

23 Marion Gibbs and Jane Lang, *Bishops and Reform, 1215–1272* (London, 1934), pp. 131–73; Helen Birkett, 'The Pastoral Application of the Lateran IV Reforms in the Northern Province, 1215–1348', *Northern History*, 43 (2006), pp. 199–219.

24 For different views see Lawrence, 'English Parish', pp. 661–6; Jeffrey H. Denton, 'The Competence of the Parish Clergy in Thirteenth-Century England', in *The Church and Learning in Later Medieval Society*, ed. Caroline Barron and Jenny Stratford (Donington, 2002), pp. 273–85.

25 Leonard Boyle, '*Summae Confessorum*', in *Les Genres Littéraires dans les Sources Théologiques et Philosophiques Médiévales: Définition, Critique et Exploitation* (Louvain-la-Neuve, 1982), pp. 227–37; Pierre Michaud-Quantin, *Sommes de Casuistique et Manuels de Confession au Moyen Age (XII–XVI siècles)* (Louvain, 1962); Leonard Boyle, *Pastoral Care, Clerical Education and Canon Law, 1200–1400* (London, 1981).

26 Thomas of Chobham, *Summa Confessorum*, ed. F. Broomfield (Louvain, 1968), p. lxxvi.

27 Flint, *Rise of Magic*, Harmening, *Superstitio* and Bernadette Filotas, *Pagan Survivals, Superstitions and Popular Cultures in Early Medieval Pastoral Literature* (Toronto, 2005).

28 Most notably Baumann, *Aberglaube für Laien*.

29 G. R. Owst, '*Sortilegium* in English Homiletic Literature of the Fourteenth Century', in *Studies Presented to Sir Hilary Jenkinson*, ed. J. Conway Davies (London, 1957), pp. 272–303.

30 Harmening, *Superstitio*, p. 318; Filotas, *Pagan Survivals*, p. 51.

31 See ch. 3, ref. 21.

Chapter 1: Predicting the Future and Healing the Sick: Magic and the Natural World

1 'Experimenta pro furtis: Si uis scire quis ille sit qui res tuas furatus sit, scribe hec nomina in cera uirginea et tene ea super caput tuum cum manu tua sinistra, et in sopno [sic] tuo uidebis illum qui fecerat furtum: + agios crux + agios crux + agios crux domini. In nomine patris etc. Item si quis tibi aliquid furatus fuerit uel susspicionem super aliquod habueris, ita poteris scire: perquire spumam argenti que proicitur de argento quando funditur, et cum albumine oui illam fortiter tere. Postea in aliquo pariete depinge talem oculum. Postea conuoca omnes de quibus tibi susspicio fit. Statim ut accesserint, oculum dextrum illorum qui rei fuerint uidebis lacrimantem.' OBL MS e.Mus 219, f. 186r.

2 Robert Bartlett, *The Natural and the Supernatural in the Middle Ages* (Cambridge, 2008), pp. 29–32.

3 Ibid., p. 66.

4 Stuart Jenks, 'Astrometeorology in the Middle Ages', *Isis*, 74 (1983), p. 194.

5 See Luke Demaitre, 'The Art and Science of Prognostication in Early University Medicine', *Bulletin of the History of Medicine*, 77 (2003), pp. 765–88.

6 Thomas of Chobham, *Summa Confessorum*, ed. F. Broomfield (Louvain, 1968), pp. 477–8.

7 '*ut quando canis ululat in domo, creditur quod inde sit aliquis cito moriturus et quando pica garrit in tecto, creditur quod aliquis hospes sit cito superuenturus.*' Ranulph Higden, *Speculum Curatorum*, CUL MS Mm.i.20, f. 37v.

8 '*Si quis inueniat ferrum equi vel clauum ferri vulgariter dicit, "Bene valebo isto die."*' Robert Rypon, *Sermons*, BL MS Harley 4894, f. 33v.

9 Augustine, *De Doctrina Christiana*, ed. and trans. R.P.H. Green (Oxford, 1995), pp. 93–9; Gratian, *Decretum*, ed. E. Friedberg, *Corpus Iuris Canonici*, vol. 1 (Leipzig, 1879, repr. Graz, 1959), 26.2.6.

10 Augustine, *De Doctrina Christiana*, p. 99.

11 John Bromyard, *Summa Praedicantium* (Nuremberg, 1518), 'Sortilegium' 3, f. 356v.

12 For one version see A. Lecoy de la Marche, ed., *Anecdotes Historiques, Légendes et Apologues tirés du Recueil Inédit d'Etienne de Bourbon* (Paris, 1877), p. 315.

13 On Trewythian see Sophie Page, 'Richard Trewythian and the Uses of Astrology in Late Medieval England', *Journal of the Warburg and Courtauld Institutes*, 64 (2001), pp. 193–228.

14 Rosemary Horrox, ed. and trans., *The Black Death* (Manchester, 1994), p. 159.

15 '*Si quis consideratione astrorum utatur ad precognoscendum futuros casuales vel fortuitos eventus, vel etiam ad precognoscendum futura opera hominum per certitudinem, procedet hec ex falsa opinione et vana, et tunc opinio demonis se immiscet, unde erit divinatio superstitiosa et illicita. Si vero aliquis utatur consideratione astrorum ad precognoscendum futura que ex celestibus causantur corporibus, puta siccitates et pluvias et alia huiusmodi, non erit illicita divinatio.*' John of Freiburg, *Summa Confessorum* (Lyons, 1518), 1.11.5, f. 31r. On John see Leonard Boyle, 'The *Summa Confessorum* of John of Freiburg and the Popularization of the Moral Teaching of St Thomas and Some of his Contemporaries', in Boyle, *Pastoral Care, Clerical Education and Canon Law* (London, 1981), article III.

16 Hilary M. Carey, *Courting Disaster: Astrology at the English Court and University in the Later Middle Ages* (Basingstoke, 1992), p. 14.

17 Page, 'Richard Trewythian', pp. 200–6.

18 Ibid., p. 206.

19 '*Januarius: Uentos ualidos, habundanciam frugum et bellum . . . December: Habundanciam* [my emendation: MS reads '*habundam*'] *frugum et annone, pacem et concordiam in populo.*' OBL MS Rawlinson D.939, part 3. On this MS see John B. Friedman, 'Harry the Haywarde and Talbat his Dog: An Illustrated Girdlebook from Worcestershire', in *Art into Life: Collected Papers from the Kresge Art Museum Medieval Symposia*, ed. Carol Garrett Fisher and Kathleen L. Scott (East Lansing, 1995), pp. 115–53.

20 'Si dies nativitatis domini in die dominica euenerit, erit bona yemps et quatragesima ventosa, sicca estas. Vites bone erunt et oues multiplicate sane in illo anno erunt. Pax erit, mel erit bonum et multi sani [my emendation: MS reads 'sanes'] morientur. Si in die lune, yemps mutabilis erit, quatragesima bona, estas ventosa et de pluribus [. . .] auferret [my emendation: MS reads 'aufert']. Vites non erunt bone.' BL MS Harley 206, f. 9v.

21 'Sic errant qui in hancellis noui anni vel septimane vel diei nolunt vicinis aliquid concedere nisi hansellum prius ceperint. Ignem vetant vicinis dum parit vacca, vel aura fovit pullos et huiusmodi, vel seminare incipiunt [my emendation: MS says 'inceperint'] in traductionibus sponsarum et etiam in funeribus mortuorum.' Richard of Wetheringsett, Summa, CUL MS Ii.iv.12, pp. 168–9. On Richard see Joseph Goering, 'The Summa "Qui bene present" and its Author', in Literature and Religion in the Later Middle Ages: Philological Studies in Honor of Siegfried Wenzel, ed. Richard G. Newhauser and John A. Alford (Binghamton, NY, 1995), pp. 143–59.

22 Gratian, Decretum, 26.7.14, 26.7.16; John Mirk's Festial, ed. Susan Powell, Early English Texts Society, original ser. 334 (Oxford, 2009), vol. I, p. 44.

23 S. Wenzel, ed. and trans., Fasciculus Morum: a Fourteenth-Century Preacher's Handbook (University Park, PA, 1989), p. 579.

24 'in primo anni ponunt fabas iuxta ignem ad prenoscendum commencionem aliquorum.' Higden, Speculum Curatorum, f. 37r; Stephen Wilson, The Magical Universe: Everyday Ritual and Magic in Pre-Modern Europe (London and New York, 2000), pp. 387–8.

25 See ch. 6, ref. 22.

26 Raymond of Peñafort, Summa de Paenitentia, ed. X. Ochoa and A. Diez (Rome, 1976), col. 391.

27 Linda E. Voigts and Michael R. McVaugh, 'A Latin Technical Phlebotomy and its Middle English Translation', Transactions of the American Philosophical Society, 74 (1984), p. 5.

28 BL MS Harley 209, f. 1v.

29 'Sed talia nullo modo sunt obseruanda, quoniam aspectus orbis beniuolus aut maliuolus non habet ita generalem infixam et determinatam influentiam, cum influentia varietur secundum diuersitatem et cursus diuersorum aspectuum et diuersorum radiorum descendencium. Et ita non possunt concurrere determinate semper in aliquo certo die mensis.' John of Mirfield, Florarium Bartholomei, CUL MS Mm.ii.10, ff. 239r–v. On Mirfield see Carole Rawcliffe, 'The Hospitals of Later Medieval London', Medical History, 28 (1984), p. 9.

30 '"Michi tamen accidit," ait ipsemet de Gordonia, "quod computauerim diligenter horam in qua precise luna esset in Geminis. Et postea volui facere fleubotomiam michi ipsi in illa eadem hora, sed non eram memor. Et tunc quando totum fuit paratum occurrit memorie mee quod tunc fuerit hora illa mala prius a me notata, sed nolui propter hoc dimittere; immo feci fleubotomiam et nunquam melius mihi fuit."' John of Mirfield, Florarium Bartholomei, f. 239v. See also Luke Demaitre, Doctor Bernard de Gordon: Professor and Practitioner (Toronto, 1980), p. 164.

31 Augustine, *De Doctrina Christiana*, pp. 91–3.

32 '*In his que fiunt ad aliquos effectus corporales inducendos, considerandum est utrum naturaliter videantur posse tales effectus causare, et sic non erit illicitum. Si autem naturaliter non videantur tales effectus causare posse, consequens est quod pertineat ad quedam pacta cum demonibus inita . . . Hoc autem specialiter apparet in hoc cum adhibentur aliqui caracteres vel nomina ignota vel alie quecumque varie observationes quas manifestum est naturaliter efficaciam non habere.*' John of Freiburg, *Summa*, 1.11.11, ff. 31v–32r.

33 '*Quondam Londoniis quidam* [my emendation: edition reads '*quidem*'] *dicebatur curari a quartana per imaginem leonis auream secundum certas constellationes factam.*' Alexander Carpenter, *Destructorium Viciorum* (Paris, 1516), 6.52; Robert Holcot, *In Librum Sapientiae Regis Salomonis Praelectiones* (Basel, 1586), p. 530.

34 See Joseph Shatzmiller, 'In Search of the "Book of Figures": Medicine and Astrology in Montpellier at the Turn of the Fourteenth Century', *AJS Review*, 7 (1982), pp. 383–407.

35 Jean-Patrice Boudet, *Entre science et nigromance: astrologie, divination et magie en l'Occident médiéval* (Paris, 2006), p. 123.

36 Frank Klaassen, 'English Manuscripts of Magic, 1300–1500: A Preliminary Survey', in *Conjuring Spirits: Texts and Traditions of Medieval Ritual Magic*, ed. Claire Fanger (Stroud, 1998), p. 7.

37 Joan Evans, *Magical Jewels of the Middle Ages Particularly in England* (Oxford, 1922), p. 112.

38 Thomas of Chobham, *Summa Confessorum*, p. 478.

39 '*Dicit Lincolniensis quod quedam herbe habent virtutem sanatiuam et portari possunt cum euangelio vel orationis dominice verbis vel simboli, ita tamen quod nihil aliud intendatur nisi honor dei et sanitas infirmi.*' Robert Rypon, *Sermons*, f. 34r.

40 Thomas of Chobham, *Summa Confessorum*, p. 478.

41 Claire Fanger, 'Things Done Wisely by a Wise Enchanter: Negotiating the Power of Words in the Thirteenth Century', *Esoterica*, 1 (1999), pp. 97–131.

42 Carpenter, *Destructorium Viciorum*, 6.52; Holcot, *In Librum Sapientiae*, p. 627.

43 *Dives and Pauper*, ed. Priscilla Heath Barnum, Early English Texts Society, original ser. vol. 275 (London, 1976), vol, I, pp. 159–61.

44 '*Diversi sunt experti quod quedam negocia malos eventus denunciant, sicut obviare lepori est malum et obviare bufoni significat bonum.*' '*Multi experiuntur quod inchoare labores vel itinera certis diebus, puta feria tertia, est periculosum et taediosum.* Holcot, *In Librum Sapientiae*, pp. 626, 529.

45 Thomas of Chobham, *Summa Confessorum*, p. 479.

Chapter Two: Charms, Prayers and Prophecies: Magic and Religion

1 '*Sancta Maria carminauit filium suum a morsu alphorum et a morsu hominum et coniunxit os ad os, et sanguinem ad sanguinem, et iuncturam ad iuncturam,*

et sic puer conualuit.' John Bromyard, *Summa Praedicantium* (Nuremberg, 1518) 'Sortilegium' 7, f. 357v.

2 Jonathan Roper, *English Verbal Charms* (Helsinki, 2005), p. 96.

3 '*Quis christianus non diceret ista verba mendosa et contra fidem esse catholicam . . .?*' '*Dicunt tam facientes quam consentientes quod sancta verba dicunt dei et sancte Marie et aliorum sanctorum et orationes multas.*' Bromyard, *Summa,* 'Sortilegium' 7, f. 357v.

4 Jacobus de Voragine, *The Golden Legend*, trans. W. G. Ryan, (Princeton, NJ 1993), vol. II, pp. 52, 217, vol. I, p. 103.

5 Jean-Claude Schmitt, 'Appropriating the Future', in *The Future in the Middle Ages*, ed. J. A. Burrow and Ian Wei (Woodbridge, 2000), pp. 10–11.

6 William E. Klingshirn, 'Defining the Sortes Sanctorum: Gibbon, Du Cange and Early Christian Lot Divination', *Journal of Early Christian Studies*, 10 (2002), p. 95.

7 Gratian, *Decretum*, ed. E. Friedberg, *Corpus Iuris Canonici*, vol. I (Leipzig, 1879, repr. Graz, 1959), 26.2.1–4.

8 Klingshirn, 'Defining the Sortes Sanctorum', pp. 102–3.

9 *Decretals of Gregory IX* 5.21.3 in E. Friedberg, ed., *Corpus Iuris Canonici*, vol. II.

10 Catherine Rider, 'Magic and Unorthodoxy in Late Medieval English Pastoral Manuals', in *The Unorthodox Imagination in Late Medieval Britain*, ed. Sophie Page (Manchester, 2010), p. 103.

11 Robert Bartlett, *Trial by Fire and Water: the Medieval Judicial Ordeal* (Oxford, 1986), pp. 86–90.

12 Raymond of Peñafort, *Summa de Paenitentia*, ed. X. Ochoa and A. Diez (Rome, 1976), col. 390.

13 Thomas of Chobham, *Summa Confessorum*, ed. F. Broomfield (Louvain, 1968), p. 467.

14 '*non credo quod hodie locum habeat sors in electionibus.*' William of Rennes, glosses printed in Raymond of Peñafort, *Summa de Penitentia* (Rome, 1603, repr. Farnborough, 1964), p. 104.

15 W. L. Braekman, 'Fortune-Telling by the Casting of Dice', *Studia Neophilologica*, 52 (1980), p. 6.

16 Ibid., p. 13.

17 Steven F. Kruger, *Dreaming in the Middle Ages* (Cambridge, 1992), pp. 50–53.

18 Ibid., p. 15.

19 '*stultum est.*' '*Multos errare fecerunt somnia.*' Richard of Wetheringsett, *Summa*, p. 170; Peraldus, *Summa*, p. 242.

20 Bromyard, *Summa*, 'Sortilegium' 4, f. 357r.

21 Robert Rypon, *Sermons*, BL MS Harley 4894, f. 34v.

22 Robert Holcot, *In Librum Sapientiae Regis Salomonis Praelectiones* (Basel, 1586), p. 666; Alexander Carpenter, *Destructorium Viciorum* (Paris, 1516), 6.50.

23 Holcot, *In Librum Sapientiae*, pp. 666–7; Carpenter, *Destructorium Viciorum*, 6.50.

24 '*Prima quod divinatio per somnia est licita. Secunda quod talis divinatio non est ab omnibus somniis expectanda. Tertia quod divinatio per somnia est mul-*

tum periculosa.' Carpenter, *Destructorium Viciorum,* 6.50; Holcot, *In Librum Sapientiae,* p. 667.

25 Bromyard, *Summa,* 'Sortilegium' 4, ff. 356v, 357r.

26 Thomas of Chobham, *Sermones,* ed. Franco Morenzoni, *Corpus Christianorum Continuatio Mediaevalis,* vol. LXXXII/A (Turnhout, 1993), p. 237; Robert Rypon, *Sermons,* f. 34r.

27 Jacobus de Voragine, *Golden Legend,* vol. I, pp. 44–5, 98.

28 Gratian, *Decretum,* 26.5.3.

29 Thomas of Chobham, *Summa Confessorum,* p. 477; Raymond of Peñafort, *Summa,* col. 391.

30 Skemer, *Binding Words,* pp. 199–212.

31 William of Rennes, glosses printed in Raymond of Peñafort, *Summa,* pp. 104–5; Catherine Rider, 'Medical Magic and the Church in Thirteenth-Century England', *Social History of Medicine,* 24 (2011), pp. 96–8.

32 See ch. 1, ref. 32.

33 Lea Olsan, 'Charms and Prayers in Medieval Medical Theory and Practice', *Social History of Medicine,* 16 (2003), pp. 349, 352–4.

34 Carole Rawcliffe, *Medicine and Society in Later Medieval England* (Stroud, 1995), p. 95.

35 Tony Hunt, *Popular Medicine in Thirteenth-Century England* (Cambridge, 1990), pp. 26–9.

36 Olsan, 'Charms', p. 360.

37 T. S. Holmes, ed., *The Register of John Stafford, Bishop of Bath and Wells, 1425–1443* (London, 1915–16), p. 227.

38 Catherine Rider, *Magic and Impotence in the Middle Ages* (Oxford, 2006), pp. 163–4, p. 202.

39 Hunt, *Popular Medicine,* p. 88; BL MS Harley 273, f. 85v.

40 Hunt, *Popular Medicine,* p. 96.

41 William Hale, *A Series of Precedents and Proceedings in Criminal Causes extending from the Year 1475 to 1640* (1st edn 1847, repr. Edinburgh, 1973), p. 102.

42 Eamon Duffy, *Marking the Hours: English People and Their Prayers, 1240–1570* (New Haven and London, 2006), ch. 5.

43 *'Salua crux Christi salua me a presenti angustia pestilentie que salutatrix nostra es.' 'Quidam monaco abbate de Corube in comitate Lincolniensis angelus apparuit et imprimebat manu eius ex precepto Ihesu Christi hanc figuram.'* London, Wellcome Library MS 404, f. 32v.

44 Eamon Duffy, *The Stripping of the Altars: Traditional Religion in England, 1400–1580* (New Haven, CT, and London, 1992), pp. 292–8.

45 William of Rennes, glosses in Raymond of Peñafort, *Summa,* p. 105; Rider, 'Medical Magic', p. 98.

46 E. M. Elvey, ed., *The Courts of the Archdeaconry of Buckingham, 1483–1523* (Welwyn Garden City, 1975), p. 257.

47 *'Non verbis cuiuscunque conditionis dedit virtutem sanatiuam, sed ubi ordo vel sanctitas hoc meretur dicentis. Quia sicut in verbis sacramentalibus effectus*

verborum plus ex virtute verborum quam ex sanctitate dependet proferentis, ita econverso in orationibus et verbis sanatiuis et ad miracula pertinentibus: effectus plus dependet ex orantis seu loquentis sanctitate quam ex verborum virtute.' Bromyard, *Summa*, 'Sortilegium' 7, f. 357v.

48 Ibid., 2, f. 356r.

49 S. Wenzel, ed. and trans., *Fasciculus Morum: a Fourteenth-Century Preacher's Handbook* (University Park, PA, 1989), p. 577; '*Invocationes etiam quas vetule faciunt pro infirmitatibus curandis.*' Carpenter, *Destructorium Viciorum*, 6.52.

50 Karen Jones and Michael Zell, '"The Divels Speciall Instruments": Women and Witchcraft before the Great Witch Hunt', *Social History*, 30 (2005), p. 52.

51 Raymond of Peñafort, *Summa*, col. 387.

52 Owen Davies, *Cunning Folk: Popular Magic in English History* (London, 2003), pp. 85–8.

53 '*Si enim sanctitate homines sanarent et iumenta, vel spiritu prophetico futura predicerent, vel spiritu sancto furem dicerent ad correctionem, tam viui quam mortui essent tolendi sicut alii sancti . . . tunc tota ecclesia erraret que docet quod non sunt credendi nec colendi . . . Illi namque sancti cum omnibus aliis virtutibus et abstinentiis et munda vita etiam humilitatem talem habuerunt quod fugierunt loca illa in quibus miracula fecerunt ne de laude populi vanam haberent gloriam. Isti vero ubi maiorem habent populi laudem et lucra libentius se conferunt et morantur. Quo facto etiam si sancti prius fuissent, sanctitatem illam amitterent quam sub humilitate non custodiunt.*' Bromyard, *Summa*, 'Sortilegium' 7, 357v–358r.

54 '*nolunt aliquid facere vel dicere nisi aliqua certa eis portent, sicut panem, farinam, sal et huiusmodi vel pecuniam. Omnes etiam illa arte utentes ut communiter sunt indigentes, ex quo presumitur quod artem illam exercent propter lucrum acceptum vel speratum.*' Ibid., 2, f. 356r.

55 Corinne Saunders, *Magic and the Supernatural in Medieval English Romance* (Woodbridge, 2010), p. 153.

Chapter Three: Flying Women, Fairies and Demons

1 T. S. Holmes, ed., *The Register of John Stafford, Bishop of Bath and Wells, 1425–1443* (London, 1916), vol. II, p. 226.

2 Claude Jenkins, 'Cardinal Morton's Register', in *Tudor Studies*, ed. R. W. Seton-Watson (London, 1924), pp. 72–3. See also Kathleen Kamerick, 'Shaping Superstition in Late Medieval England', *Magic, Ritual and Witchcraft*, 3 (2008), p. 31.

3 A. T. Bannister, 'Visitation Returns of the Diocese of Hereford in 1397, I', *English Historical Review*, 44 (1929), p. 287.

4 C. S. Watkins, *History and the Supernatural in Medieval England* (Cambridge, 2007), chs 5–6.

5 Helen Cooper, *The English Romance in Time* (Oxford, 2004), ch. 4; Corinne Saunders, *Magic and the Supernatural in Medieval English Romance* (Woodbridge, 2010), ch. 5.

6 Werner Tschacher, 'Der Flug durch die Luft zwischen Illusionstheorie und Realitätsbeweis: Studien zum sog. Kanon Episcopi und zum Hexenflug', *Zeitschrift der Savigny-Stiftung für Rechtsgeschichte*, kan. Abt 85 (1999), p. 243.

7 Gratian, *Decretum*, ed. E. Friedberg, *Corpus Iuris Canonici*, vol. 1 (Leipzig, 1879, repr. Graz, 1959), 26.5.12. Translation based on Alan Kors and Edward Peters, *Witchcraft in Europe, 400–1700* (2nd edn, Philadelphia, 2001), p. 62.

8 Tschacher, 'Flug,' pp. 264–76.

9 See Claude Lecouteux, *Chasses Fantastiques et Cohortes de la Nuit au Moyen Age* (Paris, 1999), ch. 1.

10 Thomas de Mayo, *The Demonology of William of Auvergne: By Fire and Sword* (Lewiston, NY, and Lampeter, 2007), pp. 202–9.

11 T. F. Crane, ed., *The Exempla or Illustrative Stories from the Sermones Vulgares of Jacques de Vitry* (London, 1890), pp. 112–13.

12 BL MS Add. 33956, f. 81v; John Bromyard, *Summa Praedicantium* (Nuremberg, 1518), 'Sortilegium' 5, f. 357r.

13 '*mulieres . . . que dicunt se rapi a quodam populo et duci ad loca quedam pulchra et innota; que etiam dicunt se cum eis equitare per multa terrarum spacia in tempeste noctis silentio et loca plurima pertransire. Et qui eis credunt et quod loca quecunque clausa exeunt et intrant ad libitum.*' Bromyard, *Summa*, 'Sortilegium' 5, f. 357r.

14 '*nec a diabolo didicimus talia, nec ei credimus, sed pulchro populo.*' Ibid., 7, f. 358r.

15 Carlo Ginzburg, *The Night Battles: Witchcraft and Agrarian Cults in the Sixteenth and Seventeenth Centuries*, trans. J. and A. Tedeschi (New York, 1985), p. 7.

16 '*Si credat quod homines et umbrarii vadant. Tamen credi potest et sine peccato quod demones ita homines decipiunt quod eis videtur quod figurant in hominum figuras.*' BL MS Harley 4172, f. 17r. For earlier uses of *umbrarius* see Bernadette Filotas, *Pagan Survivals, Superstitions and Popular Cultures in Early Medieval Pastoral Literature* (Toronto, 2005), p. 43.

17 '*Si credit quod danne et umbrarii uadant et comedant . . .*'. Berengar Fredol, *Summa*, BL MS Royal 8.A.IX, f. 25v. '*Danne*' is perhaps a corruption of '*dominae*', 'ladies'.

18 '*tales vocantur phitones vel phitonisse, quales ut sepe dictum est a nonnullis, sunt in diuersis regnis que quandoque fila, quandoque funes, quandoque frena in ora homini et eos ut eis videtur transformant in figuris equorum et equitant super eos, et plerumque ut dicitur tales phitonisse transeunt in una nocte ab Anglia ad Burdecliam, ubi inebriate vino postea redeunt.*' Rypon, *Sermons*, f. 33v. *Burdeclia* may be Burdegalia, Bordeaux: the association with wine would fit this.

19 William Klingshirn, 'Isidore of Seville's Taxonomy of Magicians and Diviners', *Traditio*, 58 (2003), p. 87.

20 *The South English Legendary*, ed. Charlotte d'Evelyn and Anna J. Mill, Early English Texts Society, original ser. 236 (London, 1959), vol. II, p. 410; Alaric Hall, *Elves in Anglo-Saxon England* (Woodbridge, 2007), pp. 141–2.

21 Siegfried Wenzel, ed. and trans. *Fasciculus Morum: A Fourteenth-Century Preacher's Manual* (University Park, PA, 1989), p. 579.

22 Ibid.

23 Layamon, *Brut or Hystoria Brutonum*, ed. and trans. W.R.J. Barron and S. C. Weinberg (Harlow, 1995), p. 733.

24 *Sir Orfeo*, ed. A. J. Bliss (Oxford, 1954), pp. 16–18.

25 Hall, *Elves*, p. 115.

26 See ch. 2, ref. 1.

27 Jenkins, 'Cardinal Morton's Register', p. 73.

28 See Ginzburg, *Night Battles*; Gustav Henningsen, 'The Ladies from Outside: An Archaic Pattern of the Witches' Sabbath', in *Early Modern European Witchcraft: Centres and Peripheries*, ed. Bengt Ankarloo and Gustav Henningsen (Oxford, 1990), pp. 191–215; Wolfgang Behringer, *Shaman of Oberstdorf: Chonrad Stoeckhlin and the Phantoms of the Night*, trans. H. C. Erik Midelfort (Charlottesville, VA, 1998); Diane Purkiss, *Troublesome Things: A History of Fairies and Fairy Stories* (London, 2000), pp. 85–115.

29 Behringer, *Shaman of Oberstdorf*, pp. 17–18.

30 *Fasciculus Morum*, ed. Wenzel, p. 579.

31 '*In alio seculo nullus populus esse creditur nisi bonus vel malus. Bonus sicut illi in celo vel in purgatorio; mali sicut demones et damnati. Sed primi eis non possunt sic illudere, quia ipsemet fatentur quod eas verberant vel infirmas faciunt interdum quando cum eis loquuntur. Boni autem post mortem malum non faciunt. Nec dicere possunt quod sint anime damnatorum, quia ille in inferno sunt et exire non possunt ad libitum.*' Bromyard, *Summa*, 'Sortilegium' 5, f. 357r.

32 Watkins, *History*, pp. 206–8.

33 Elizabeth Williams, 'A Damsell by Herselfe Alone: Images of Magic and Femininity from Lanval to Sir Lambewell', in *Romance Reading on the Book*, ed. J. Fellows, R. Field, G. Rogers and J. Weis (Cardiff, 1996), p. 160.

34 *Sir Orfeo*, ed. Bliss, pp. 34–5; Saunders, *Magic*, p. 203.

35 M. R. James, 'Twelve Medieval Ghost Stories', *English Historical Review*, 37 (1922), p. 417; abridged translation in Andrew Joynes, *Medieval Ghost Stories* (Woodbridge, 2001), p. 122.

36 Lecouteux, *Chasses Fantastiques*, p. 24.

37 Jean-Claude Schmitt, *Ghosts in the Middle Ages*, trans. Teresa Lavender Fagan (Chicago, 1998), pp. 116–21.

38 Schmitt, *Ghosts*, pp. 15–16; Donald Drew Egbert, *The Tickhill Psalter and Related Manuscripts* (New York and Princeton, NJ, 1940), pp. 3–7.

39 *The Lay Folks' Catechism*, ed. T. F. Simmons and H. E. Nolloth, Early English Texts Society, original ser. 118 (London, 1901), p. 35.

40 Schmitt, *Ghosts*, pp. 135–6.

41 Ibid., p. 148; Claude Lecouteux, *Fantômes et Revenants au Moyen Age* (Paris, 1986), p. 58.

42 James, 'Twelve Medieval Ghost Stories', p. 414.

43 Ibid., pp. 418, 419; Joynes, *Medieval Ghost Stories*, pp. 123–4.

44 '*mulieres que in hac parte magis inueniuntur culpabiles quam viri.*' Bromyard, *Summa*, 'Sortilegium' 5, f. 357r; Nancy Caciola, *Discerning Spirits: Divine and Demonic Possession in the Middle Ages* (Ithaca, NY, 2003), p. 72.

45 See Caciola, *Discerning Spirits*; Dyan Elliott, *Proving Woman: Female Spirituality and Inquisitional Culture in the Later Middle Ages* (Princeton, NJ, 2004), pp. 250–63.

46 Elliott, *Proving Woman*, pp. 267–79; Purkiss, *Troublesome Things*, p. 65.

47 Caciola, *Discerning Spirits*, p. 30.

48 Diane Watt, *Secretaries of God: Women Prophets in Late Medieval and Early Modern England* (Cambridge, 1997), pp. 4–5.

49 A. T. Bannister, 'Visitation Returns of the Diocese of Hereford in 1397 (Continued)', *English Historical Review*, 44 (1929), p. 446.

50 See Catherine Rider, 'Agreements to Return from the Afterlife in Late Medieval Exempla', in *Studies in Church History 45: The Church, the Afterlife and the Fate of the Soul*, ed. P. Clarke and T. Claydon (Woodbridge, 2009), pp. 174–83.

Chapter Four: Harm and Protection

1 '*Item denunciat officio quod dicta Margeria est suspecta et diffamata de crimine sortilegii. Et dicit quidam vicinus suus habuit quatuor bonos equos in biga trahendos et cum erat maliuola eidem dixit quod non haberet equum viuum in breui tempore. Et sic statim omnes equi moriebantur.*' Maidstone, Centre for Kentish Studies, Drb/Pa/1, f. 379r. On other accusations see Karen Jones and Michael Zell, '"The Divels Speciall Instruments": Women and Witchcraft before the Great Witch Hunt', *Social History*, 30 (2005), p. 51.

2 '*Et dictus Nicholaus dicit* [my emendation: MS reads '*de dicit*'] *quod ipsa Margeria diffamauit et frequenter vilipendit uxorem suam.*' Centre for Kentish Studies Drb/Pa/1, f. 379r.

3 Richard Kieckhefer, *European Witch Trials: Their Foundations in Popular and Learned Culture, 1300–1500* (London, 1976), p. 48; Robin Briggs, *Witches and Neighbours: The Social and Cultural Context of European Witchcraft* (2nd edn, Oxford, 2002), p. 10.

4 Gratian, *Decretum*, ed. E. Friedberg, *Corpus Iuris Canonici*, vol. I (Leipzig, 1879, repr. Graz, 1959), 26.5.14. For Isidore's version and translation see William Klingshirn, 'Isidore of Seville's Taxonomy of Magicians and Diviners', *Traditio*, 58 (2003), p. 85.

5 Gratian, *Decretum*, 26.5.12.

6 Ibid., 26.5.13.

7 *Dives and Pauper*, ed. Priscilla Heath Barnum, Early English Texts Society, original ser. 275 (London, 1976), vol. I, pp. 158–9.

8 Thomas of Chobham, *Summa Confessorum*, ed. F. Broomfield (Louvain, 1968), p. 473.

9 Ibid., pp. 485, 486.

10 '*Si sortilegas consuluit, uel ad ipsas misit, uel munera dedit talibus ut ipsarum sortilegia meliorarentur in aliquo uel grauarentur* [my emendation: both MSS

read '*melioraretur*' and '*grauararetur*'] . . . *Si crediderit aliquam rem infirmari uel deteriorari propter loquelam uel uisum aliorum scilicet ouersene.*' BL MS Add. 30508 ff. 169r–v; '*scilicet forspekem*', 'that is, forspoken', added in BL MS Add. 22570, f. 200v.

11 Siegfried Wenzel, ed. and trans., *Fasciculus Morum: A Fourteenth-Century Preacher's Manual* (University Park, PA, 1989), p. 579.

12 G. L. Kittredge, *Witchcraft in Old and New England* (Cambridge, MA, 1929), pp. 77–8.

13 Miri Rubin, *Corpus Christi: The Eucharist in Late Medieval Culture* (Cambridge, 1991), p. 338.

14 Thomas of Chobham, *Summa Confessorum*, p. 184.

15 BL MS Add. 33956, f. 83r. On the collection see Annette Kehnel, 'The Narrative Tradition of the Franciscan Friars in the British Isles: Introduction to the Sources', *Franciscan Studies*, 63 (2005), pp. 498–500.

16 Robert Mannyng of Brunne, *Handlyng Synne*, ed. Idelle Sullens (Binghamton, NY, 1983), p. 16.

17 Kittredge, *Witchcraft*, p. 166.

18 Mannyng, *Handlyng Synne*, p. 17.

19 Augustine, *The City of God Against the Pagans*, trans. R. W. Dyson (Cambridge, 1998), pp. 843–4; Jan Veenstra, 'The Ever-Changing Nature of the Beast: Cultural Change, Lycanthropy and the Question of Substantial Transformation (from Petronius to Del Rio)', in *The Metamorphosis of Magic from Late Antiquity to the Early Modern Period*, ed. Jan Bremmer and Jan Veenstra (Leuven, 2002), pp. 145–6.

20 William of Malmesbury, *The History of the English Kings*, ed. and trans. R.A.B. Mynors, R. M. Thomson and M. Winterbottom (Oxford, 1998), vol. I, pp. 292–3.

21 Ranulph Higden, *Speculum Curatorum*, CUL MS Mm.i.20, ff. 40r–v.

22 Augustine, *City of God*, p. 843.

23 William of Malmesbury, *History*, vol. I, p. 293.

24 '*Item uestigia Christianorum obseruat cespitem quoque uestigiorum et inde machinatus fuerit mortem alicuius reus est homicide. Qui uero non fecerit set fieri posse crediderit, per xx. dies penitenciam faciat.*' William de Montibus, *Speculum Penitentie*, OBL MS Bodley 654, f. 112v.

25 Fernando Salmón and Montserrat Cabré, 'Fascinating Women: the Evil Eye in Medical Scholasticism', in *Medicine from the Black Death to the French Disease*, ed. R. French, J. Arrizabalaga, A. Cunningham and L. García-Ballester (Aldershot, 1998), pp. 53–84; Brian Lawn, ed., *The Prose Salernitan Questions* (London, 1979), pp. 63, 98.

26 '*Secundo modo invidia, et sic est etiam possibilis, sicut multiplex experiencia docet.*' Astesanus of Asti, *Summa de Casibus* (Venice, 1478), 1.15.

27 On this case see H. A. Kelly, 'English Kings and the Fear of Sorcery', *Mediaeval Studies*, 39 (1977), pp. 219–29; Jessica Freeman, 'Sorcery at Court and Manor: Margery Jourdemayne, the Witch of Eye next Westminster', *Journal of Medieval History*, 30 (2004), pp. 343–57.

28 *Leges Henrici Primi*, ed. and trans. L. J. Downer (Oxford, 1972), pp. 226–7.

29 *Calendar of the Patent Rolls preserved in the Public Record Office: Henry VI, 1422–9* (Norwich, 1901), p. 363.

30 F. Pollock and F. W. Maitland, *The History of English Law before the Time of Edward I* (2nd edn, Cambridge, 1968), vol. II, p. 554.

31 Robin Briggs, *Witches and Neighbours: The Social and Cultural Context of European Witchcraft* (2nd edn, Oxford, 2002), p. 6; J. A. Sharpe, *Instruments of Darkness: Witchcraft in England, 1550–1750* (London, 1996), p. 63.

32 Catherine Rider, *Magic and Impotence in the Middle Ages* (Oxford, 2006), p. 25.

33 J. Raine, ed., *Depositions and Other Ecclesiastical Proceedings from the Courts of Durham*, (London, 1845), p. 27.

34 R. Finucane, *Miracles and Pilgrims: Popular Beliefs in Medieval England* (London, 1977), p. 73; Rider, *Magic*, pp. 160–85.

35 Robin Briggs, 'Many Reasons Why: Witchcraft and the Problem of Multiple Explanation', in *Witchcraft in Early Modern Europe*, ed. Jonathan Barry, Marianne Hester and Gareth Roberts (Cambridge, 1996), pp. 55–6.

36 Jan Veenstra, *Magic and Divination at the Courts of Burgundy and France* (Leiden, 1998), pp. 21–8; Hilary M. Carey, *Courting Disaster: Astrology at the English Court and University in the Later Middle Ages* (Basingstoke, 1992), p. 17.

37 Keith Thomas, *Religion and the Decline of Magic* (London, 1971), pp. 186–7.

38 Michael Bailey, 'The Disenchantment of Magic: Spells, Charms and Superstition in Early European Witchcraft Literature', *American Historical Review*, 111 (2006), pp. 394–401.

39 See above, ref. 4.

40 '*Sed hoc contigit quod huiusmodi per mortale peccatum subiciuntur diabolo. Si enim castitatem haberent, demones circa uoluntates eorum nil possent.*' Odo of Cheriton, *Sermones de Sanctis*, CUL MS Kk.i.11, Sermon for St John the Baptist's Day, f. 116r.

41 Mannyng, *Handlyng Synne*, p. 208.

42 E. F. Jacob, ed., *The Register of Henry Chichele, Archbishop of Canterbury, 1414–1443* (Oxford, 1947), vol. IV, pp. 206–7; Margaret Archer, ed., *The Register of Philip Repingdon, 1405–19* (Lincoln, 1982), vol. III, p. 289.

43 Eamon Duffy, *Marking the Hours: English People and their Prayers, 1240–1570* (New Haven, CT, 2006), pp. 76–8.

44 Thomas, *Religion*, ch. 2; R. W. Scribner, 'Cosmic Order and Daily Life: Sacred and Secular in Pre-Industrial German Society', in Scribner, *Popular Culture and Popular Movements in Reformation Germany* (London, 1987), pp. 6–9.

45 C. S. Watkins, *History and the Supernatural in Medieval England* (Cambridge, 2007), pp. 113–14; Kathleen Kamerick, 'Shaping Superstition in Late Medieval England', *Magic, Ritual and Witchcraft*, 3 (2008), p. 48.

46 Duffy, *Stripping of the Altars*, pp. 277–87.

47 Bailey, 'Disenchantment of Magic', pp. 396–7.

48 Maria Helena da Rocha Pereira, ed., *Obrás Medicas de Pedro Hispano* (Coimbra, 1973), pp. 237–9.

49 Tony Hunt, *Popular Medicine in Thirteenth-Century England* (Cambridge, 1990), p. 39.

50 Peter Murray Jones and Lea T. Olsan, 'Middleham Jewel: Ritual, Power and Devotion', *Viator*, 31 (2000), pp. 249–90.

51 Joan Evans, *Magical Jewels of the Middle Ages Particularly in England* (Oxford, 1922), pp. 121–39.

52 Thomas, *Religion*, p. 498.

53 Jonathan Barry, 'Introduction: Keith Thomas and the Problem of Witchcraft', in *Witchcraft*, ed. Barry, Hester and Roberts, pp. 12–13.

Chapter Five: Channelling the Stars and Summoning Demons: Magical Texts

1 Siegfried Wenzel, ed. and trans., *Fasciculus Morum: A Fourteenth-Century Preacher's Manual* (University Park, PA, 1989), pp. 691–3.

2 On this see Lucy Freeman Sandler, *Omne Bonum: A Fourteenth-Century Encyclopaedia of Universal Knowledge* (London, 1996).

3 Richard Kieckhefer, *Forbidden Rites: A Necromancer's Manual of the Fifteenth Century* (Stroud, 1997), pp. 13, 114.

4 Richard Kieckhefer, *Magic in the Middle Ages* (Cambridge, 1989), pp. 153–4; Frank Klaassen, 'English Manuscripts of Magic, 1300–1500: A Preliminary Survey', in *Conjuring Spirits: Texts and Traditions of Medieval Ritual Magic*, ed. Claire Fanger (Stroud, 1998), pp. 6–7; Jean-Patrice Boudet, *Entre science et nigromance: astrologie, divination et magie en l'Occident médiéval* (Paris, 2006), p. 389.

5 Boudet, *Entre Science*, pp. 252, 459–64.

6 Edward Peters, *The Magician, the Witch and the Law* (Philadelphia, 1978), pp. 89–90; Boudet, *Entre Science*, pp. 214–20.

7 Charles Burnett, 'Talismans: Magic as Science? Necromancy among the Seven Liberal Arts', in Charles Burnett, *Magic and Divination in the Middle Ages* (Aldershot, 1996), pp. 10–13.

8 Nicolas Weill-Parot, *Les 'images astrologiques' au moyen âge et à la Renaissance: Spéculations intellectuelles et pratiques magiques* (Paris, 2002), p. 84.

9 Juris G. Lidaka, trans., 'The Book of Angels, Rings, Characters and Images of the Planets; attributed to Osbern Bokenham', in *Conjuring Spirits*, ed. Fanger, p. 51.

10 Julien Véronèse, *L'Ars Notoria au Moyen Age* (Florence, 2007), p. 16; Claire Fanger and Nicholas Watson, eds, 'The Prologue to John of Morigny's Liber Visionum: Text and Translation,' *Esoterica*, 3 (2001), p. 178.

11 Klaassen, 'English Manuscripts', pp. 4, 18–19, 21.

12 Kieckhefer, *Forbidden Rites*, p. 149.

13 Robert Mathiesen, 'A Thirteenth-Century Ritual to Attain the Beatific Vision from the *Sworn Book* of Honorius of Thebes', in *Conjuring Spirits*, ed. Fanger, pp. 147–8.

14 '*Respondeo secundum Thomam . . . quod Ars Notoria omnino illicita est et christiano fugienda. Hec enim ars est per quam quidam nituntur scientiam*

acquirere sed omnino inefficax est et fiunt ibi quedam pacta implicita cum demone.' John of Freiburg, *Summa Confessorum* (Lyons, 1518), 1.11.10, f. 31v.

15 '*Respondeo secundum Thomam . . . ymagines quas astronomicas vocant fieri illicitum est, et ex opere demonum habent effectum, cuius signum est, quia necesse est eis inscribi quedam caracteres qui naturaliter nihil operantur. Unde fiunt ibi tacita pacta cum demonibus. In ymaginibus autem nigromanticis fiunt expresse invocationes demonum.*' Ibid., 1.11.12, f. 32r.

16 Norman Cohn, *Europe's Inner Demons: the Demonization of Christians in Medieval Christendom* (3rd edn, London, 1993), pp. 113–14.

17 Leonard Boyle, 'The *Summa Confessorum* of John of Freiburg and the Popularization of the Moral Teaching of St Thomas and Some of his Contemporaries', in Boyle, *Pastoral Care, Clerical Education and Canon Law* (London, 1981), pp. 258–65.

18 G. R. Owst, '*Sortilegium* in English Homiletic Literature of the Fourteenth Century', in *Studies Presented to Sir Hilary Jenkinson*, ed. J. Conway Davies (London, 1957), p. 279.

19 '*Quantum ad culturam ymaginum, sciendum est quod error est sentire de lapidibus gemmis ymaginibus quod ipsa possint dare hominibus bona que solius dei sunt, utpote invincibilitatem, gratiositatem, amorem, temperanciam, invisibilitatem. Nam secundum omnes philosophos nulla virtus potest aliquid dare quod sit seipsa maius et nobilius . . . Similis error est eorum qui putauerunt ymagines stellarum, aut specula suspensa sculpta vel fusa sub ascensu alicuius planete talem virtutem posse recipere et refundere.*' Ranulph Higden, *Speculum Curatorum*, CUL MS Mm.i.20, f. 36r.

20 See ch. 1, ref. 33.

21 Alexander Carpenter, *Destructorium Viciorum* (Paris, 1516), 6.48; Robert Holcot, *In Librum Sapientiae Regis Salomonis* (Basel, 1586), p. 625.

22 W. R. Childs, '"Welcome, my Brother": Edward II, John of Powderham and the Chronicles, 1318', in *Church and Chronicle in the Middle Ages*, ed. Ian Wood and G. A. Loud (London, 1991), pp. 150–54.

23 '*in necromantia videntur fieri characteres et alia signa per que* [my emendation: edition reads '*que per*'] *demones videntur artari ad comparendum et ad respondendum ad interrogata. Qui et aliter non videntur velle vera dicere nisi ad hoc artarentur dictis vel factis incantatorum et coniuratorum postquam etiam eis comparuerint quasi inferioribus et ad faciendum imperium illorum obligantur.*' John Bromyard, *Summa Praedicantium* (Nuremberg, 1518), 'Sortilegium' 1, f. 356r.

24 See ch. 4, ref. 11.

25 *Dives and Pauper*, ed. Priscilla Heath Barnum, Early English Texts Society, original ser. vol. 275 (London, 1976), vol, I, p. 156.

26 '*necromantici sancti non sunt nec miracula facere possunt.*' Bromyard, *Summa*, 'Sortilegium' 1, f. 356r.

27 Peters, *Magician*, p. 28; J. T. Welter, ed., *Le Speculum Laicorum* (Paris, 1914), p. 104.

28 A. G. Little, ed., *Liber Exemplorum ad Usum Praedicantium* (Aberdeen, 1908),

p. 22; trans. in David Jones, *Friars' Tales: Thirteenth-Century Exempla from the British Isles* (Manchester, 2011), pp. 48–9.

29 BL MS Add. 33956, f. 83r; Welter, *Speculum Laicorum*, p. 35.

30 D. L. d'Avray, *The Preaching of the Friars: Sermons Diffused from Paris before 1300* (Oxford, 1985), p. 202.

31 Welter, *Speculum Laicorum*, p. 54.

32 '*Quidam clericus in hiis malis artibus in Hispania edoctus rediens in Angliam cum quodam rustico impetuoso et audaci ut inuocaret demones. Circulum in biuio semel intrauerunt* [my emendation: MS reads '*intrauit*'] *et in illa nocte demones in specie equorum et aliarum bestiarum apparuerunt.*' Odo of Cheriton, *Sermones in Epistolas*, sermon for Ascension Day, Lincoln Cathedral Library MS 11, f. 101r.

33 d'Avray, *Preaching*, pp. 200–1.

34 Kieckhefer, *Forbidden Rites*, pp. 47–8, 51–3; Frank Klaassen, 'Learning and Masculinity in Manuscripts of Ritual Magic of the Later Middle Ages and Renaissance', *Sixteenth-Century Journal*, 38 (2007), pp. 64–9.

35 Little, *Liber Exemplorum*, p. 22; trans. Jones, *Friars' Tales*, p. 49.

36 *The St Albans Chronicle: the Chronica Maiora of Thomas Walsingham*, ed. and trans. J. Taylor, W. Childs and L. Watkiss (Oxford, 2003), vol. I, pp. 47–9.

37 E. F. Jacob, ed., *The Register of Henry Chichele, Archbishop of Canterbury, 1414–1443* (Oxford, 1945), vol. III, pp. 54–6.

38 Frank Klaassen, 'The Middleness of Ritual Magic', in *The Unorthodox Imagination in Late Medieval Britain*, ed. Sophie Page (Manchester, 2010), p. 141.

Chapter Six: Arguing Against Magic

1 Thomas of Chobham, *Summa de Arte Praedicandi*, ed. F. Morenzoni, *Corpus Christianorum Continuatio Mediaevalis*, vol. LXXXII (Turnhout, 1988), p. 166.

2 Alexander Murray, 'Confession as a Historical Source in the Thirteenth Century', in *The Writing of History in the Middle Ages*, ed. R.H.C. Davis and J. M. Wallace-Hadrill (Oxford, 1981), pp. 285–90.

3 D. L. d'Avray, *Medieval Marriage Sermons: Mass Communication in a Culture without Print* (Oxford, 2001), pp. 29–30.

4 Joseph Goering, 'The Summa of Master Serlo and Thirteenth-Century Penitential Literature', *Mediaeval Studies*, 40 (1978), p. 301; '*Caveat tamen predicator ne . . . mulieres doceat remedia que ipse nesciunt si credit quod ea facture sint.*' Guilelmus Peraldus, *Summa Virtutum ac Vitiorum* (Mainz, 1618), Pride, part 3, ch. 36, p. 244.

5 Franco Mormando, *The Preacher's Demons: Bernardino of Siena and the Social Underworld of Early Renaissance Italy* (Chicago, 1999), pp. 56, 71.

6 Siegfried Wenzel, *Latin Sermon Collections from Later Medieval England* (Cambridge, 2005), p. 242.

7 Alexander Murray, 'Confession before 1215', *Transactions of the Royal Historical Society*, 6th ser. vol. 6 (1993), p. 63; Norman Tanner and Sethina

Watson, 'Least of the Laity: the Minimum Requirements for a Medieval Christian', *Journal of Medieval History*, 32 (2006), pp. 407–8.

8 Eamon Duffy, *The Stripping of the Altars: Traditional Religion in England, 1400–1580* (New Haven, CT, 1992), p. 60.

9 J. Shinners and W. Dohar, ed., *Pastors and the Care of Souls in Late Medieval England* (Notre Dame, IN, 1998), p. 37; J. Goering and D. Taylor, 'The *Summulae* of Bishops Walter de Cantilupe (1240) and Peter Quinel (1287)', *Speculum*, 67 (1993), pp. 576–94.

10 '*Si aliquando credidit maleficiis* [my emendation: ms reads '*maleficis*'], *sortilegiis et auguriis, incantationibus demonum et huiusmodi.*' BL MS Add. 24660, f. 5v.

11 '*Si fidem adibuerit sortilegiis et diuinacionibus per astra uel per sompnia, uel alia quecumque instrumenta. Debet etiam confiteri si aliquando demones inuocauerit per incantaciones uerborum, per inscripciones caractarum* [sic], *per immolaciones sacrificiorum uel consimilium.*' BL MS Add. 24660, f. 131v.

12 *Councils and Synods with Other Documents relating to the English Church part II, A.D., 1205–1313*, ed. F. M. Powicke and C. R. Cheney (Oxford, 1964), p. 1062; trans. Shinners and Dohar, *Pastors*, p. 172.

13 '*Deinde circa finem querere poteris de sortilegiis et superstitionibus. Si aliqua talia fecit uel fieri procurauit, sicut multa ualde que fiunt a pluribus in alligaturis, uerbis, uanis inscriptionibus et multis ac uariis obseruationibus. Item specialiter si per astra uel sompnia aut per auguria uoluit prescire ea ad que se huiusmodi non extendunt, puta ad actus humanos subiacentes libero arbitrio. Item si usus est aliquibus litteris uel scripsit in quibus fit aliqua adiuratio uel inuocatio demonum uel in quibus continentur nomina ignota uel aliqui caracteres preter signum crucis, huiusmodi enim illicita sunt. Facias enim specialiter sortilegia que fecit exprimere et modum dicere et cum quibus rebus fecerit et cum qua intentione, huiusmodi enim frequenter fiunt cum rebus immundissimis et cum periculo uite aliquorum, quandoque etiam cum sacramentis et aliis rebus sacris, quod grauissimum peccatum est. Item quere si aliqua talia docuerit uel ad talia aliquem induxit. Facias quantum potes reuocare.*' John of Freiburg, *Confessionale*, BL MS Add. 19581, f. 187v.

14 Ibid., ff. 190v, 192r.

15 '*Si demoni uel creature diuinum cultum exhibuit sacrificando uel sortilegia faciendo, seu prestigiatores aut sortilegos consulendos, quod est transgredi primum mandatum.*' Worcester Cathedral Library MS Q.61, f. 1v.

16 John Bossy, 'Moral Arithmetic: Seven Sins into Ten Commandments' in *Conscience and Casuistry in Early Modern Europe*, ed. E. Leites (Cambridge, 1988), p. 230.

17 Powicke and Cheney, *Councils and Synods*, p. 902; trans. Shinners and Dohar, *Pastors*, p. 129.

18 *The Lay Folks' Catechism*, ed. T. F. Simmons and H. E. Nolloth, Early English Texts Society, original ser. 118 (London, 1901), pp. 34–5.

19 '*in quo prohibentur omnes ydolatrie et incantaciones ac omnia sortilegia.*' CUL MS Ii.iii.8, f. 45v. On this manuscript see Wenzel, *Latin Sermon Collections*, pp. 175–81.

20 *John Mirk's Festial*, ed. Susan Powell, Early English Texts Society, original ser. 334 (Oxford, 2009), vol. I, p. 44; see also chapter 1, ref. 21.

21 '*omnia sacrilegia et diuinaciones quibus falsi christiani solent intendere, querentes in diuersis operacionibus experimenta futurorum.*' OBL MS Bodley 440, f. 5r.

22 '*In hac nocte solent filie diaboli exercere maleficia et sortilegia.*' Odo of Cheriton, *Sermones de Sanctis*, CUL MS Kk.i.11, f. 114v. On Midsummer see Stephen Wilson, *The Magical Universe: Everyday Ritual and Magic in Pre-Modern Europe* (London and New York, 2000), pp. 40–42.

23 *Mirk's Festial*, part I, ed. T. Erbe, Early English Texts Society, extra ser. 96 (London, 1905), pp. 208–10. For Cyprian see ch. 4, ref. 41.

24 Mary Aquinas Devlin, ed., *The Sermons of Thomas Brinton, Bishop of Rochester (1373–1389)* (London, 1954), vol. I, p. 190.

25 H. Leith Spencer, *English Preaching in the Later Middle Ages* (Oxford, 1993), p. 319; Albert C. Friend, 'Master Odo of Cheriton', *Speculum*, 23 (1948), pp. 641–58.

26 Odo of Cheriton, *Sermones in Epistolas*, sermon for Ascension Day, Lincoln Cathedral Library MS 11, ff. 100v–101r.

27 For differing views see Wenzel, *Latin Sermon Collections*, p. 68 and Margaret Harvey, *Lay Religious Life in Late Medieval Durham* (Woodbridge, 2006), p. 129.

28 Powicke and Cheney, *Councils and Synods*, pp. 900–1; Shinners and Dohar, *Pastors*, pp. 127–32.

29 See ch. 5, ref. 32, ch. 2, ref. 21.

30 Miri Rubin, *Corpus Christi: the Eucharist in Late Medieval Culture* (Cambridge, 1991), p. 341.

31 BL MS Burney 361, f. 149r. On the manuscript see Annette Kehnel, 'The Narrative Tradition of the Medieval Franciscan Friars on the British Isles: Introduction the Sources', *Franciscan Studies*, 63 (2005), pp. 501–2.

32 See ch. 4, ref. 15.

33 Robert Rypon, *Sermons*, BL MS Harley 4894, ff. 33r–v, 34v.

34 Ibid., BL MS Harley 4894, f. 34v. For the *phitonissae* see ch. 3, ref. 18.

35 '*De diuinatoribus, auguriis et nigromanciis et de mulieribus sortiariis raro inueniuntur quod bono fine uitam suam concludant, quoniam aut uiui a demonibus rapiuntur, aut subitanea morte suffocantur, aut obstinati in malicia moriuntur.*' Odo of Cheriton, *Sermones de Sanctis*, ff. 114v–116r (f. 115 is an interpolation on another topic).

36 Siegfried Wenzel, ed. and trans., *Fasciculus Morum: A Fourteenth-Century Preacher's Manual* (University Park, PA, 1989), pp. 583–5.

37 D. L. d'Avray, *The Preaching of the Friars: Sermons Diffused from Paris before 1300* (Oxford, 1985), p. 127.

38 '*huiusmodi mulieres solent esse multum pronae ad sortilegia vel pro se, vel pro aliquibus casibus, vel pro filiis cum infirmantur, vel pro animalibus suis ut a lupis custodiantur, et similibus.*' Humbert of Romans, *De Eruditione Praedicatorum*, in *Maxima Bibliotheca Veterum Patrum*, ed. M. de la Bigne (Lyons, 1677), vol. XXV, p. 505.

39 Ibid., p. 487.

40 '*Scolares incredibilibus fidem adhibent que statim sicut imponibilia abiicere debuerant, ut quod constellationes argumento nostro inferant, quod talis effectus sit circa tales caracteres vel ad talem inuocationem vel figure aspectionem.*' Guibert of Tournai, *Sermones ad Omnes Status* (Lyons 1511), f. 70r.

41 T. F. Crane, ed., *The Exempla or Illustrative Stories from the Sermons Vulgares of Jacques de Vitry* (London, 1890), p. 112.

42 Jole Agrimi and Chiara Crisciani, 'Savoir Médical et Anthropologie Religieuse: les Représentations et les Fonctions de la Vetula (xiiie–xve siècle)', *Annales*, 48 (1993), pp. 1,289–95.

43 Richard Kieckhefer, *Magic in the Middle Ages* (Cambridge, 1989), pp. 56–7.

44 See ch. 1, ref. 12.

45 '*nam quidam tam fatui, quam viri quam mulieres, plus credunt talibus truffis quam scripturis vel sanctorum dictis, plus vetule quam doctori optimo theologie.*' Robert Rypon, *Sermons*, ff. 34v–35r.

46 John Bromyard, *Summa Praedicantium*, 'Sortilegium' 8, f. 358r.

47 A. H. Thomas, ed., *Calendar of Plea and Memoranda Rolls of the City of London, 1364–1381* (Cambridge, 1929), p. 188.

Chapter Seven: Action Against Magic

1 On these developments see Michael Bailey, 'From Sorcery to Witchcraft: Clerical Conceptions of Magic in the Later Middle Ages', *Speculum*, 76 (2001), pp. 960–90; Alain Boureau, *Satan Hérétique: Naissance de la Démonologie dans l'Occident Médiéval* (Paris, 2004).

2 Jean-Patrice Boudet, *Entre science et nigromance: astrologie, divination et magie en l'Occident médiéval* (Paris, 2006), pp. 454–5.

3 Michael D. Bailey, 'Concern over Superstition in Late Medieval Europe', in *The Religion of Fools? Superstition Past and Present*, ed. S. A. Smith and Alan Knight, *Past and Present*, Supplement 3 (Oxford, 2008), p. 117.

4 On Bernardino see ch. 6, ref. 5.

5 Jan. R. Veenstra, *Magic and Divination at the Courts of Burgundy and France* (Leiden, 1998), pp. 58–77.

6 On this see Bailey, 'Sorcery to Witchcraft'.

7 On these studies see Kathrin Utz Tremp, 'Witches' Brooms and Magic Ointments: Twenty Years of Witchcraft Research at the University of Lausanne (1989–2009)', *Magic, Ritual and Witchcraft*, 5 (2010), pp. 173–87.

8 Georg Modestin, *Le Diable chez l'Evêque: Chasse aux Sorciers dans le Diocèse de Lausanne* (Lausanne, 1999), pp. 5–6; Arno Borst, 'The Origins of the Witch-Craze in the Alps', in Arno Borst, *Medieval Worlds: Barbarians, Heretics and Artists in the Middle Ages*, trans. Eric Hansen (Cambridge, 1991), p. 109; Laurence Pfister, *L'Enfer sur Terre: Sorcellerie à Dommartin (1498)* (Lausanne, 1997), p. 33.

9 Hans Peter Broedel, *The Malleus Maleficarum and the Construction of Witchcraft: Theology and Popular Belief* (Manchester, 2003), pp. 16–18.

10 H. A. Kelly, 'English Kings and the Fear of Sorcery', *Mediaeval Studies*, 39 (1977), p. 207.

11 Michael D. Bailey and Edward Peters, 'A Sabbat of Demonologists: Basel, 1431–1440', *The Historian*, 65 (2003), p. 1,377.

12 '*Generaliter fere* [my emendation: MS reads '*fare*'] *ab omnibus queri possunt . . . an fecerit artes sorciarias docuerit uel consenserit.*' OBL MS Rawlinson C.4, ff. 7r–v.

13 Joseph Goering, ed., 'The Summa de Penitentia of Magister Serlo', *Mediaeval Studies*, 38 (1976), p. 26.

14 '*Sortilogus* [sic] *xl diebus peniteat. Si clericus fuerit, officio vel beneficio potest privari. Si laicus fuerit, privetur communione ecclesie.*' William of Pagula, *Oculus Sacerdotis*, CUL MS Gg.iv.10, f. 52v.

15 See ch. 6, ref. 7.

16 '*Sed ista non aduertunt quamplures confessores moderni . . . maxime de ordinibus mendicancium qui de singulis casibus sibi confessatis se intromittunt absoluendo indistincte et hoc male. Deus est testis.*' OBL MS Selden Supra 39, f. 9r.

17 *Councils and Synods with Other Documents relating to the English Church part II, AD., 1205–1313*, ed. F. M. Powicke and C. R. Cheney (Oxford, 1964), p. 33.

18 Ian Forrest, 'William Swinderby and the Wycliffite Attitude to Excommunication', *Journal of Ecclesiastical History*, 60 (2009), p. 264.

19 D. L. d'Avray, *Medieval Religious Rationalities: a Weberian Analysis* (Cambridge, 2010), pp. 45–6.

20 T. S. Holmes, ed., *The Register of John Stafford, Bishop of Bath and Wells, 1425–1443* (London, 1916), vol. II, p. 104.

21 Thomas of Chobham, *Summa Confessorum*, ed. F. Broomfield (Louvain, 1968), pp. lv–lvi; Powicke and Cheney, *Councils and Synods*, pp. 68, 146, 210.

22 W. Sparrow Simpson, 'Visitations of Churches Belonging to St Paul's Cathedral, 1249–52', *Camden Miscellany*, 9 (1895); W. Sparrow Simpson, *Visitations of Churches Belonging to St Paul's Cathedral in 1297 and 1458*, Camden Society, new ser. 55 (London, 1895).

23 A. T. Bannister, 'Visitation Returns of the Diocese of Hereford in 1397', *English Historical Review*, 44 (1929), pp. 279–89, 444–53 and *English Historical Review*, 45 (1930), pp. 92–101, 444–63. Weston, p. 282.

24 Powicke and Cheney, *Councils and Synods*, pp. 1,349–50.

25 Anne Neary, 'The Origins and Character of the Kilkenny Witchcraft Case of 1324', *Proceedings of the Royal Irish Academy*, 83C (1983), pp. 333–50; Norman Cohn, *Europe's Inner Demons: the Demonization of Christians in Medieval Christendom* (3rd edn, London, 1993), pp. 135–41.

26 Margaret Archer, ed., *The Register of Bishop Philip Repingdon, 1405–1419* (Hereford, 1963–5), vol. I, p. xxxiii.

27 Holmes, *Register of John Stafford*, pp. 103–8.

28 Kelly, 'English Kings', p. 220.

29 Archer, *Register of Philip Repingdon*, vol. III, pp. 194–6.

30 See ch. 3, ref. 1.

31 Jones and Zell, 'Divels Speciall Instruments', p. 51; Houlbrooke, 'Magic and Witchcraft', p. 118.

32 William Brown, ed., *The Register of William Wickwane, Lord Archbishop of York, 1279–1285* (Durham, 1907), pp. 22–4.

33 Ibid., p. 211.

34 William Brown, ed., *The Register of John Le Romeyn, Lord Archbishop of York, 1286–1296* (Durham, 1913), vol. I, p. 158.

35 F. Donald Logan, *Runaway Religious in Medieval England, c. 1240–c. 1540* (Cambridge, 1996), pp. 132–3.

36 '*idem dominus Willelmus sortilegium commisit utendo videlicet coniurationibus et incantationibus per quas nitebatur et sollicitauit Katerinam uxorem Henrici Molle de Ffulbourn ad cameram ipsius noctanter venire, ut sic eam in adulterio opprimeret violenter.*' CUL Ely Diocesan Records, D/2/1, f. 84v.

37 Ibid., f. 87r.

38 Ibid., f. 22r.

39 William Hale, *A Series of Precedents and Proceedings in Criminal Causes extending from the Year 1475 to 1640* (1st edn 1847, repr. Edinburgh, 1973), p. 7.

40 '*Comparet Christina East et producit compurgatrices super crimine adulterii quod ipsa Christina fuisset communis meretrix . . . Item purgauit se eadem Christina super crimine sortilegii ei ut asserit nequiter et maliciose imposito videlicet quod ipsa esset et est una hagge.*' Maidstone, Centre for Kentish Studies, Drb/Pa/2, f. 29r.

41 Houlbrooke, 'Magic and Witchcraft', pp. 122–3.

42 Archer, *Register of Philip Repingdon*, vol. III, p. 195.

43 Sandra Lee Parker and L. R. Poos, 'A Consistory Court from the Diocese of Rochester, 1363–4', *English Historical Review*, 106 (1991), p. 655.

44 Hale, *Precedents*, p. 36.

45 Margaret Lynch, trans., *Life, Love and Death in North-East Lancashire, 1510 to 1537* (Manchester, 2006), p. 95.

46 L. R. Poos, ed. and trans., *Lower Ecclesiastical Jurisdiction in Late Medieval England* (Oxford, 2001), pp. 352–3.

47 Lynch, *Life, Love and Death*, p. 53.

48 E. M. Elvey, ed., *The Courts of the Archdeaconry of Buckingham, 1483–1523* (Welwyn Garden City, 1975), pp. 257–8.

49 Owen Davies, *Cunning Folk: Popular Magic in English History* (London, 2003), pp. 12–13.

50 See ch. 4, ref. 33.

51 Hale, *Precedents*, pp. 77–8.

52 L. Poos, 'Sex, Lies and the Church Courts of Pre-Reformation England', *Journal of Interdisciplinary History*, 25 (1995), p. 594.

53 Houlbrooke, 'Magic and Witchcraft', pp. 129–30.

54 Jones and Zell, 'Divels Speciall Instruments', p. 51.

55 Parker and Poos, 'Consistory Court', p. 654.

56 Poos, trans., *Lower Ecclesiastical Jurisdiction*, 463.

57 Robin Briggs, 'Many Reasons Why: Witchcraft and the Problem of Multiple Explanation', in *Witchcraft*, ed. Barry, Hester and Roberts (Cambridge, 1996), pp. 55–6.

Conclusion: Religion and Magic: Medieval England and Beyond

1 Frank Klaassen, 'Learning and Masculinity in Manuscripts of Ritual Magic of the Later Middle Ages and Renaissance', *Sixteenth-Century Journal*, 38 (2007), p. 62.

2 Richard Kieckhefer, *Magic in the Middle Ages* (Cambridge, 1989), pp. 56–7.

3 See for example Carlo Ginzburg, *The Night Battles: Witchcraft and Agrarian Cults in the Sixteenth and Seventeenth Centuries*, trans. J. and A. Tedeschi (New York, 1985); Guido Ruggiero, *Binding Passions: Tales of Magic, Marriage and Power at the End of the Renaissance* (New York, 1993); David Gentilcore, *From Bishop to Witch: The System of the Sacred in Early Modern Terra d'Otranto* (Manchester, 1992); Mary O'Neil, 'Magical Healing, Love Magic and the Inquisition in Late Sixteenth-Century Modena', in *Inquisition and Society in Early Modern Europe*, ed. S. Haliczer (London, 1987), pp. 88–114.

4 William Shiels, 'Nature and Modernity: J. C. Atkinson and Rural Ministry in England, *c.* 1850–1900', in *God's Bounty? The Churches and the Natural World* (Studies in Church History, vol. 46), ed. Peter Clarke and Tony Claydon (Woodbridge, 2010), pp. 385–7.

5 David Gentilcore, *Bishop to Witch*, pp. 15–16.

6 See Introduction, ref. 4–7.

7 Kathleen Kamerick, 'Shaping Superstition in Late Medieval England', *Magic, Ritual and Witchcraft*, 3 (2008), p. 30.

8 O'Neil, 'Magical Healing', p. 89.

9 E. E. Evans-Pritchard, *Witchcraft, Oracles and Magic Among the Azande* (2nd edn, Oxford, 1960), p. 84.

10 Heidi Breuer, *Crafting the Witch: Gendering Magic in Medieval and Early Modern England* (New York, 2009), p. 97.

Select Bibliography

Manuscript Primary Sources

Anonymous Charms, Experiments and Divinatory Materials

London, British Library (hereafter BL) MS Harley 206
BL MS Harley 273
London, Wellcome Library MS 404
Oxford, Bodleian Library (hereafter OBL) MS e.mus 219
OBL MS Rawlinson D.939

Anonymous Sermons

Cambridge University Library (hereafter CUL) MS ii.iii.8
OBL MS Bodley 440

Anonymous Treatises on Confession

BL MS Add. 24660
BL MS Add. 30508
BL MS Harley 2272
BL MS Harley 4172
Worcester Cathedral Library MS Q.61

Treatises on Confession

Berengar Fredol, *Summa*, BL MS Royal 8.A.IX
Exempla, BL MS Add. 33956
John of Freiburg, *Confessionale*, BL MS Add. 19581
John of Mirfield, *Florarium Bartholomei*, CUL MS Mm.ii.10
Odo of Cheriton, *Sermones in Epistolas*, Lincoln Cathedral Library MS 11
——, *Sermones de Sanctis*, CUL MS Kk.i.11
Ranulph Higden, *Speculum Curatorum*, CUL MS Mm.i.20
Richard of Wetheringsett, *Summa*, CUL MS ii.iv.12
Robert Rypon, *Sermones*, BL MS Harley 4894
William of Pagula, *Oculus Sacerdotis*, CUL MS Gg.iv.10

Printed Primary Sources

Archer, Margaret, ed., *The Register of Bishop Philip Repingdon, 1405–1419*
    (Hereford, 1963), 3 vols
Augustine, *De Doctrina Christiana*, ed. and trans. R.P.H. Green (Oxford, 1995)
Barnum, Priscilla Heath, ed., *Dives and Pauper*, Early English Texts Society 275
    (London, 1976)
Bromyard, John, *Summa Praedicantium* (Nuremberg, 1518)
Carpenter, Alexander, *Destructorium Viciorum* (Paris, 1516)
Elvey, E. M., ed., *The Courts of the Archdeaconry of Buckingham, 1483–1523*
    (Welwyn Garden City, 1975)
Gratian, *Decretum*, in *Corpus Iuris Canonici*, ed. E. Friedberg, vol. I (Leipzig, 1879,
    repr. Graz, 1959)
Guibert of Tournai, *Sermones ad Omnes Status* (Lyons, 1511)
Hale, William, *A Series of Precedents and Proceedings in Criminal Causes extending
    from the Year 1475 to 1640; extracted from the Act-Books of Ecclesiastical Courts
    in the Diocese of London* (1st edn 1847, repr. Edinburgh, 1973)
Holcot, Robert, *In Librum Sapientiae Regis Salomonis Praelectiones* (Basel, 1586)
Holmes, T. S., ed., *The Register of John Stafford, Bishop of Bath and Wells, 1425–1443*
    (London, 1915)
Humbert of Romans, *De Eruditione Praedicatorum*, in *Maxima Bibliotheca
    Veterum Patrum*, ed. M. de la Bigne (Lyons, 1677), vol. xxv
Jacob, E. F., ed., *The Register of Henry Chichele, Archbishop of Canterbury,
    1414–1443* (Oxford, 1945), 4 vols
James, M. R., ed., 'Twelve Medieval Ghost Stories', *English Historical Review*, 37
    (1922), pp. 413–22
John of Freiburg, *Summa Confessorum* (Lyons, 1518)
Little, A. G., ed., *Liber Exemplorum ad Usum Praedicantium* (Aberdeen, 1908),
    trans. David Jones, *Friars' Tales: Thirteenth-Century Exempla from the British
    Isles* (Manchester, 2011)
Lynch, Margaret, trans., *Life, Love and Death in North-East Lancashire, 1510 to 1537*
    (Manchester, 2006)
Peraldus, Guilelmus, *Summa Virtutum ac Viciorum* (Mainz, 1618)
Poos, L. R., ed., *Lower Ecclesiastical Jurisdiction in Late Medieval England* (Oxford,
    2001)
Powicke, F. M. and Cheney, C. R., eds, *Councils and Synods with Other Documents
    relating to the English Church part II, A.D. 1205–1313* (Oxford, 1964)
Raymond of Peñafort, *Summa de Paenitentia*, ed. X. Ochoa and A. Diez (Rome, 1976)
Robert Mannyng of Brunne, *Handlyng Synne*, ed. Idelle Sullens (Binghamton, NY,
    1983)
Thomas of Chobham, *Summa Confessorum*, ed. F. W. Broomfield (Louvain, 1968)
Welter, J. T., ed., *Le Speculum Laicorum* (Paris, 1914)
Wenzel, S., ed. and trans., *Fasciculus Morum: A Fourteenth-Century Preacher's
    Handbook* (University Park, PA, 1989)
William of Rennes, glosses on Raymond of Peñafort's *Summa*, printed in

Raymond of Peñafort, *Summa de Penitentia* (Rome, 1603, repr. Farnborough, 1964)

Secondary Sources

Bailey, Michael, 'A Late-Medieval Crisis of Superstition?', *Speculum*, 84 (2009), pp. 633–61

——, 'Concern over Superstition in Late Medieval Europe', in *The Religion of Fools? Superstition Past and Present*, ed. S. A. Smith and Alan Knight, Supplement 3 (2008), pp. 115–33

——, 'The Disenchantment of Magic: Spells, Charms and Superstition in Early European Witchcraft Literature', *American Historical Review*, 111 (2006), pp. 383–404

——, 'From Sorcery to Witchcraft: Clerical Conceptions of Magic in the Later Middle Ages', *Speculum*, 76 (2001), pp. 960–90

Barry, Jonathan, 'Introduction: Keith Thomas and the Problem of Witchcraft', in *Witchcraft in Early Modern Europe: Studies in Culture and Belief*, ed. Jonathan Barry, Marianne Hester and Gareth Roberts (Cambridge, 1996), pp. 1–45

Bartlett, Robert, *The Natural and the Supernatural in the Middle Ages* (Cambridge, 2008)

Baumann, Karin, *Aberglaube für Laien: zur Programmatik und Überlieferung mittelalterlicher Superstitionenkritik* (Würzburg, 1989)

Boudet, Jean-Patrice, *Entre science et nigromance: Astrologie, divination et magie en l'Occident médiéval* (Paris, 2006)

Boureau, Alain, *Satan Hérétique: Naissance de la démonologie dans l'Occident Médiéval* (Paris, 2004)

Boyle, Leonard, *Pastoral Care, Clerical Education and Canon Law, 1200–1400* (London, 1981)

——, 'Summae confessorum', in *Les Genres littéraires dans les sources théologiques et philosophiques médiévales: Définition, critique et exploitation* (Louvain-la-Neuve, 1982), pp. 227–37

Briggs, Robin, 'Many Reasons Why: Witchcraft and the Problem of Multiple Explanation', in *Witchcraft in Early Modern Europe: Studies in Culture and Belief*, ed. Jonathan Barry, Marianne Hester and Gareth Roberts (Cambridge, 1996), pp. 49–63

Briggs, Robin, *Witches and Neighbours: The Social and Cultural Context of European Witchcraft* (2nd edn, Oxford, 2002)

Burnett, Charles, 'Talismans: Magic as Science? Necromancy among the Seven Liberal Arts', in Charles Burnett, *Magic and Divination in the Middle Ages* (Aldershot, 1996), pp. 1–15

Cameron, Euan, *Enchanted Europe: Superstition, Reason and Religion, 1250–1750* (Oxford, 2010)

Cohn, Norman, *Europe's Inner Demons: The Demonization of Christians in Medieval Christendom* (3rd edn, London, 1993)

Cooper, Helen, *The English Romance in Time: Transforming Motifs from Geoffrey of*

Monmouth to the Death of Shakespeare (Oxford, 2004)

Davies, Owen, *Cunning Folk: Popular Magic in English History* (London, 2003)

d'Avray, D. L., *The Preaching of the Friars: Sermons Diffused from Paris before 1300* (Oxford, 1985)

de Mayo, Thomas B., *The Demonology of William of Auvergne: By Fire and Sword* (Lewiston, NY, 2007)

Duffy, Eamon, *Marking the Hours: English People and their Prayers, 1240–1570* (New Haven, CT, and London, 2006)

——, *The Stripping of the Altars: Traditional Religion in England, c. 1400–c. 1580* (New Haven, CT, 1992)

Filotas, Bernadette, *Pagan Survivals, Superstitions and Popular Cultures in Early Medieval Pastoral Literature* (Toronto, 2005)

Flint, Valerie, *The Rise of Magic in Early Medieval Europe* (Oxford, 1991)

Geertz, Hildred, 'An Anthropology of Religion and Magic, I', *Journal of Interdisciplinary History*, 6 (1975), pp. 71–89

Goering, Joseph, *William de Montibus: the Schools and the Literature of Pastoral Care* (Toronto, 1992)

Harmening, Dieter, *Superstitio: Überlieferungs- und theoriegeschichtliche Untersuchungen zurkirchlich-theologischen Aberglaubensliteratur des Mittelalters* (Berlin, 1979)

Houlbrooke, Ralph A., 'Magic and Witchcraft in the Diocese of Winchester, 1491–1570', in *Cross, Crown and Community: Religion, Government and Culture in Early Modern England, 1400–1800*, ed. D. Trim and P. Balderstone (Bern, 2004), pp. 113–41

Hunt, Tony, *Popular Medicine in Thirteenth-Century England* (Cambridge, 1990)

Jolly, Karen, *Popular Religion in Late Saxon England* (Chapel Hill, NC, 1996)

Jolly, Karen, Catharina Raudvere and Edward Peters, *Witchcraft and Magic in Europe: The Middle Ages* (London, 2002)

Jones, Karen, and Michael Zell, '"The Divels Speciall Instruments": Women and Witchcraft before the Great Witch Hunt', *Social History*, 30 (2005), pp. 45–63

——, Peter Murray, and Lea T. Olsan, 'Middleham Jewel: Ritual, Power and Devotion', *Viator*, 31 (2000), pp. 249–90

Kamerick, Kathleen, 'Shaping Superstition in Late Medieval England', *Magic, Ritual and Witchcraft*, 3 (2008), pp. 29–53

Kelly, H. A., 'English Kings and the Fear of Sorcery', *Mediaeval Studies*, 39 (1977), pp. 206–38

Kieckhefer, Richard, *Forbidden Rites: A Necromancer's Manual of the Fifteenth Century* (Stroud, 1997)

——, *Magic in the Middle Ages* (Cambridge, 1989)

——, 'The Specific Rationality of Medieval Magic', *American Historical Review*, 99 (1994), pp. 813–36

Kittredge, G. L., *Witchcraft in Old and New England* (Cambridge, MA, 1929)

Klaassen, Frank, 'English Manuscripts of Magic, 1300–1500: A Preliminary Survey', in *Conjuring Spirits: Texts and Traditions of Medieval Ritual Magic*, ed. Claire Fanger (Stroud, 1998), pp. 3–31

——, 'Learning and Masculinity in Manuscripts of Ritual Magic of the Later
 Middle Ages and Renaissance', *Sixteenth-Century Journal*, 38 (2007), pp. 49–76

——, 'The Middleness of Ritual Magic' in *The Unorthodox Imagination in Late
 Medieval Britain*, ed. Sophie Page (Manchester, 2010), pp. 131–65

Klingshirn, William, 'Defining the Sortes Sanctorum: Gibbon, Du Cange and
 Early Christian Lot Divination', *Journal of Early Christian Studies*, 10 (2002),
 pp. 77–130

——, 'Isidore of Seville's Taxonomy of Magicians and Diviners', *Traditio*, 58
 (2003), pp. 59–90

Michaud-Quantin, Pierre, *Sommes de Casuistique et Manuels de Confession au
 Moyen Age (xii–xvi siècles)* (Louvain, 1962)

Neary, Anne, 'The Origins and Character of the Kilkenny Witchcraft Case of 1324',
 Proceedings of the Royal Irish Academy, lxxxiii, section c (1983), pp. 333–50

Olsan, Lea, 'Charms and Prayers in Medieval Medical Theory and Practice', *Social
 History of Medicine*, 16 (2003), pp. 343–66

Owst, G. R., '*Sortilegium* in English Homiletic Literature of the Fourteenth
 Century', in *Studies Presented to Sir Hilary Jenkinson*, ed. J. Conway Davies
 (London, 1957), pp. 272–303

Rider, Catherine, 'Medical Magic and the Church in Thirteenth-Century England',
 Social History of Medicine, 24 (2011), pp. 92–107

——, *Magic and Impotence in the Middle Ages* (Oxford, 2006)

Salmón, Fernando, and Montserrat Cabré, 'Fascinating Women: the Evil Eye in
 Medical Scholasticism', in *Medicine from the Black Death to the French
 Disease*, ed. Roger French et al. (Aldershot, 1998), pp. 53–84

Saunders, Corinne, *Magic and the Supernatural in Medieval English Romance*
 (Woodbridge, 2010)

Schmitt, Jean-Claude, *Ghosts in the Middle Ages*, trans. Teresa Lavender Fagan
 (Chicago, 1998)

Skemer, D., *Binding Words: Textual Amulets in the Middle Ages* (University Park,
 pa, 2006)

Thomas, Keith, *Religion and the Decline of Magic* (London, 1971)

——, 'An Anthropology of Religion and Magic, ii', *Journal of Interdisciplinary
 History*, 6 (1975), pp. 91–109

Tschacher, Werner, 'Der Flug durch die Luft zwischen Illusionstheorie und Realitätsbeweis: Studien zum sog. Kanon Episcopi und zum Hexenflug', *Zeitschrift der
 Savigny-Stiftung für Rechtsgeschichte*, kan. Abt. 85 (1999), pp. 225–76

Watkins, C. S., *History and the Supernatural in Medieval England* (Cambridge, 2007)

Weill-Parot, Nicolas, *Les 'images astrologiques' au moyen âge et à la Renaissance:
 Spéculations intellectuelles et pratiques magiques* (Paris, 2002)

Wenzel, Siegfried, *Latin Sermon Collections from Later Medieval England: Orthodox
 Preaching in the Age of Wyclif* (Cambridge, 2005)

Acknowledgements

Many people have contributed to the writing of this book in different ways. Much of the research was done during a Junior Research Fellowship at Christ's College, Cambridge, and the uninterrupted time I had there has contributed greatly to the results. The writing was done at the University of Exeter, and I am grateful to my colleagues there for their continued interest and for a period of research leave, and to my 'Magic in the Middle Ages' Special Subject classes for making me think harder about many aspects of medieval magic. Michael Leaman at Reaktion Books suggested writing the book in its current form and he and an anonymous reader made many helpful comments on earlier versions. The British Academy's Neil Ker Memorial Fund provided funding for a related project on confession manuals which enabled me to travel to look at manuscripts in Lincoln and Worcester. Jonathan Barry, Simon Barton, David d'Avray, Chris Fletcher, Ian Forrest, Sarah Hamilton, Sophie Page, Laura Sangha and Alex Walsham gave much helpful feedback on drafts of chapters. My parents read the entire manuscript and helped to compile the bibliography. Finally, Laurence Bassett has lived with a great deal of medieval magic talk over the years and it is to him that this book is dedicated.

Photo Acknowledgements

The author and publishers wish to express their thanks to the below sources of illustrative material and/or permission to reproduce it.

Bibliothèque Nationale de France, Paris (MS Fr. 12476, f. 105v): 10; The Bodleian Libraries, The University of Oxford (photos courtesy The Bodleian Libraries): 3 (MS e. Mus 219, f. 186r), 5 (MS Rawlinson D.939, part III), 13 (MS Rawlinson D.252, f. 28v), 15 (MS Rawlinson D.10, f. 1r); The British Library, London: 4 (MS Sloane 428, f. 55r), 7 (MS Arundel 157, f. 4v), 8 (MS Harley 273, f. 85v), 12 (MS Royal 6.E.VI, f. 396v), 16 (MS Royal 10 D. VIII, f. 280r); photos © The British Library Board: 1, 4, 7, 8, 12, 16; British Museum, London (photo © Trustees of the British Museum): 6; Cambridgeshire Record Office (MS WR CR, f. 68r – photo © Cambridgeshire Archives, Cambridge): 17; from *The Famous History of the Lancashire Witches Containing the manner of their becoming such; their enchantments, spells, revels, merry pranks, raising of storms and tempests, riding on winds, &c. The entertainments and frolics which have happened among them . . .* (London, (?)1780): 1; from *The History of Witches and Wizards: Giving a true Account of all their Tryals in England, Scotland, Sweedland, France and New England; with their Confession and Condemnation. Collected from Bishop Hall, Bishop Morton, Sir Matthew Hale, Dr Glanvil, Mr Emlin, Dr Horneck, Dr Tilson, Mr Baxter, Mr Hodges, Corn. Agrippa. By W. P.* (London, (?)1720): 2; New York Public Library, Astor, Lenox and Tilden Foundations (Spencer Collection; Psalterium, fol. 43r): 10; Wellcome Library, London: 9 (MS 404, f. 32v); photos Wellcome Library, London: 2, 9; York Museums Trust (Yorkshire Museum), York (photo © York Museums Trust): 11.

Index